Plantandink

MAKE YOUR OWN PLANT-BASED INK

Judith Rosema

SEARCH PRESS

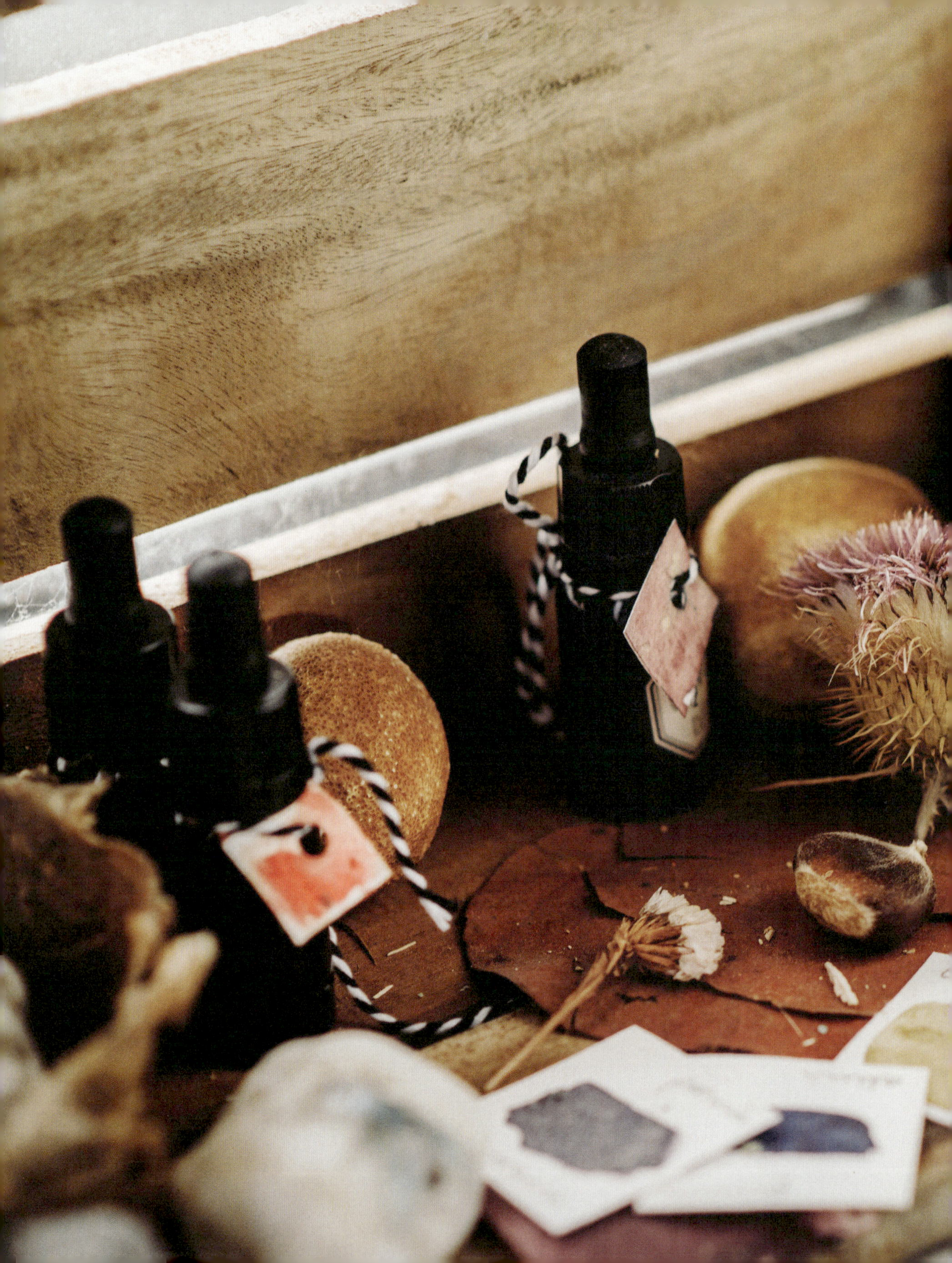

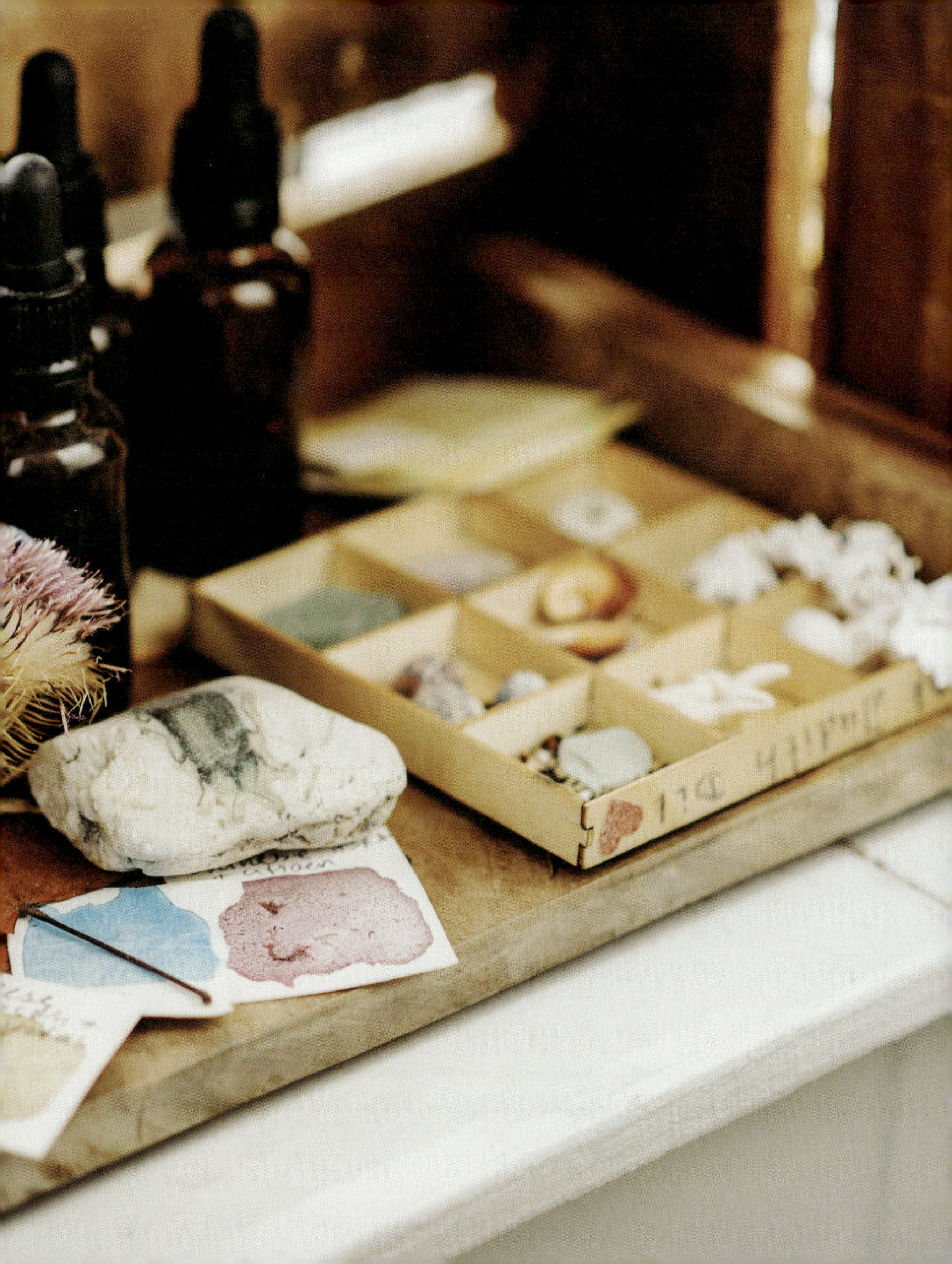

Contents

Dye plants / tutorials

Ink / tutorials

SPRING

SUMMER

Paint, chalk and printing ink / tutorials

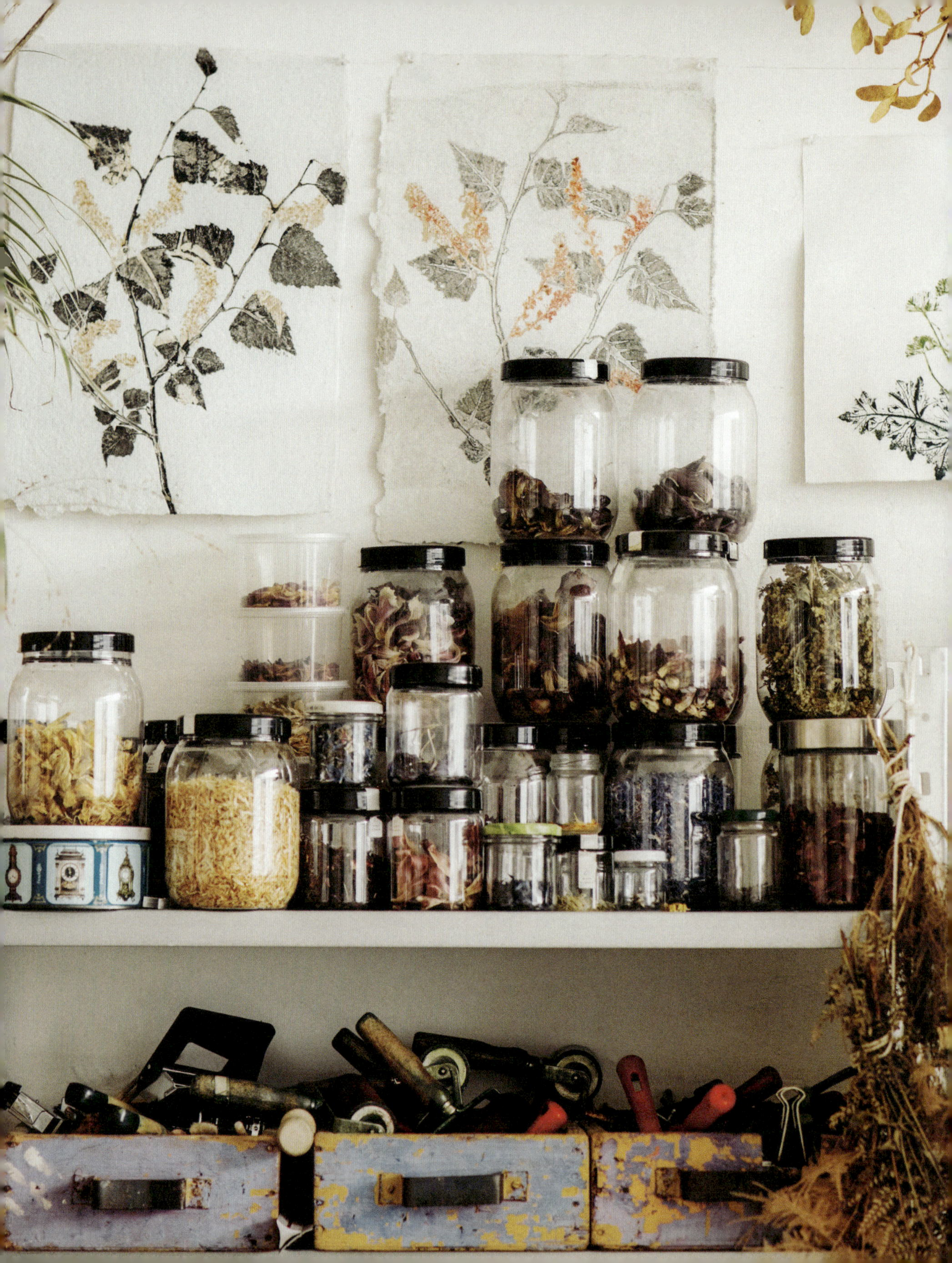

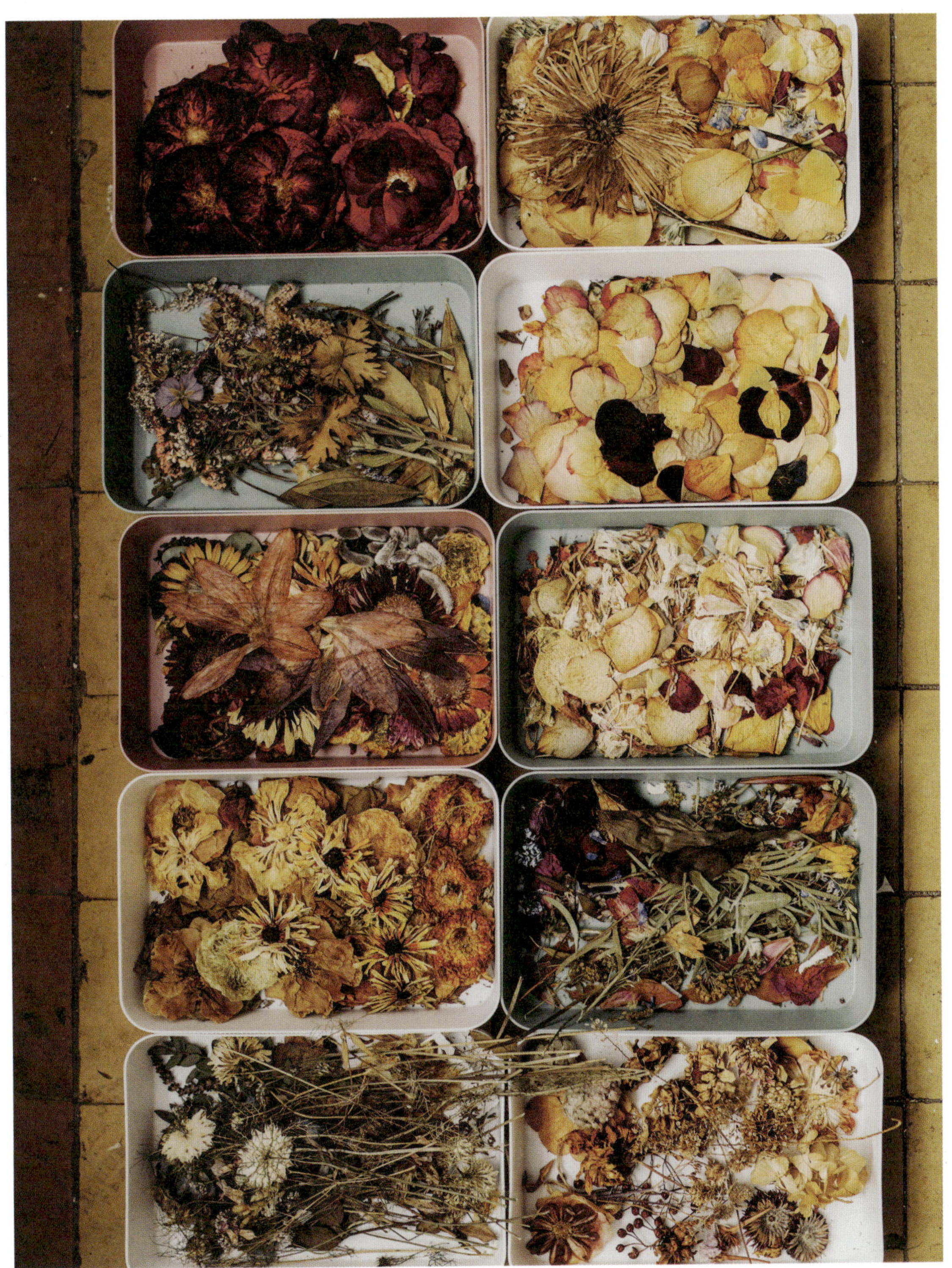

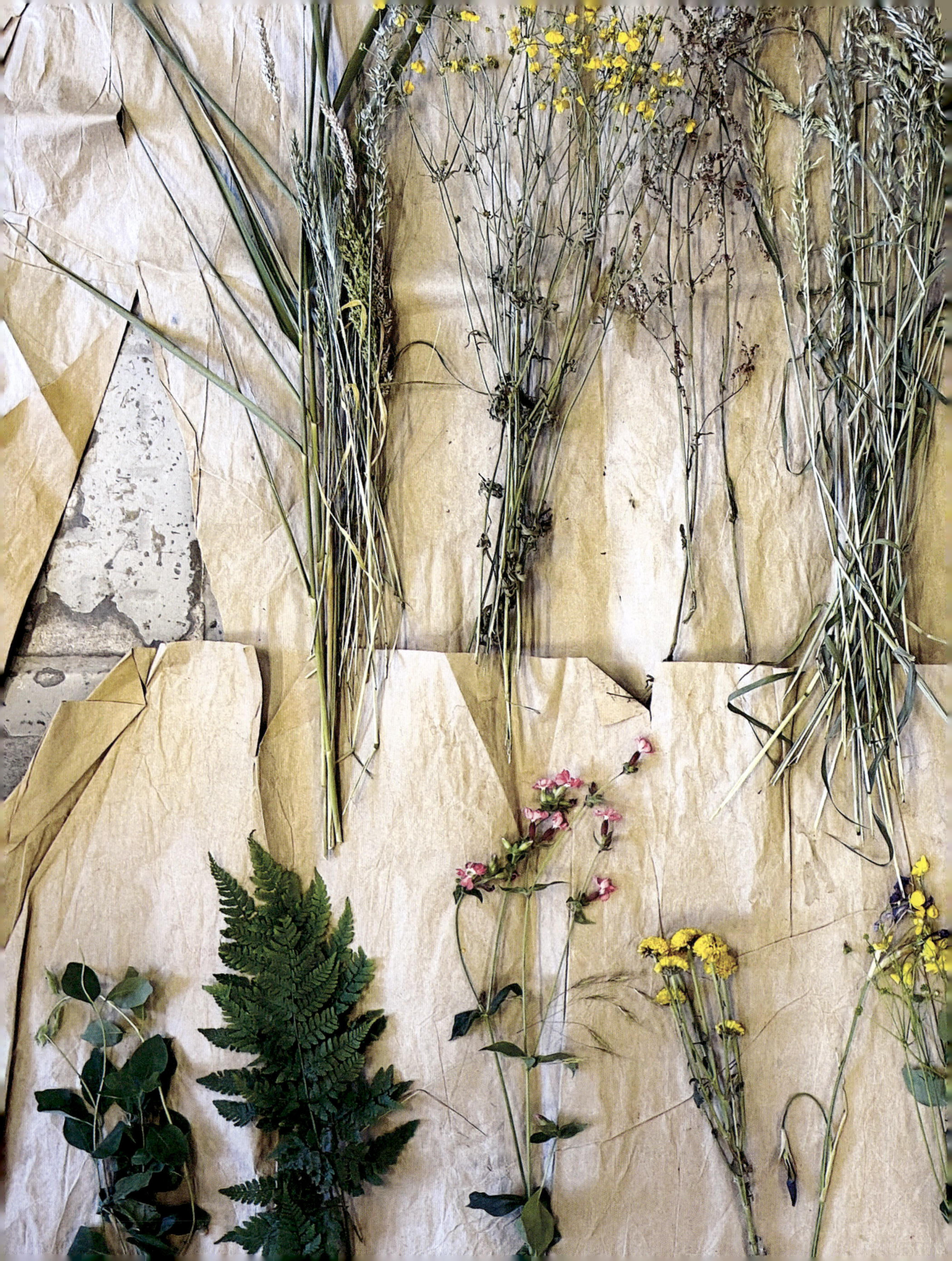

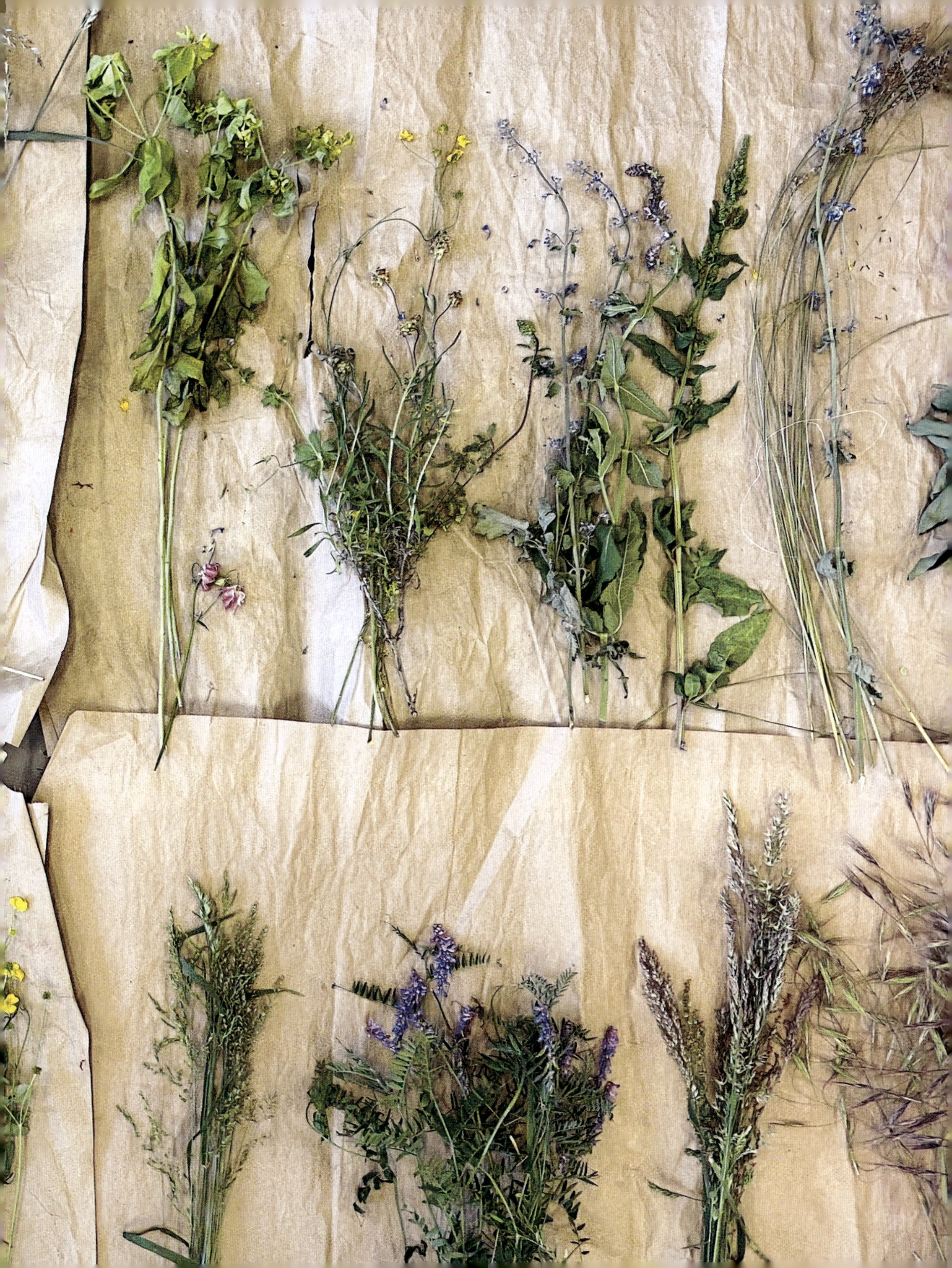

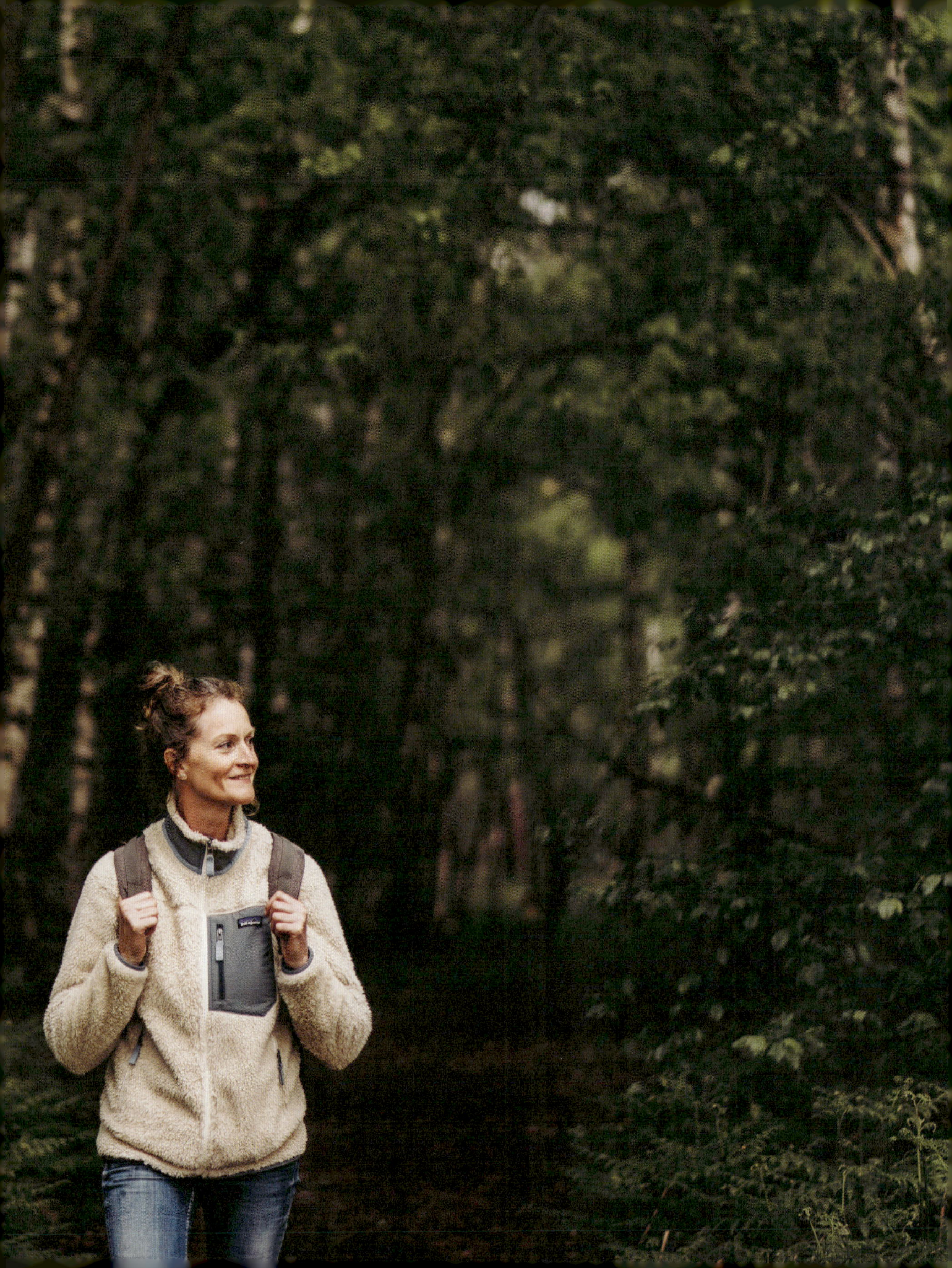

My love for ink and nature

I trained to become a visual artist at the Academy of Art and Design in Den Bosch in the Netherlands. During my time there, I discovered the printmaking studio, which is where my love for ink and paper began. The studio offered the opportunity to work with several printing presses and learn many printing techniques: lithography, screen-printing, etching, wood and lino printing. When the head of the workshop saw how enthusiastic I was, he taught me all about graphic techniques and it was from him that I learned all the ins and outs of the trade. There are so many ways to print on paper – it's amazing! From that point on, I never looked back.

After my time at the academy, I took the art world by storm. I held exhibitions both at home and abroad, mainly showcasing black-and-white drawings, lithographs, etchings and woodcuts. They were dark pieces of work with a raw edge to them, simultaneously vulnerable yet powerful in a poetic way. At the time they were hugely expressive, but this dark side to my work changed overnight when I had a child. All of a sudden, colour re-entered my work. Motherhood changed my outlook on the world. I started looking into sustainability. I became increasingly aware of the levels of suffering that we, as human beings, inflict upon the world. I refused to play my part in this for any longer. Both in my work and in my everyday life, nature became increasingly important.

Although flora and fauna had always been inspirational to me and played a part in many of my drawings, their influence was indirect to start with. That is until one day, my daughter dyed her face yellow with a dandelion. This was the start of a whole new wonderful world of colour – nature's palette. At the time, my daughter was about four years old. She picked a dandelion, smelled it and then rubbed it on her face. The dye from the flower turned her eyebrows yellow and the soft fuzz on her face took on a yellowish glow. I looked at her in amusement, full of wonder; she had no idea how yellow she was! I remember thinking how interesting it was that dandelion creates a yellow dye.

I knew about dye plants, such as woad, madder, weld and the more commonly found indigo, from looking in books, but to grow these plants you need a garden. So that's when I decided to look for colours in nature, which also turned out to be a lot of fun! After all, dandelions aren't true dye plants. Through this book, I'm going to take you on a journey into nature in search of wild plants that are full of colour. While you're on this journey I hope that you, like me, develop a passion for natural paints and inks. In doing so, you will find that using your homemade products for drawing only increases the love and attention with which you approach your work. Enjoy the creative power found within nature and within you.

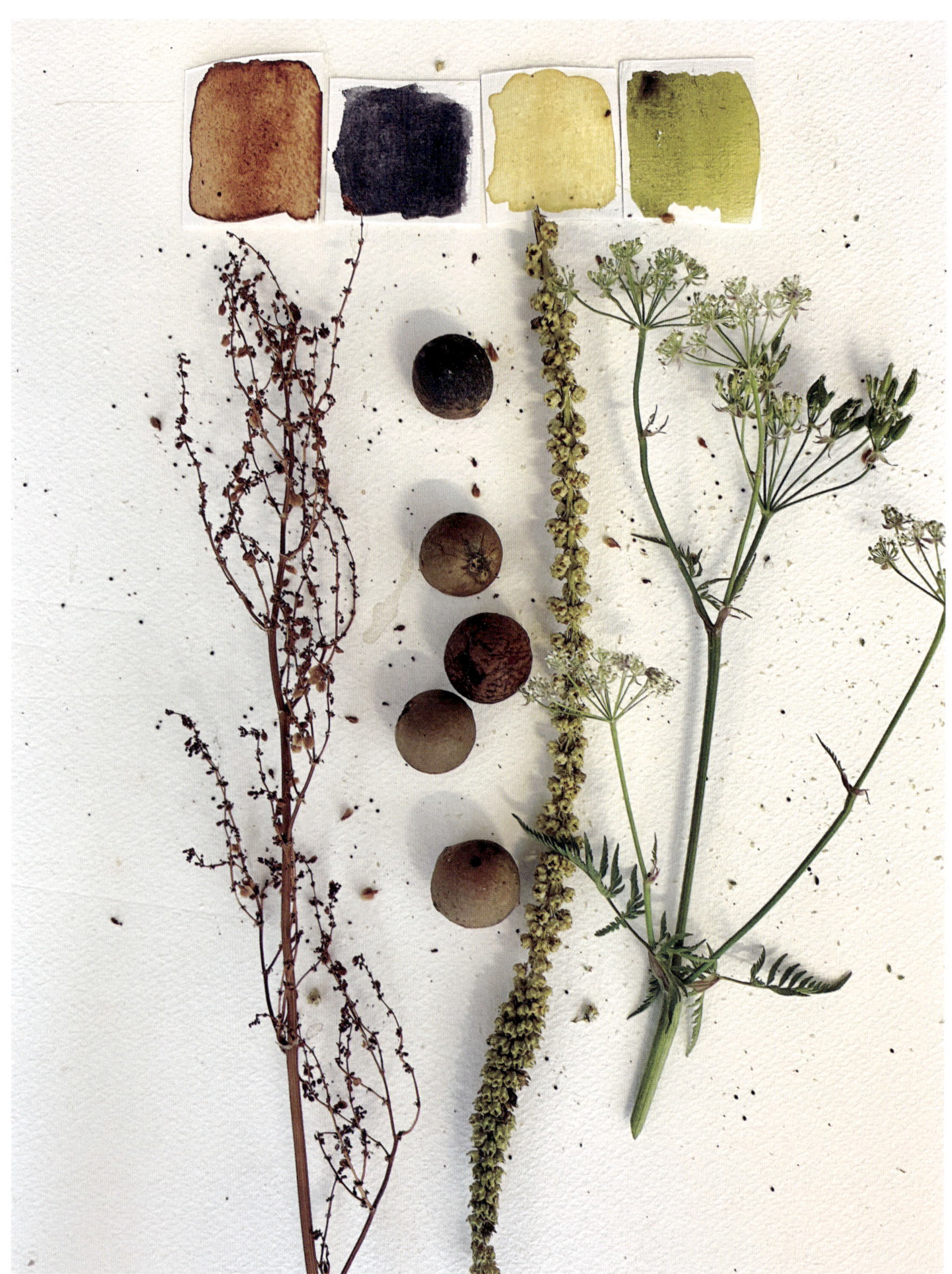

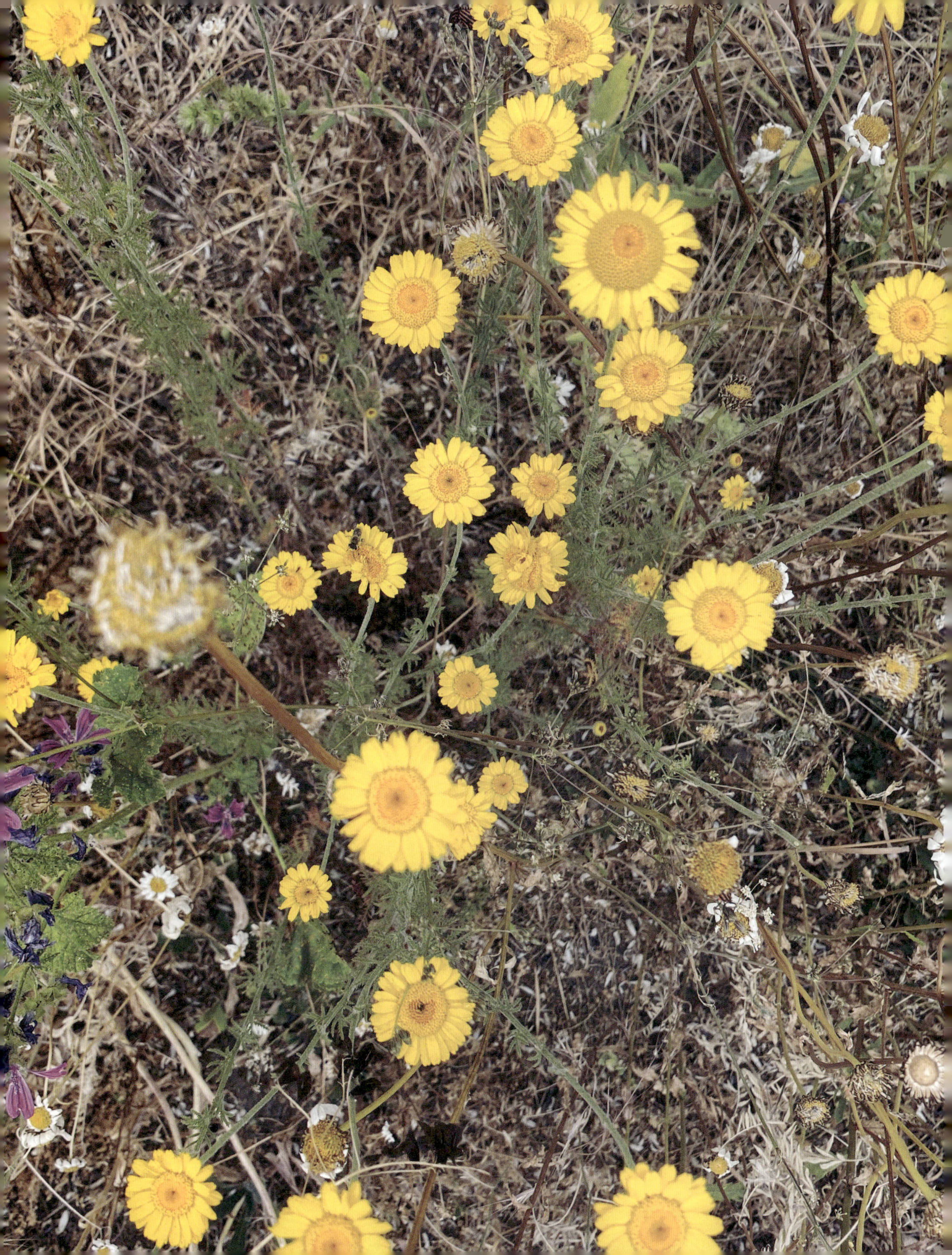

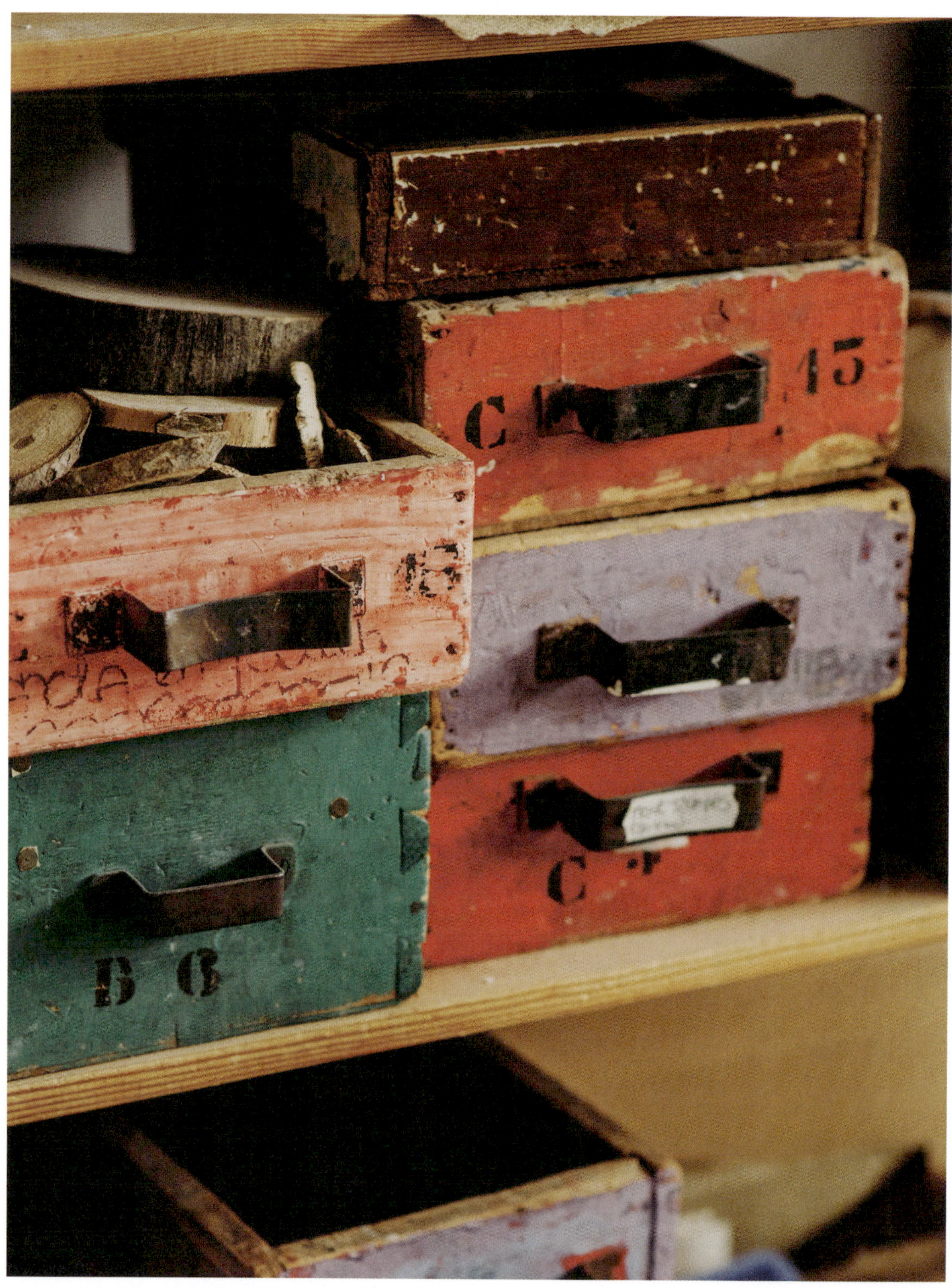

The history of paper and ink

There is an intrinsic link between paper and ink. The first type of paper was papyrus, which was made by the Egyptians. It is from this word that we get the word 'paper'.

PAPYRUS AND PARCHMENT

Papyrus was made from the stems of the papyrus plant (*Cyperus papyrus*). This is a grassy plant that grows in abundance along the banks of the River Nile in Egypt. The stalks of the plant were cut into strips and braided together to form sheets. Using the sticky sap from the plant, the sheets could then be glued together. These first sheets of paper were created about 5,000 years ago. Papyrus was fragile: it was easily torn, did not respond well to humid environments and could easily be damaged by insects that ate it. Since Egypt has a dry climate, it has meant that a good number of papyrus sheets have been preserved.

However, because the climate was not so dry everywhere else, the search for other writing materials went on. In around 2700BC, the Greeks made parchment using animal skins. Parchment is named after the Turkish city of Pergamon where it is said the material was first developed. In order to make parchment, steaming water was poured onto animal skins to make them supple, before all remnants of hair roots and flesh were stripped away. After this, they were stretched out over a wooden frame and treated with pumice and lime to achieve a flat surface. Parchment was more expensive but lasted much longer than papyrus.

Paper as we know it today was invented in China as far back as AD 105 by an official at the Imperial Court, called Ts'ai Lun. One day, Ts'ai Lun watched as a wasp built a nest. He noticed that the wasp was chewing petals so that they formed a pulp and was then using the pulp to build a nest. Once this pulp dried, the result was a solid nest – a paper structure. By mashing together bamboo reed fibres, the bark of the mulberry tree and rags with a hammer, Ts'ai Lun was able to replicate the process. He then added water to the pulp to dilute it, before stretching it and laying it out to dry. Once the pulp had fully dried to form a sheet, the material could be written on. In fact, the process of making paper has not really changed that much over the intervening years.

Today, papermakers still use plant fibres to create a pulp, before diluting it with water and scooping the pulp into a thin layer using a mesh frame. This wet sheet is laid on a felt cloth, pressed and then hung out to dry.

INK

A reed pen or brush dipped in ink made from carbon particles was used to write on papyrus. This ink was invented in around 2500BC, and it was an invention that would prove to be invaluable. Ink was invented in both China and Egypt at around the same time and the methods used were quite similar.

In around AD 400, the Romans used iron salt and gallnuts (also known as gall apples or oak apples) to create an ink that they called *atramentum librarium*. This ink was actually used until the end of the Middle Ages. Gallnuts, just like the oak tree upon which they are formed, contain a large amount of tannic acid. Over time, the combination of this tannic acid with an oxidation process (as a result of the iron in the ink) could literally burn the letters into the paper. This is called ink corrosion and plant-based paper in particular was susceptible to this; parchment, however, was better able to withstand it.

In the Middle Ages, monks created beautiful manuscripts on parchment using a quill pen and iron gall ink. Since much of their work involved copying texts, many stories from antiquity have been preserved. On page 57, you can find the recipe for this historical ink.

The Chinese made ink using carbon (in the form of soot) and water. They ground the soot particles into a very fine dust and then mixed in some water. The soot particles stayed floating around in the water; once they were dry, they stuck to the paper like a brittle film. This ink was sold in powder form. In order to make the ink better adhere to the paper, bone glue or shellac was later added to act as a binder. While bone glue did not turn the ink indelible, shellac did.

Today, it is possible to purchase two types of 'Chinese ink' in shops. Chinese or Japanese ink is made from soot that contains bone glue and it is not waterproof. East Indian ink or India ink is made from soot that contains shellac and is, therefore, indelible. Both come in liquid form in either a jar or a bottle. It is also possible to purchase Chinese ink in the form of an ink stick. A specific technique called *sumi* has been developed for use with *sumi* ink sticks: to create liquid ink, the ink stick is rubbed in a few drops of water on an ink stone. This is seen as an act of meditation that takes place before drawing. The ink is deep black in colour and colourfast since carbon is not degraded by UV light.

THE ART OF LETTERPRESS PRINTING

In China, the art of printing with blocks of wood – known as block printing – has been around since approximately AD 800. Images, and occasionally words, were carved into these blocks, meaning China was able to print material in print runs long before the West. In Europe, letterpress printing using loose letters made from lead was invented by Johannes Gutenberg in the 15th century. One of the advantages of working with loose letters was that the letters could be reused after printing. Gutenberg also developed the first printing ink, which was oil-based and – unlike the *atramentum* ink – rarely smudged during the printing process. In order to print books, it was necessary to use paper that easily absorbed ink; the type of paper that had long been made in China was particularly suited for this purpose.

HAND-MADE PAPER

Nomadic people such as the Arabs introduced the knowledge of papermaking to the West in around AD 1600. From that point on, the making of paper continued to increase in popularity. Early mills in the UK were established in Hertford, Dartford and Buckinghamshire, then in the first half of the 17th century more appeared near Edinburgh and in Staffordshire, Oxfordshire and Surrey. It takes a lot of water to make paper, so they were built near water courses.

The paper was made using fragments and pieces of rags that were placed in tubs of water. Powered by a water wheel, large wooden mallets knocked into the pieces of rags all day long, gradually turning them into pulp. This pulp was then scooped out from the tubs using scooping frames and laid out on sheets made from felt. The felt sheets and paper were then piled up together and positioned under a blocking press, allowing most of the moisture to be squeezed out of the paper. After this, the rags were hung up to allow them to dry. Once they were dry, it was possible to separate the paper from the felt and the paper was then ready to use.

The 19th century was an era of industrialization and millers proved to be no match for the modern paper industry. They either closed down the mills or started to convert some of them into laundries. The UK currently has 47 modern paper mills, producing around 4 tonnes of paper, but only one water mill – Two Rivers Paper Company in West Somerset.

SYNTHETIC INK

The development of the chemical industry in the late 19th century also brought about changes to ink. In actual fact, it was by pure chance that the Englishman William Perkin discovered synthetic ink. Perkin was undertaking laboratory work, researching a cure for malaria, when he discovered that a beautiful purple colour could be extracted from pitch. He called the colour mauve, named after the genus *malva*, or mallow, which has purple flowers (see page 64). Not long after this, the dye alizarin began to be prepared synthetically. Alizarin is the dyeing component of madder, a dye that is orange-red in colour (see page 37). Synthetic indigo (blue) was also discovered in AD 1880 by Adolf von Baeyer. Advances in chemistry superseded the use of natural dyes and this marked the end of the line for dyers working with plant-based dyes: almost without exception their businesses failed, and their knowledge of plant-based dyes disappeared with them.

'BACK TO NATURE' AND 'SLOW LIVING'

Although the 1970s saw a revival of plant-based dyeing techniques, interest waned once more. Today, however, there is a new wave of interest in working with natural products. Growing numbers of people want to get back to a simpler way of life, understanding the origins of their products and opting to create those products themselves: 'back to nature' and 'slow living' are catchwords for this. The notion of plant-based inks perfectly fits this concept, from the enjoyment derived from the ink-making process to its resolute differences compared with a fast-paced, disposable, consumer-driven society.

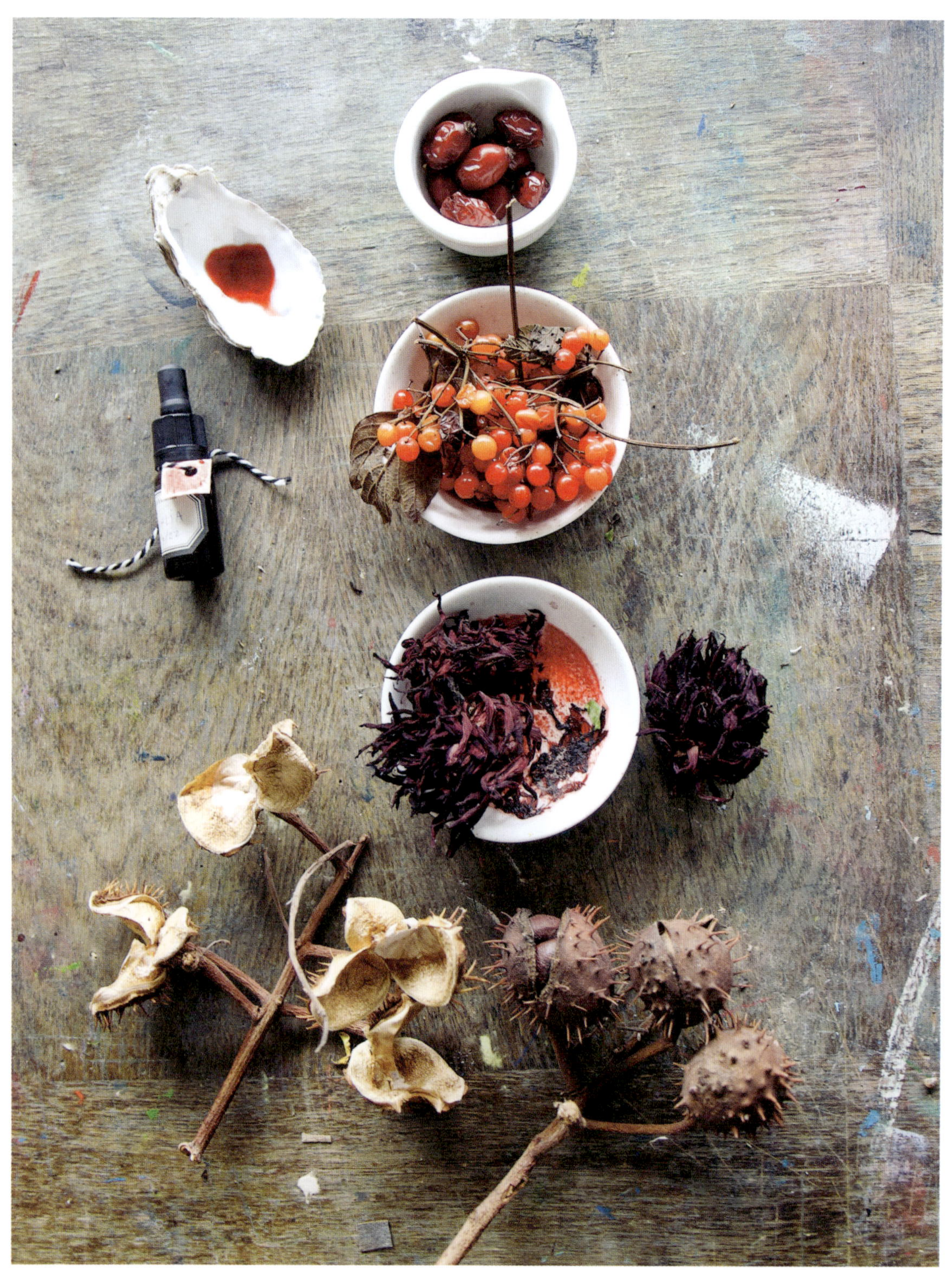

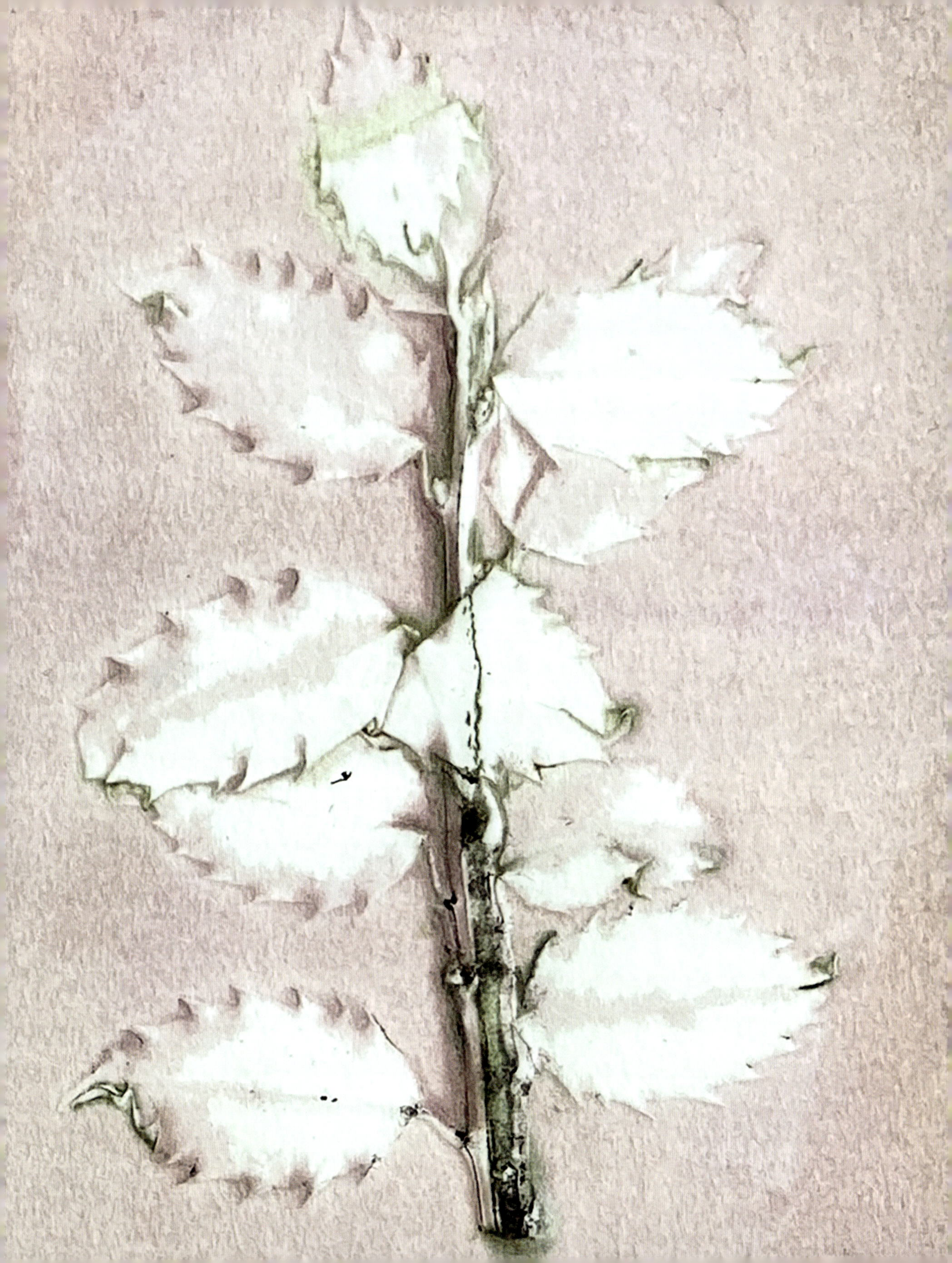

Discovering nature

The aim of this book is to open your eyes to the wondrous colours found in nature, for you to enjoy all those colours and to work creatively using natural materials. So, pack up a rucksack and head outdoors! Make sure you take paper bags and pruning shears with you and nurture your curiosity about the dyeing properties of plants. Take a few petals back with you in a paper bag – it's important not to use plastic bags for this purpose since the plastic can sometimes make the plant matter go mouldy.

Guidelines on wild foraging for the UK can be found on the website of the Woodland Trust: www.woodlandtrust.org.uk

Make a note of which plant you have picked. If you're not totally sure which plant you're looking at, apps such as PlantNet and ObsIdentify can be really helpful. You should also make a note of where you found the plant because if the plant ends up producing a beautiful colour, you'll want to be able to find your plant again!

If you buy a special notebook, then think about buying a nice one that has thick watercolour paper. That way, you can paint the colour you've created directly on a page in the notebook alongside any notes you've written – it's the start of your very own colour reference book.

The recipes in this book make about 30ml (1oz) of ink. This is the equivalent of a standard-sized pipette bottle. I have tried to describe the quantities as precisely as possible but ultimately, the amount of ink you will end up with depends on how long you allow the ink to soak and the length for which you boil it. The longer you leave it to soak, the more solid the colour will become and the longer you boil the ink to reduce it down, the thicker the ink will become. In these recipes I state the minimum number of hours but it's up to you if you decide you want to leave it for longer. Personally, I like a slightly thicker ink since it can easily be thinned out again with a drop or two of water.

This book has been written with the Northern hemisphere in mind – therefore, do bear in mind that specific growing conditions and harvesting times may vary in the Southern hemisphere.

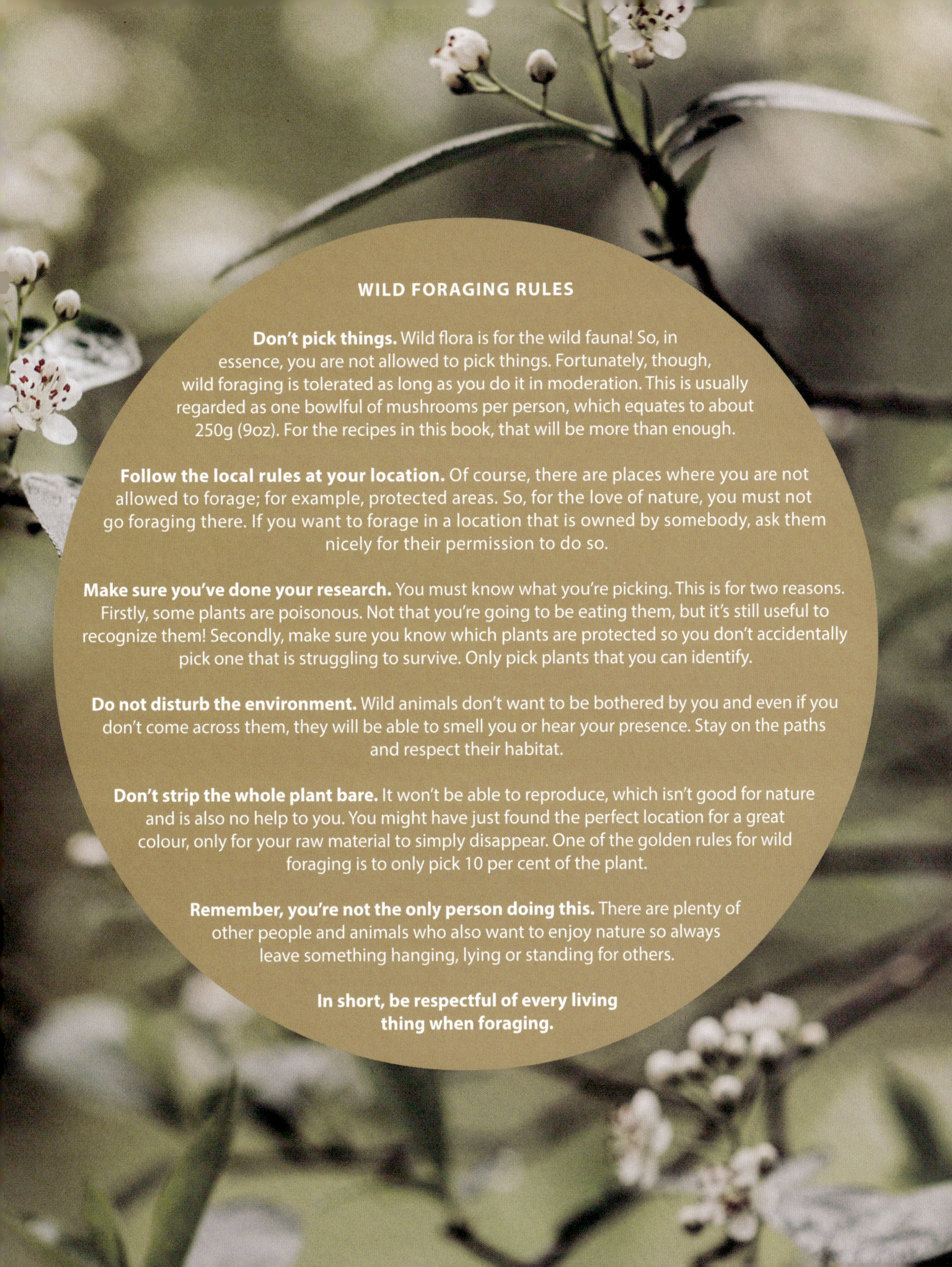

WILD FORAGING RULES

Don't pick things. Wild flora is for the wild fauna! So, in essence, you are not allowed to pick things. Fortunately, though, wild foraging is tolerated as long as you do it in moderation. This is usually regarded as one bowlful of mushrooms per person, which equates to about 250g (9oz). For the recipes in this book, that will be more than enough.

Follow the local rules at your location. Of course, there are places where you are not allowed to forage; for example, protected areas. So, for the love of nature, you must not go foraging there. If you want to forage in a location that is owned by somebody, ask them nicely for their permission to do so.

Make sure you've done your research. You must know what you're picking. This is for two reasons. Firstly, some plants are poisonous. Not that you're going to be eating them, but it's still useful to recognize them! Secondly, make sure you know which plants are protected so you don't accidentally pick one that is struggling to survive. Only pick plants that you can identify.

Do not disturb the environment. Wild animals don't want to be bothered by you and even if you don't come across them, they will be able to smell you or hear your presence. Stay on the paths and respect their habitat.

Don't strip the whole plant bare. It won't be able to reproduce, which isn't good for nature and is also no help to you. You might have just found the perfect location for a great colour, only for your raw material to simply disappear. One of the golden rules for wild foraging is to only pick 10 per cent of the plant.

Remember, you're not the only person doing this. There are plenty of other people and animals who also want to enjoy nature so always leave something hanging, lying or standing for others.

In short, be respectful of every living thing when foraging.

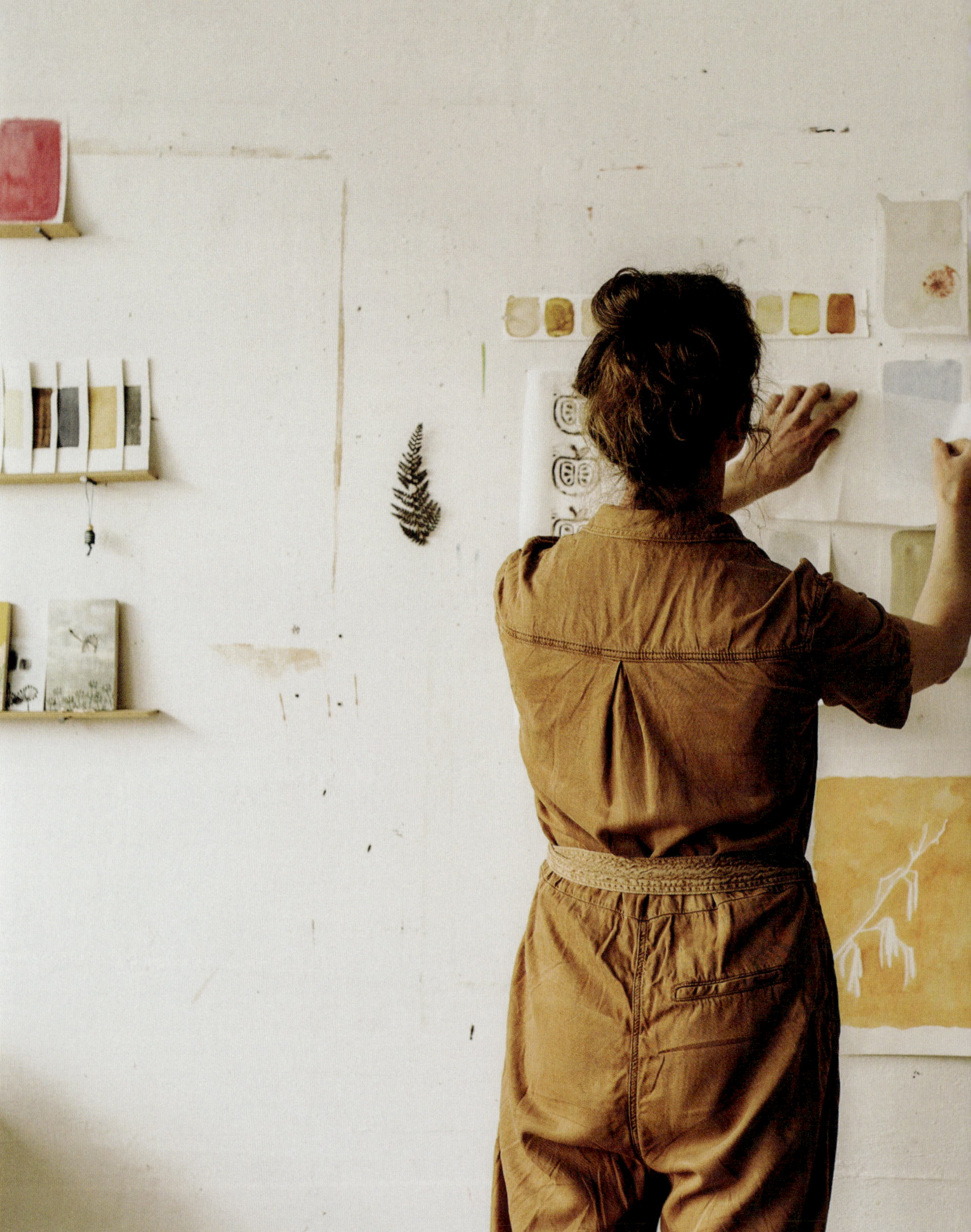

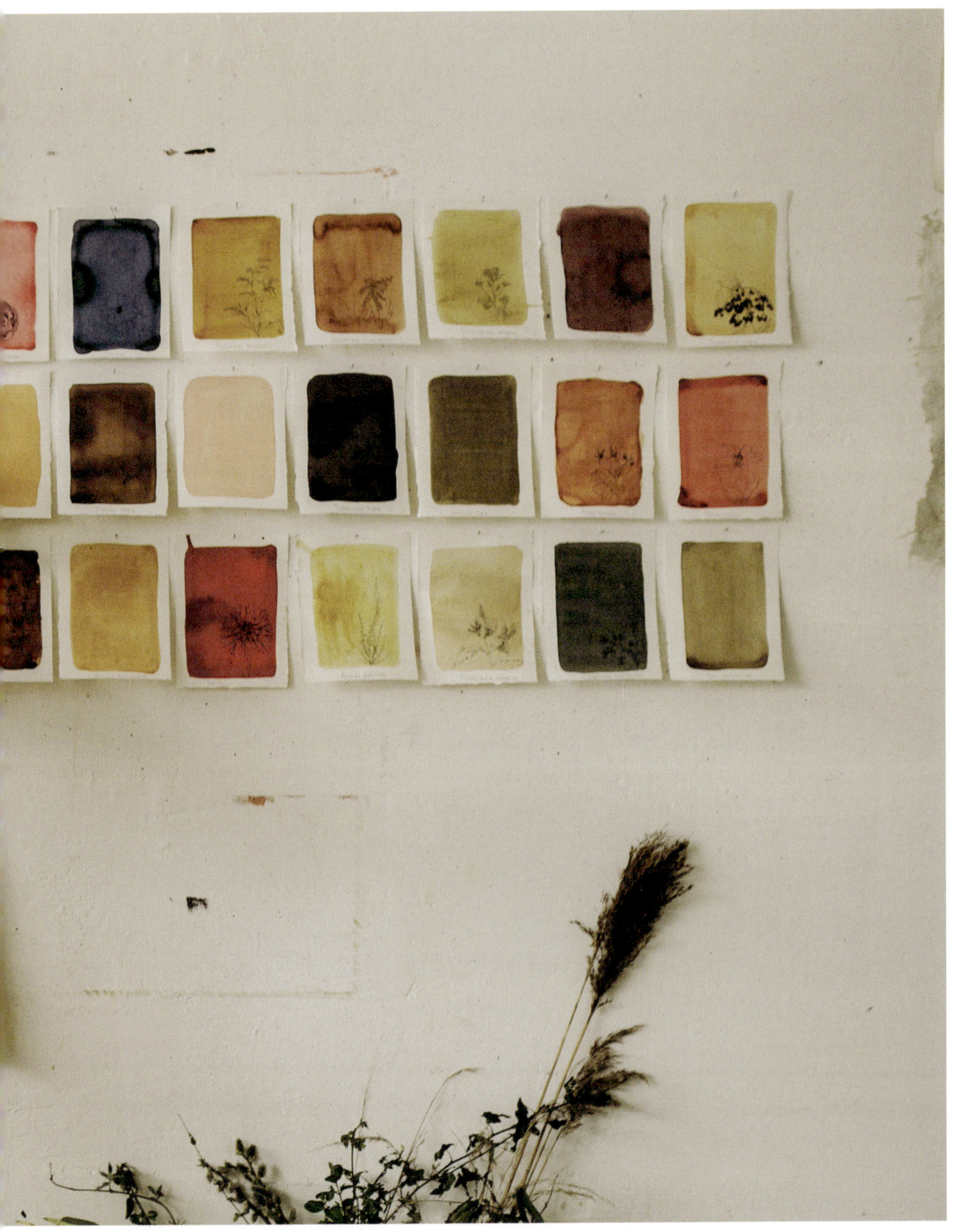

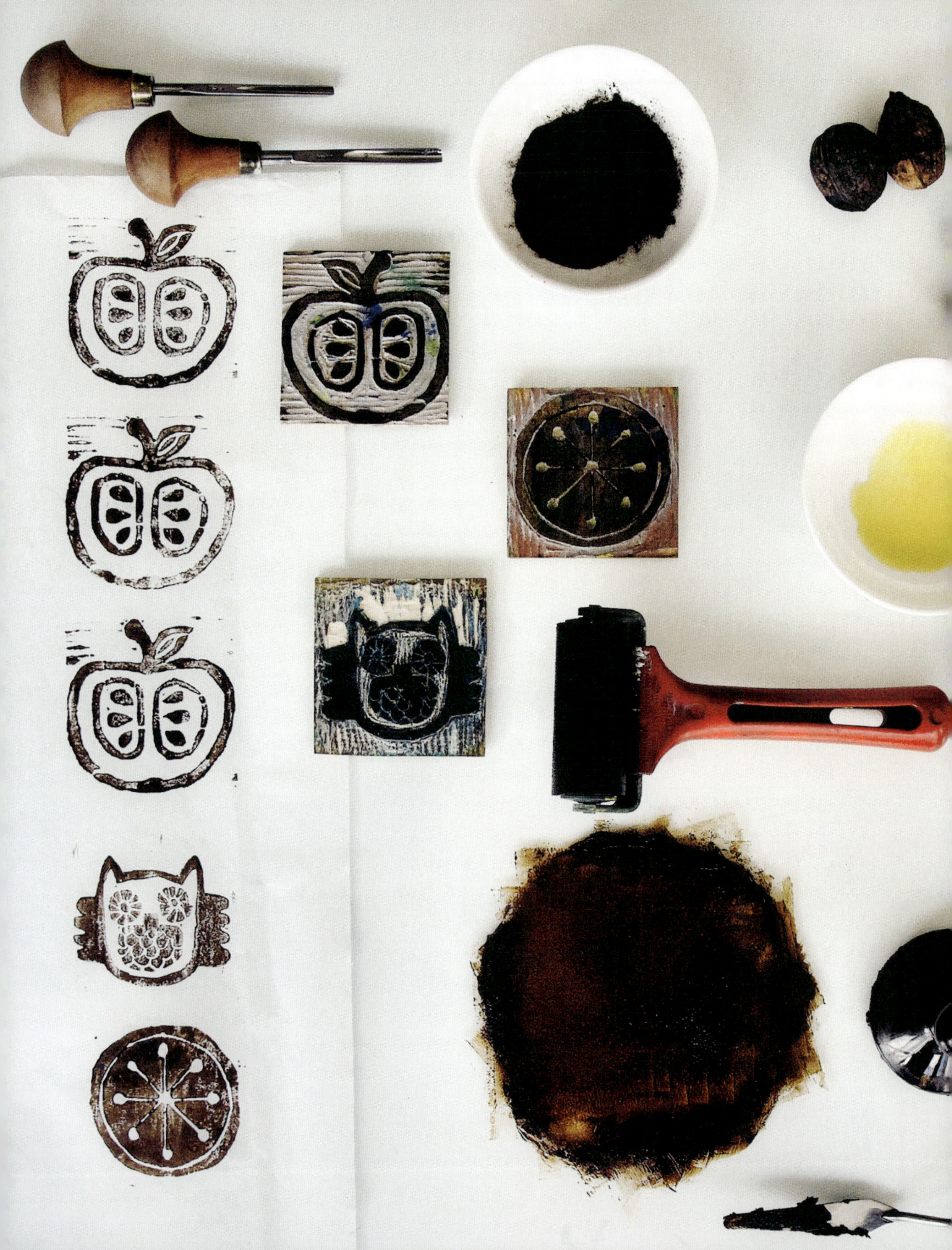

What is ink?

Ink is nothing more than coloured water that is able to adhere to your paper. In fact, you can make ink using all kinds of materials as long as they are able to release colour into the water.

GRAND TEINTS AND PETIT TEINTS

When working with plant-based paints, dyes and inks, it is important to differentiate between *grand teints and petit teints*. *Grand teints* are colours that will retain their intensity over a long period of time and will not fade quickly when applied to paper. Traditional dye plants are used to make *grand teints*; for example, woad, indigo, madder, gallnuts and weld. These are the plants traditionally used to make dye. *Petit teints* are those colours that tend to fade over time. These encompass practically all inks derived from plants that are not official dye plants, although there are a few exceptions. Each recipe in this book includes a number of plus signs to indicate whether the plant will make a *grand teint* or *petit teint*. Therefore, ++++ is the symbol for an ink that is lightfast and will remain colourfast for years, while + is the symbol for very unstable ink.

I actually like the fact that colours will eventually fade because nothing in nature lasts forever. If you want to ensure that your drawing is still exactly the same colour in ten years' time, you will need to visit an art shop to buy synthetic ink (and even that will eventually fade in time), but if you do that, you will miss out on the rather special process of making your own ink. If you make your own plant ink you will gradually develop a bond with it, something that will always benefit your artwork.

DYE PLANTS

Traditionally, painters and wool-dyers used a number of dye plants to create their paints and dyes. Three of the best-known dye plants are weld (for yellow), woad (for blue) and madder (for red): the three primary colours that can be mixed together to create all the other colours. These three dye plants produce colours that are highly lightfast (*grand teints*), which is why dyers loved working with them.

PLANT-BASED INK OR SYNTHETIC INK?

I personally prefer using plant-based ink over synthetic ink. Plant-based inks are fuller and richer in colour: they are not one uniform colour, but instead contain the whole spectrum of pigments found in abundance within the plant. Synthetic colours consist of a single hue and can sometimes clash with each other, but plant-based inks never clash since all the colours complement each other. Next time you're in a garden, take a look at all the plants around you and you'll see that it doesn't matter what you put next to what; nothing actually clashes. It is exactly the same with plant-based dyes. They are all so rich in colour that they complement and enhance one another.

Handy to keep in the house

You don't have to purchase expensive items to make your own ink. In fact, everything you need is readily available. You may have to look a little harder for pipette bottles, but they can be bought at art or craft retailers. Incidentally, there is also a list of useful addresses at the back of the book where you can purchase equipment and ingredients.

Use old pans! You don't want to cook food in the same pans you have used for brewing ink. Equally, not everybody will want to make ink in their kitchen so if you're planning to make it outdoors, a camping stove is useful.

EQUIPMENT FOR MAKING INK

- baker's twine
- camping stove (optional)
- labels
- muslin or a pair of tights
- coffee filters
- measuring cup
- knife
- mini funnel
- old pans with lids
- 100% cellulose paper
- paper bags
- paintbrush
- pipette bottles
- pipettes
- glass jars with lids (sterile)
- (pruning) shears
- hand-held blender
- pestle and mortar
- sieve

EXTRA ITEMS NEEDED FOR MAKING PIGMENTS AND PAINT

- rubber bands
- glass plate
- strip of glass
- electric whisk
- litmus paper
- palette knife
- thermometer
- tubes (empty)
- preserving jars

INGREDIENTS

To adjust or intensify the colour of the ink:

- baking soda
- citric acid, or a squeeze of lemon juice
- iron sulphate
- potash
- washing soda

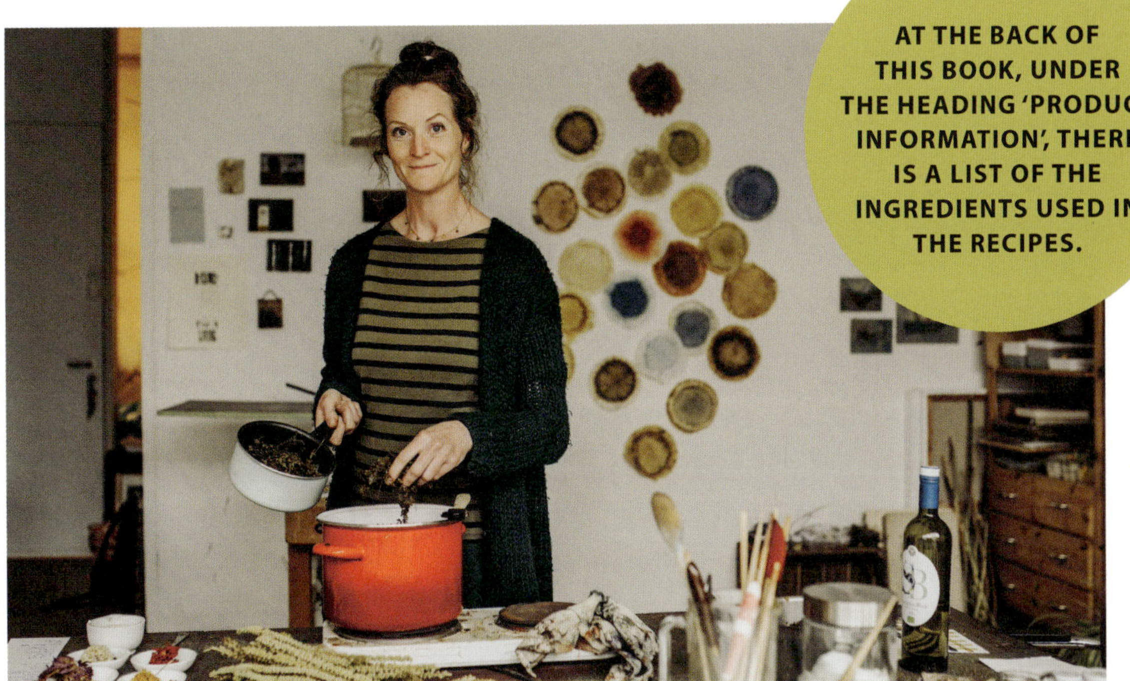

TO BOTTLE INK

• Gum arabic (acacia gum)

Gum arabic is the gummy resin of the acacia tree. It is used as a thickener in the food industry, including in making liquorice. Gum arabic can be purchased as chunks or in powder form. I buy it in chunks: although they don't dissolve as quickly as the powder form, they are purer. You can dissolve the chunks of gum by placing them in a pair of tights and suspending them in a jar of cold water. That way, you can filter out the gum directly from the scraps of acacia that stick to it. The ratio you need is 1 part gum to 2 parts water.

Gum arabic not only helps your ink to flow properly so that it is less likely to bleed on to the paper, it also helps it to adhere better. Moreover, it also ensures an even distribution of pigments in your inks and paints. Once the gum has been dissolved it is more likely to grow mould, so make sure you store it in the fridge. It will keep for about three weeks. Once the gum starts smelling sour you can tell it is no longer any good so only make as much as you will use in three weeks.

• Clove oil or whole cloves

Natural inks can go mouldy in the bottle. Cloves are a natural fungicide. You can use one drop of clove oil per 30ml (1oz) bottle. If you don't have clove oil to hand, you can also add a whole clove.

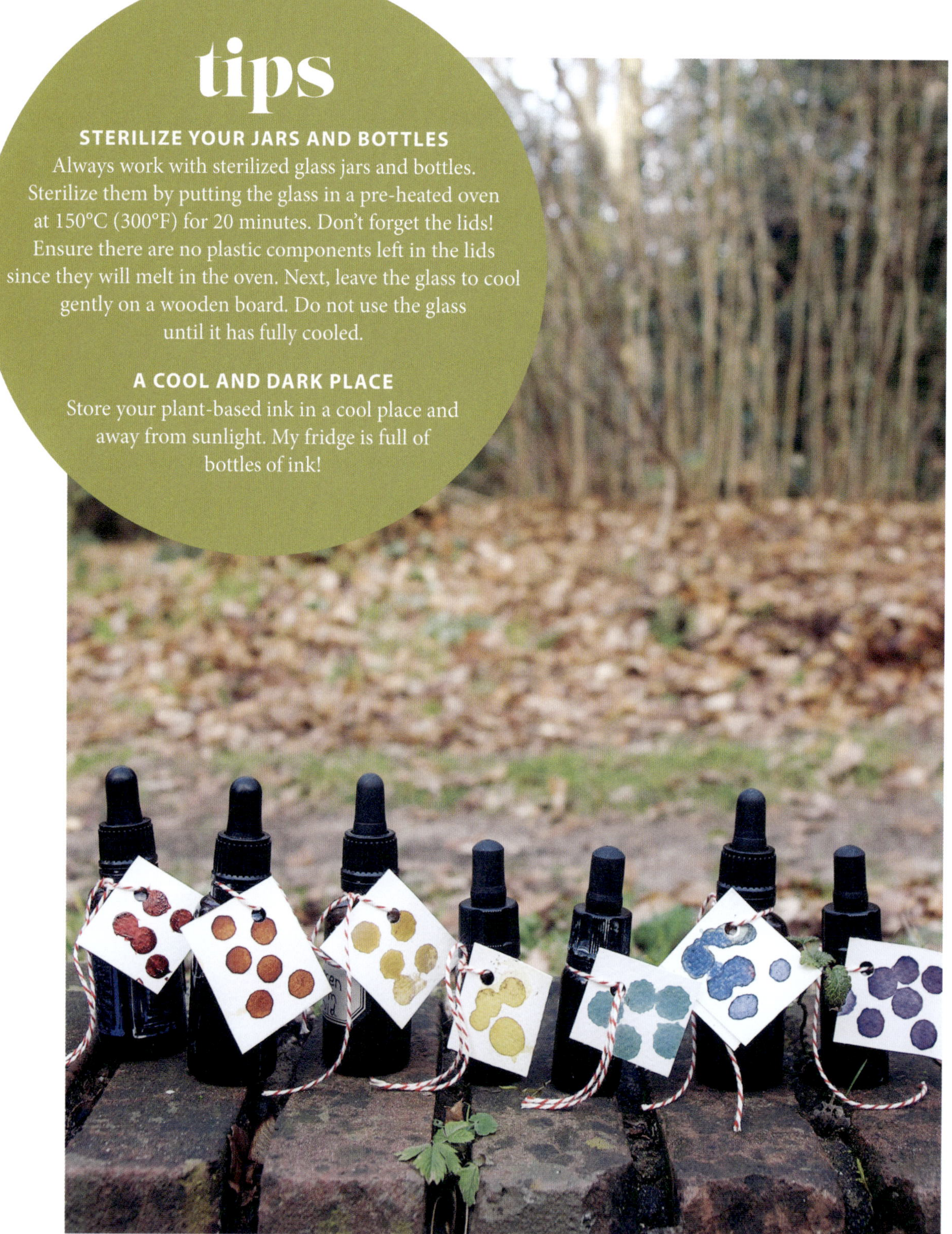

tips

STERILIZE YOUR JARS AND BOTTLES

Always work with sterilized glass jars and bottles.
Sterilize them by putting the glass in a pre-heated oven
at 150°C (300°F) for 20 minutes. Don't forget the lids!
Ensure there are no plastic components left in the lids
since they will melt in the oven. Next, leave the glass to cool
gently on a wooden board. Do not use the glass
until it has fully cooled.

A COOL AND DARK PLACE

Store your plant-based ink in a cool place and
away from sunlight. My fridge is full of
bottles of ink!

Bottling ink

Using a mini funnel makes it easier to pour the ink into a pipette bottle. Once you have done this, add gum arabic (5 drops per 30ml/1oz of ink) and clove oil (1 drop per 30ml/1oz) and your ink will then be ready to use. It is best to store the ink in a dark glass pipette bottle, which will block out UV light. By using the pipette, you can then conveniently remove the amount of ink that you need. For each bottle of plant-based ink, paint the colour of the ink on to a small card made from natural paper. Make a hole in the card and then hang it around the neck of the bottle with baker's twine or similar. This allows you to quickly see which colour ink is in the bottle. Write the name of the plant on a label and stick it on the bottle.

The basis of plant-based inks

The basis of any plant-based ink is a plant tea. This is tea that has been brewed from the leaves, flowers, fruits or roots of a plant. If a plant contains a lot of dye, it will release it into the warm water. The plants that I've included in this book contain lots of dye, but I would wholeheartedly encourage you to experiment with other plants as well. The important thing to remember when making the plant tea is that the liquid should not boil. If it does, the whole structure of the ink can change. It may become flaky and no longer flow evenly, or sometimes you end up ruining the colour.

The level of intensity of the coloured ink depends on the ratio of plants and water. Submerge the plants just under the water for the best results. If you don't have enough plant material or you have too much water, the ink will be a weak colour. The amount of ink you are left with depends on how long you allow the ink to simmer and how long you let it reduce. By reduction, I mean heating it very gently so that just the water vapour disappears. Again, it is important not to allow it to boil. Never leave the pan unattended while it is cooking. Towards the end, the process moves very quickly and it can easily burn. If you allow the liquid to reduce over a long period of time, the ink will become thicker and the colour will intensify, but you will end up with a smaller quantity of ink. I prefer working with thicker ink, which I can then dilute with water as required. It is best to use a strainer or fine sieve to separate the plants from the plant tea. I like to filter the ink using a coffee filter that I've placed in a separate coffee filter holder or clipped onto a jar using two pegs. Sometimes I don't filter the ink at all as I find that any fine pieces of plant left in the ink can add a nice texture to my paper.

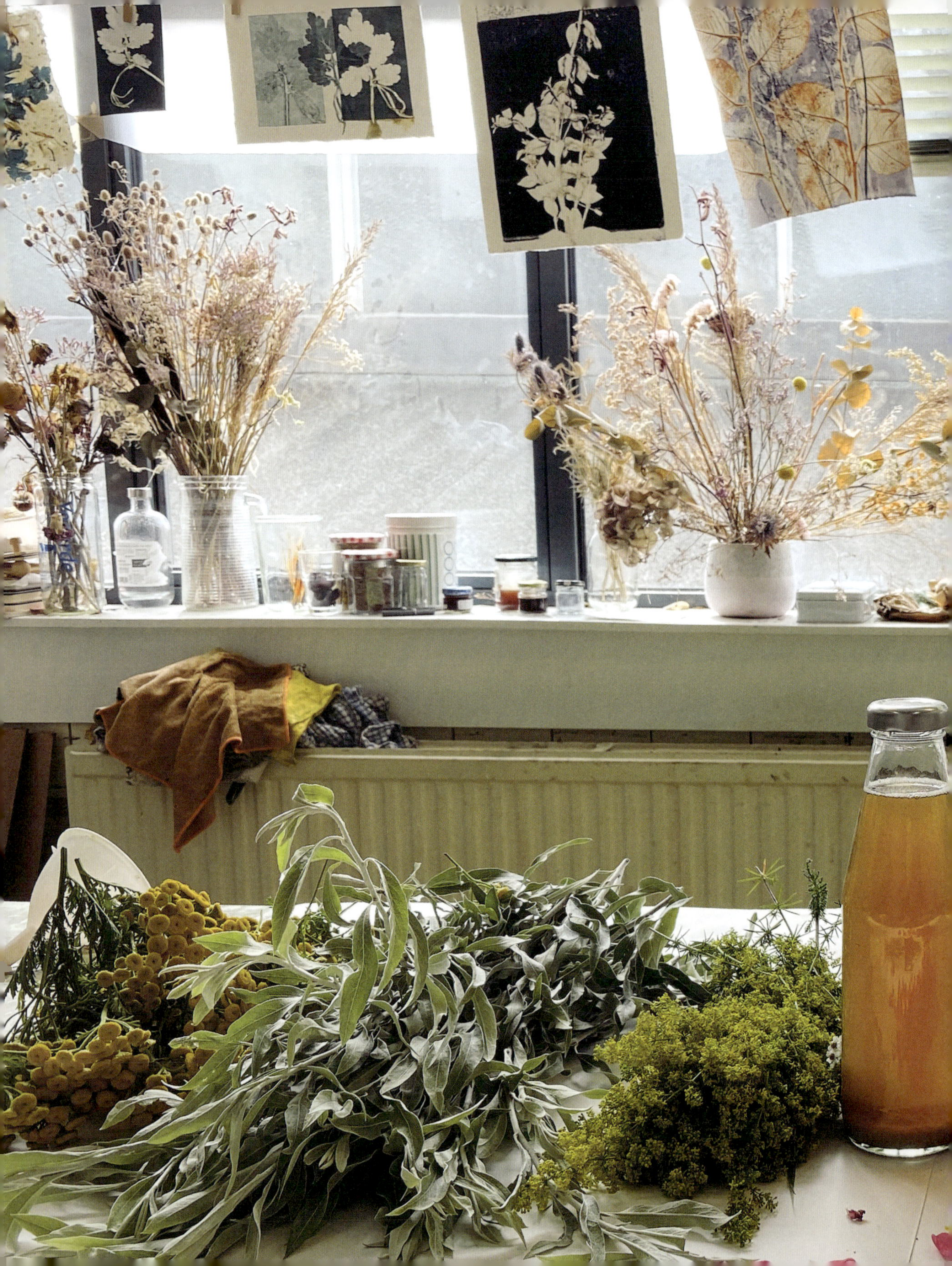

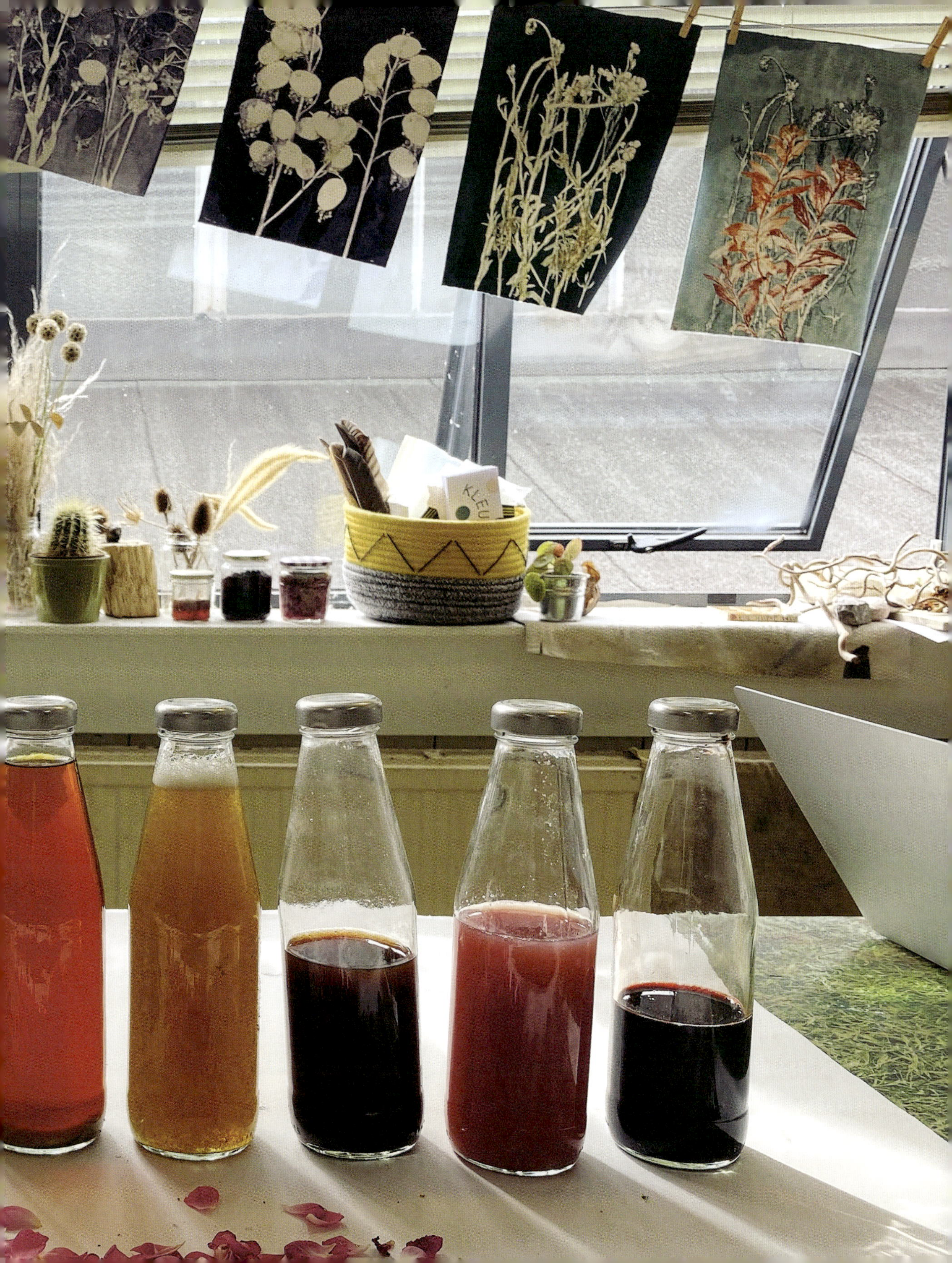

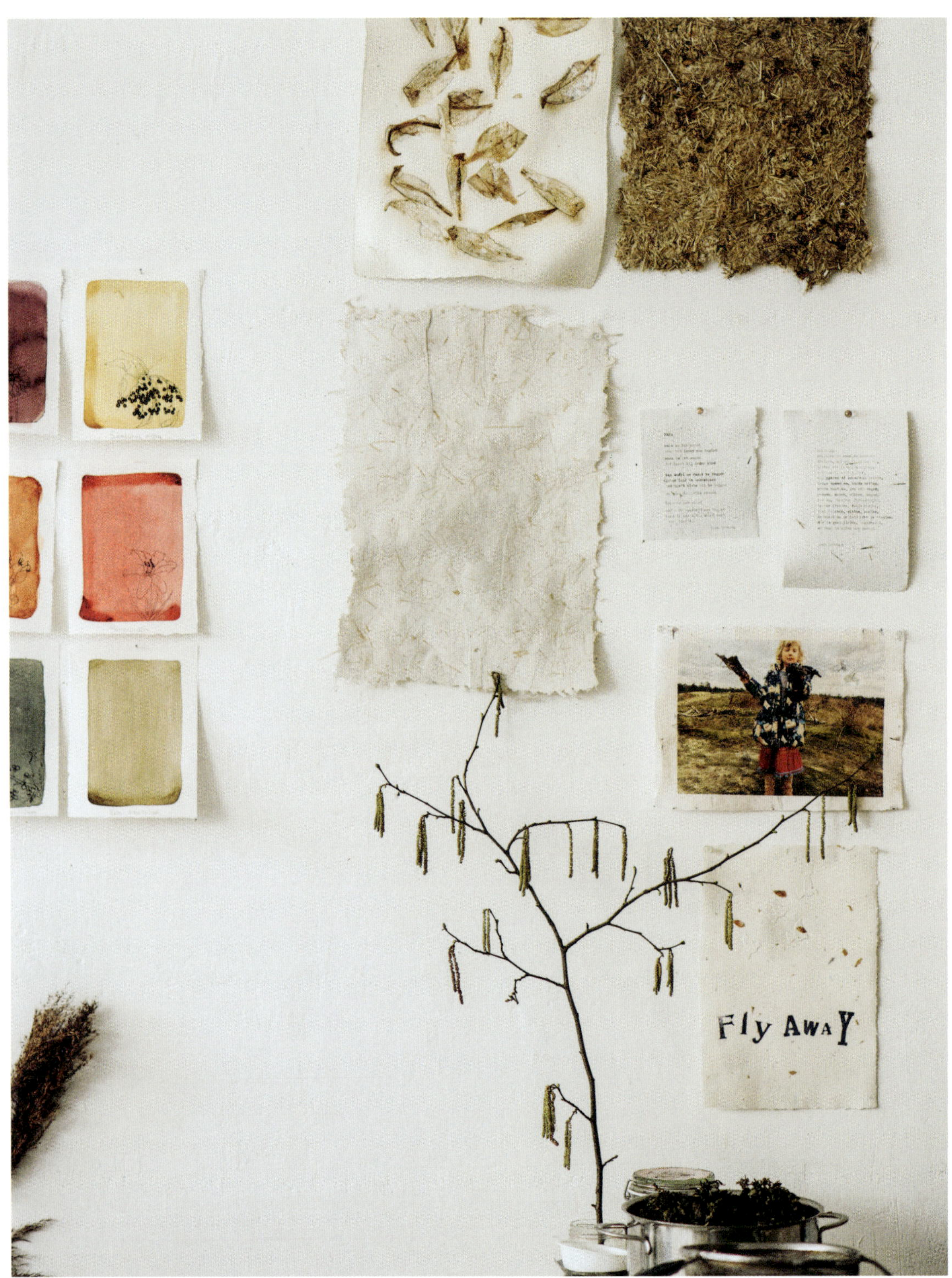

Three *golden* rules for working with plant-based inks

1 GIVE THE INK TIME TO BREATHE

Plant-based inks are living inks. Even once they've been applied to paper, they still need time to develop. At first, the inks will be watery, thin and transparent. Give plant-based inks time to adhere to your paper and in due course they will reveal their radiant colours.

2 PREVENT MOULD FORMING

Because plant-based inks are living inks, they can go mouldy. If possible, it is best to use bottles made from dark glass since this prevents UV light from penetrating. The best place to store your bottles of ink is in the fridge. If you see any fur growing on your ink, remove it straight away. The easiest way to do this is using a skewer, the tip of which you need to bend over itself so that it resembles a fish hook. Once you've removed the fur, place a fresh clove in your bottle. This won't change the colour of the ink and once applied to your paper, the ink will never go mouldy.

3 WORK ON NATURAL PAPER

Natural paper is paper that is made from 100 per cent cellulose, with no additional optical brighteners or acids. It is important to work with plant-based inks on natural paper because this will deliver the most beautiful and vibrant results. Paper that contains acid or a whitening agent will react with the ink, causing it to change colour. Always check the packaging to see if the paper is made from 100 per cent cellulose. Thick watercolour paper is lovely to work with; I work with Canson watercolour paper, which is 300gsm (140lb) and cold-pressed.

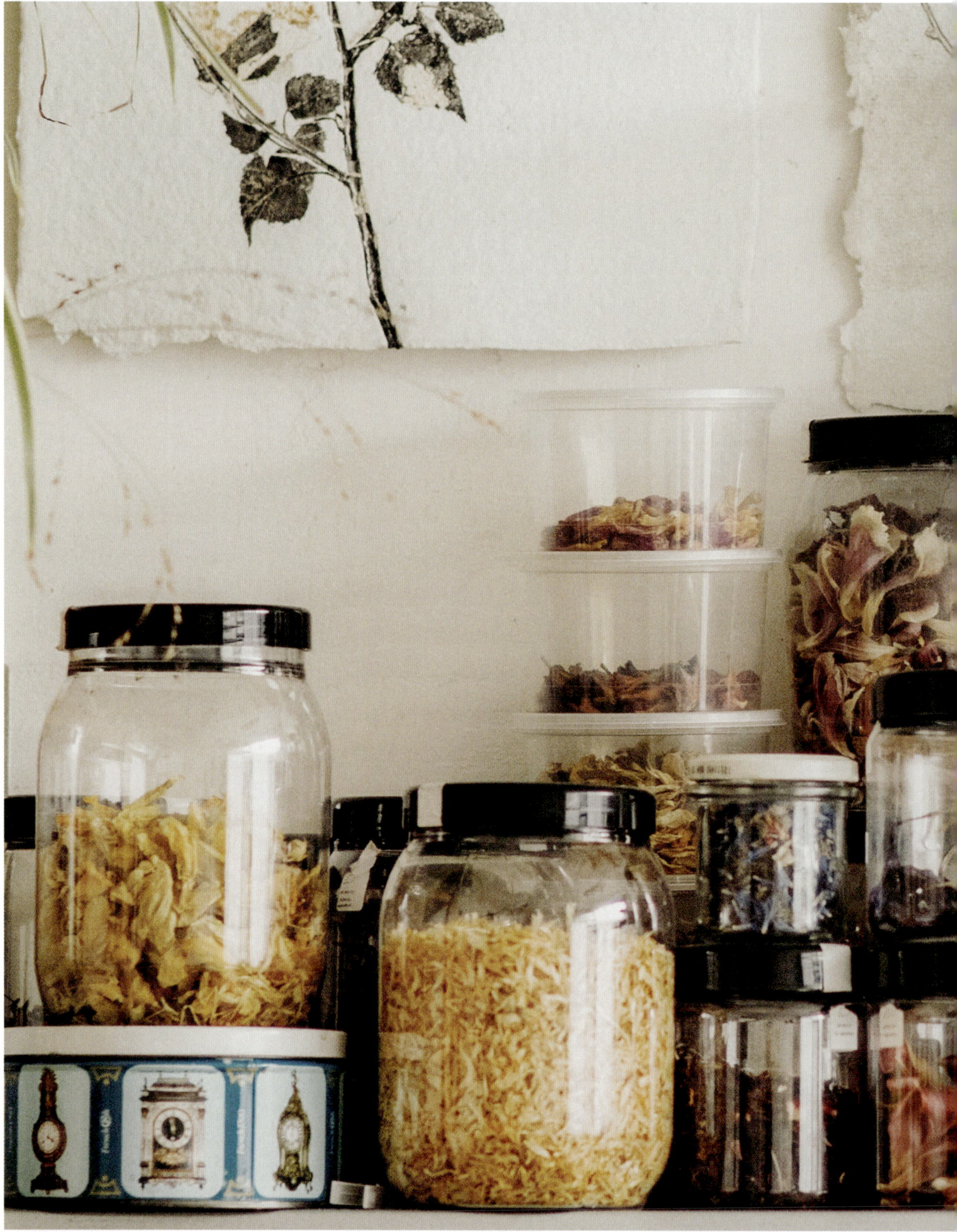

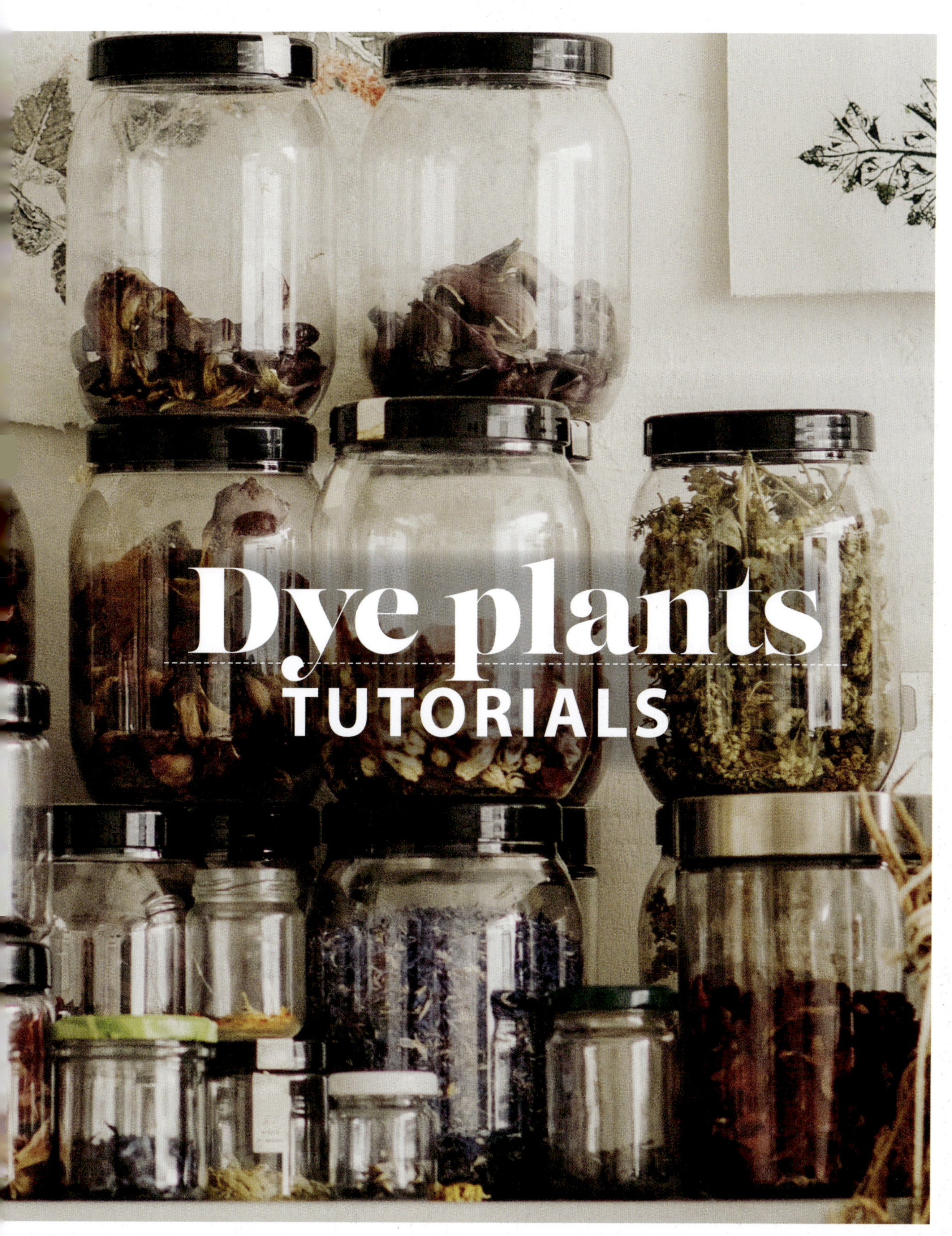

Dye plants
TUTORIALS

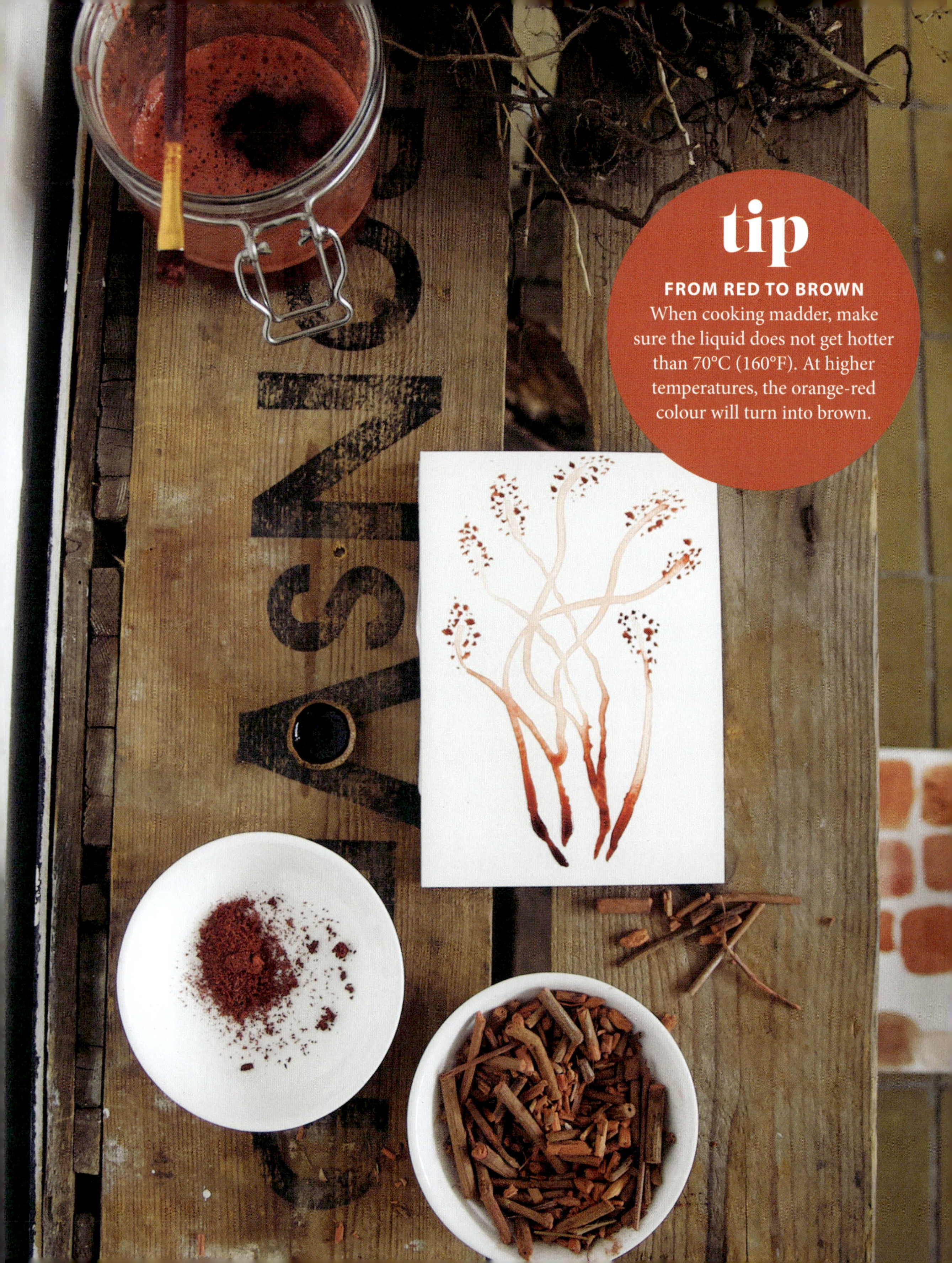

tip

FROM RED TO BROWN
When cooking madder, make
sure the liquid does not get hotter
than 70°C (160°F). At higher
temperatures, the orange-red
colour will turn into brown.

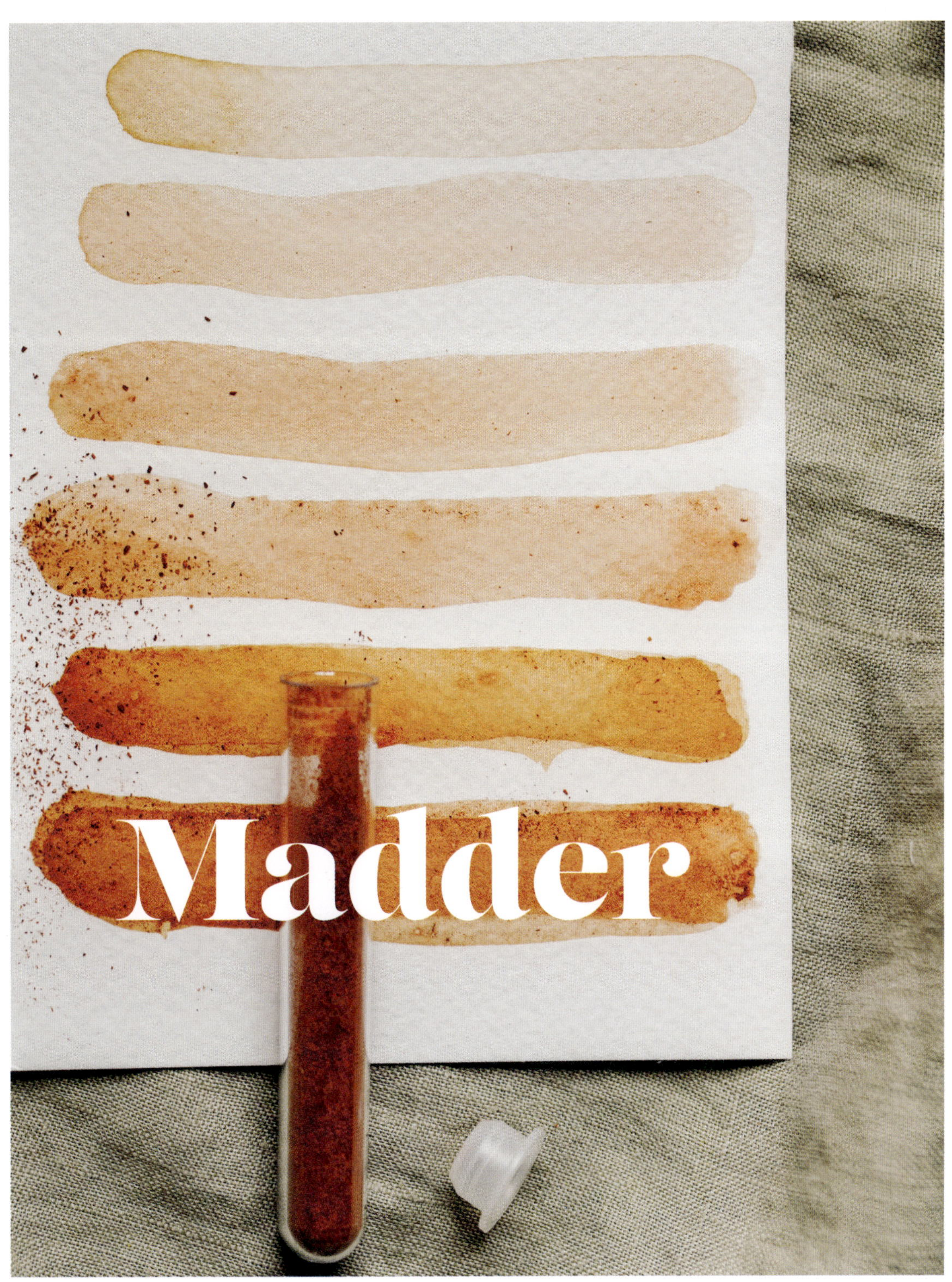
Madder

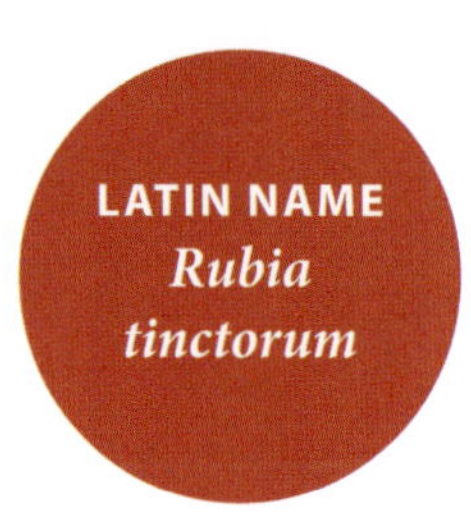

Madder

Ink from madder is lightfast ++++

The Latin word *tinctorum* means 'of dyers'. If you see this written after the name of a plant, it is a dye plant. Madder is originally from Asia, where it has been used as a dye plant since ancient times. The Egyptians also extracted dyestuff from the plant, with fabrics that had been dyed using madder even found in Tutankhamun's tomb. Madder was first seen in Europe around 1300. In around 1400, it started to be grown in France and the Netherlands. In around 1870, people discovered how to make synthetic dyes. Alizarin, the name of the red-coloured dye derived from madder, was also produced synthetically at some point, which effectively put an end to the growing of madder.

Madder is a plant that grows to heights of 60cm (23½in) and has star-shaped leaves and small yellow flowers. The dye itself is developed in the rhizomes. The plant can be harvested when it is about three years old and has developed enough dye. Once harvested, the roots should be left to dry for two years at which point, you can pulverize the roots into a powder that can be used for dyeing or painting. The red colour derived from madder is not comparable with the colour we know as red today.

Madder roots have to be left to dry for two years after harvesting before you can turn them into a powder you can dye with.

Our modern-day red is a fire-engine red, while the red derived from madder is more of an orange-red. Dried madder roots can be bought in pieces from art supply shops. You can use the pieces as they are, or you can grind them up to achieve a more intense colour.

Madder is related to bedstraw (from the genus *galium*). This little plant is found a lot more commonly in the wild than madder. Bedstraw blooms profusely with yellow or white flowers and grows quite low to the ground. Bedstraw can also be used as a dye plant, but the colour is less intense than madder and is more of a pale pink. This recipe can also be used to make ink from bedstraw. The roots can also be used fresh.

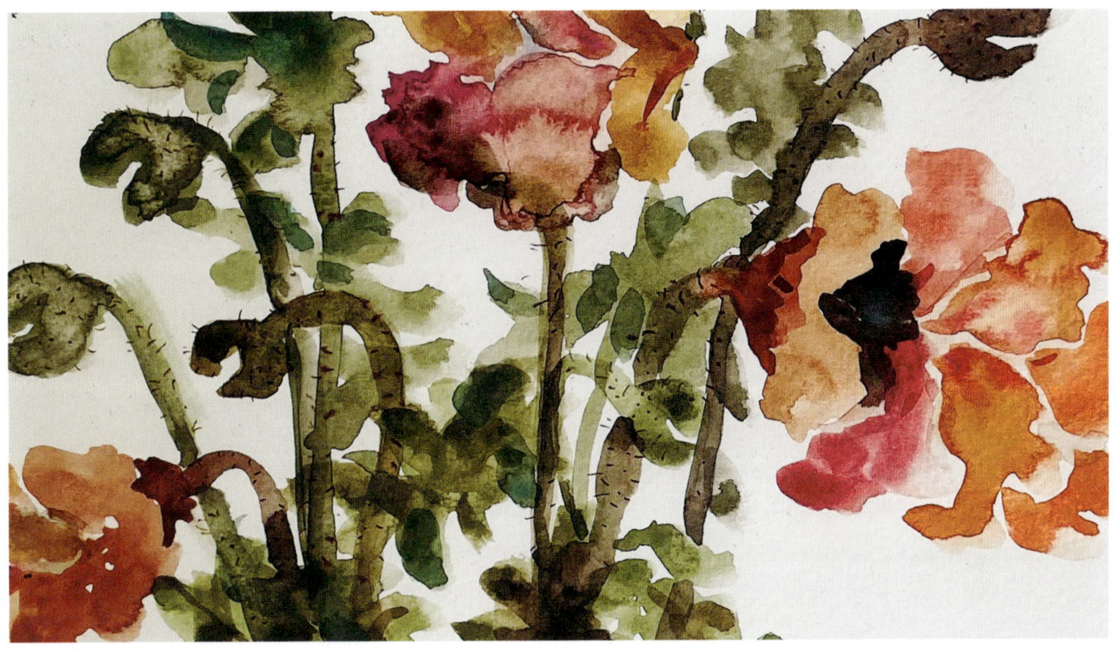

Ingredients
- 1 handful of madder root

Equipment
- old pan with lid thermometer
- sieve and bowl
- coffee filter

METHOD

1. Break the madder root into small pieces and put them in a pan.
2. Pour in just enough water to cover the madder.
3. Place the pan on the heat but turn it down as soon as the temperature reaches 70°C (160°F).
4. Place the lid on the pan and leave to steep for 1 hour.
5. Turn off the heat and then leave the pan to stand overnight with the lid on.
6. Strain the madder mixture through a sieve and collect the liquid in a bowl.
7. Rinse the pan and then pour the liquid back into it through a coffee filter.
8. Gently heat the liquid until it reaches the consistency of syrup; do not exceed 70°C (160°F).
9. Bottle the ink following the instructions on page 29.

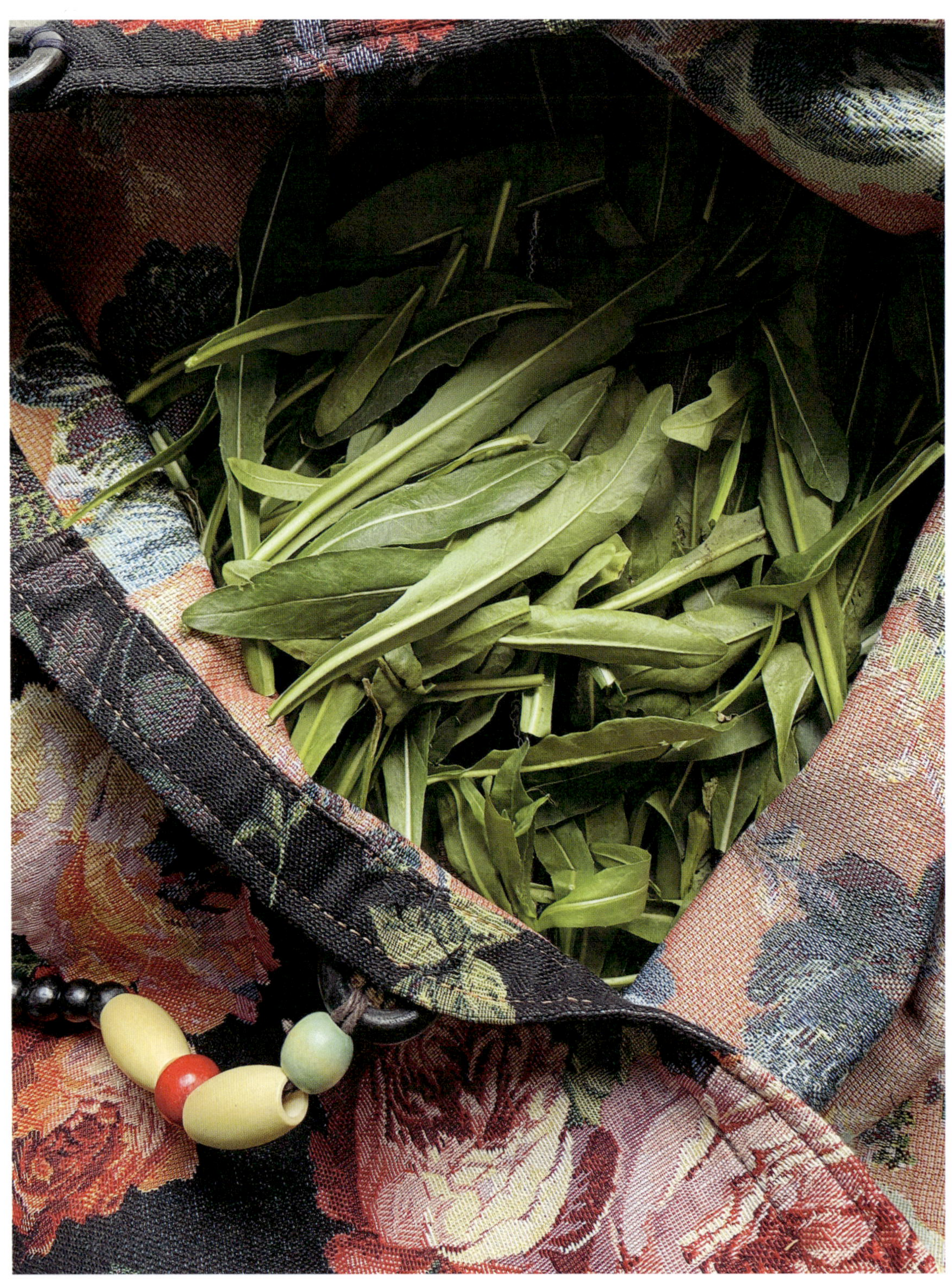

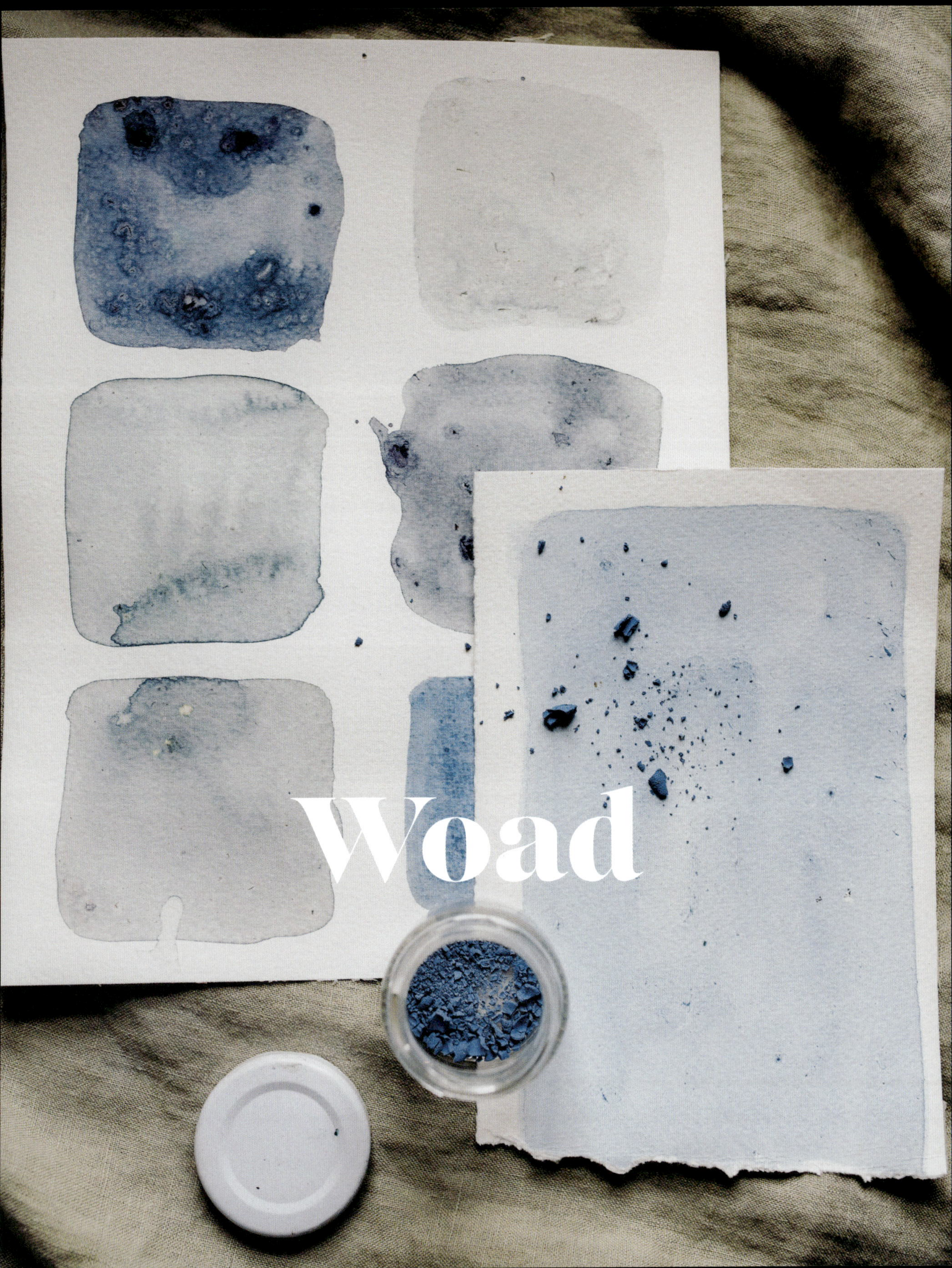

Woad

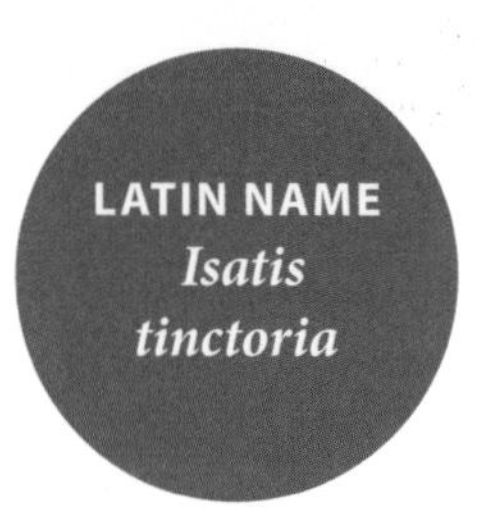

BLUE

Woad

Ink from woad is lightfast ++++

Like weld, woad has been used since prehistoric times for its dyeing properties. Initially, anything dyed by the plant will be yellow before turning blue when exposed to oxygen. Woad is a biennial plant. The leaves contain the most dye in their first year, so harvesting them during this time yields the best results. During the second year, the woad will start flowering with a cloud of yellow flowers. I think woad in flower is beautiful – it reminds me of the fine, elegant lace that my grandmother used to skilfully weave.

Until the Middle Ages, woad was used to dye textiles blue. In around 1600, the Portuguese brought back indigo with them from India. Indigo contains 30 times more dye than can be found in woad, meaning it was much cheaper to work with. In fact, woad cultivation completely collapsed faced with imports of indigo.

If you dip textiles into this yellow colour bath and then hang them up so that they are exposed to oxygen, the yellow will transform into an indelible brilliant blue.

It takes a lot of time and patience to extract blue dye from woad and the original process was a lengthy one. The leaves had to be harvested before the plant came into flower and then crushed while they were as fresh as possible. Balls were formed from the leaf pulp and laid out to dry. These dried balls could be stored for a long time, which made them useful items for trading. In fact, the trade in woad thrived until the introduction of indigo. Wool dyers processed the dry balls to make the final colour dye. As part of the process, the balls were broken into pieces and wetted with urine, which caused a fermentation process. There must have been a terrible smell! This is why dyeworks were always located on the outskirts of towns, because there were fewer neighbours to be disturbed by the stench. The leaf pulp became warm through the fermentation process but once it was cooled again, it was turned back into balls. This created a hard granular substance within the balls, and it was this substance that dyers used.

Now, if you don't need to keep woad for as long as traders in bygone years did, the process is a little simpler because you can miss out the step where you form the balls. However, you should still cook the woad leaves while they are as fresh as possible. The liquid will turn yellow. If you dip textiles into this yellow colour bath and then hang them up so that they are exposed to oxygen, the yellow will transform into an indelible brilliant blue. You can introduce oxygen to the yellow dye bath by using an electric whisk; as you do so, you will see the water turning green-blue in colour. If you then leave the water to evaporate, you will be left with a blue pigment. The recipe below gives step-by-step instructions on how to obtain the blue pigment and make paint.

Ingredients
- 2 handfuls of freshly picked woad leaves
- washing soda (optional)

Equipment
- old pan with lid
- hand-held blender
- container to fit the pan
- sieve and bowl
- coffee filter
- litmus paper
- electric whisk
- flat plastic container
- pestle and mortar

METHOD

1. Tear the woad leaves into small pieces and put them in a pan.
2. Pour in just enough water to cover the woad.
3. Using the hand-held blender, puree the woad until it turns into pulp.
4. Put the pan on the heat and simmer it gently for 15 minutes.
5. Turn off the heat and quickly chill the liquid by placing it in a bowl of cold water.
6. Strain the woad mixture through a sieve, collecting the liquid in a bowl.
7. Rinse the pan and then pour the liquid back into it through a coffee filter. It will be yellow-brown in colour.
8. Use litmus paper to check whether the pH level has reached 9; if necessary, use washing soda to increase the level.
9. Put an electric whisk in the liquid and mix it to introduce lots of oxygen. The water will now turn a teal colour with a blue foam.
10. Make it into a lake pigment (see page 138) or pour the liquid into a flat plastic container and leave it until all the water has evaporated. This could take a number of weeks. At the end of this, you will find you have blue pigment on the bottom of the container.
11. Grind this pigment in the mortar; this is the pigment you will use to make the paint.
12. Take a look at the oil paint recipes on page 149.

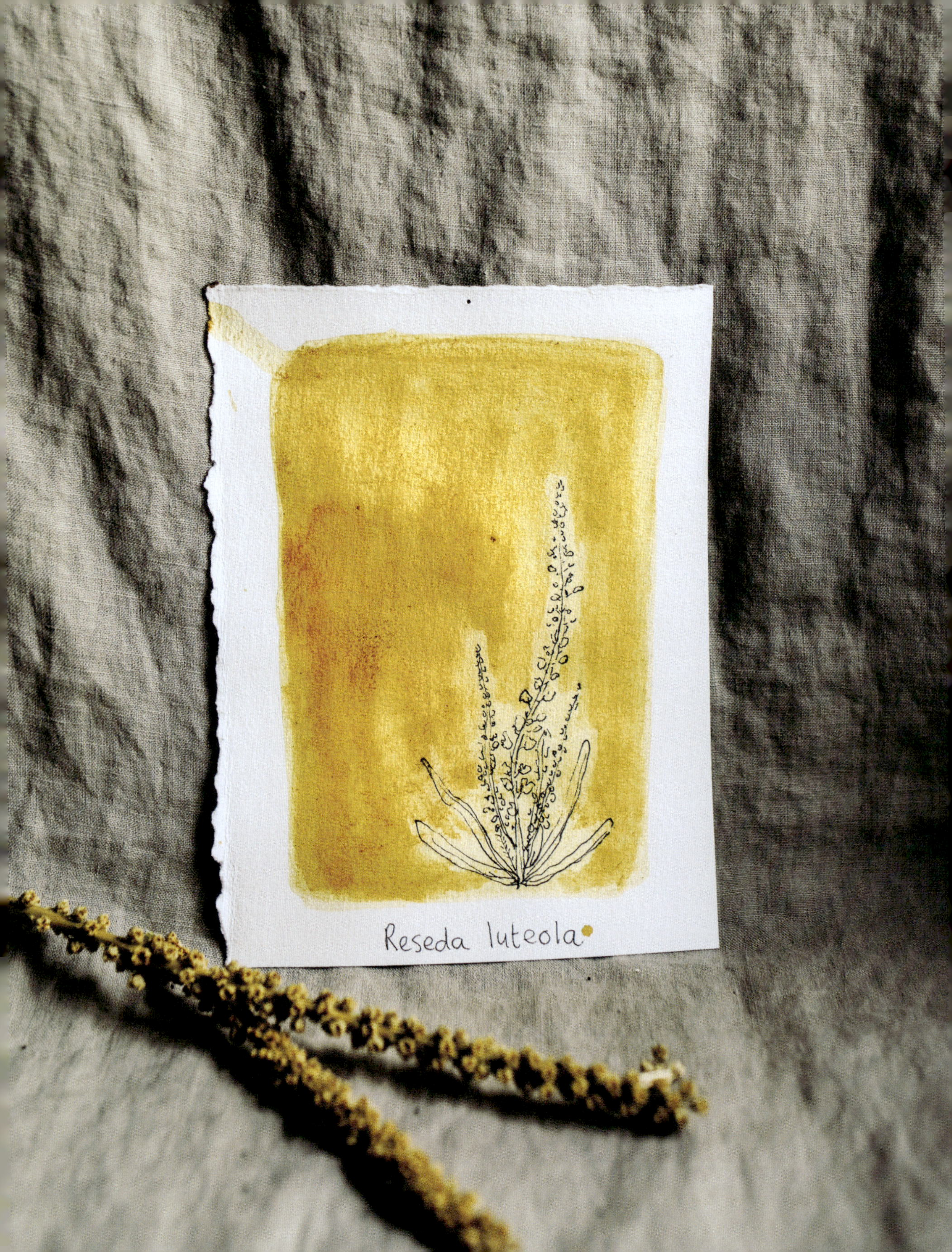

Reseda luteola

Weld

Ink from weld is lightfast +++

Weld is also known as 'dyer's rocket'. Lots of countries call weld by a name that makes reference to its dye heritage. Weld has been used as a dye plant since ancient times. In fact, the Romans gave it the name *luteola*, meaning 'yellow' because they knew that the plant could be used to dye items yellow. The paint or dye it creates is a lovely, sunny yellow colour. The plant thrives in dry, poor, sandy soil.

Weld forms a rosette of leaves on the ground, out of which a thick, erect stem grows upwards, reaching heights of up to 1m (3ft). A number of side shoots and green leaves form on the stem. The pale chartreuse-coloured flowers form clusters and bloom from June through to September along the entire length of the stem. Weld contains a high concentration of the dye luteolin, which provides the yellow colour. Luteolin is found in all parts of the plant, but mainly in the buds and seeds.

Ingredients
- 2 handfuls of weld (leaf, stem, flowers and seed)
- ½tsp washing soda (optional)

Equipment
- old pan with lid
- sieve and bowl
- coffee filter

METHOD

1. Cut the weld into very small pieces and put them in a pan.
2. Pour in just enough water to cover the weld.
3. Place the pan on the heat but turn it down as soon as the water has almost reached boiling point. Make sure it doesn't boil.
4. Place the lid on the pan and leave to steep for 3 hours.
5. Turn off the heat and then leave the pan to stand overnight with the lid on.
6. Strain the weld mixture through a sieve and collect the liquid in a bowl.
7. Rinse the pan and then pour the liquid back into it through a coffee filter.
8. Gently heat the liquid until it reaches the consistency of syrup; do not allow it to boil.
9. Add washing soda to create an extra-sunny colour.
10. Bottle the ink following the instructions on page 29.

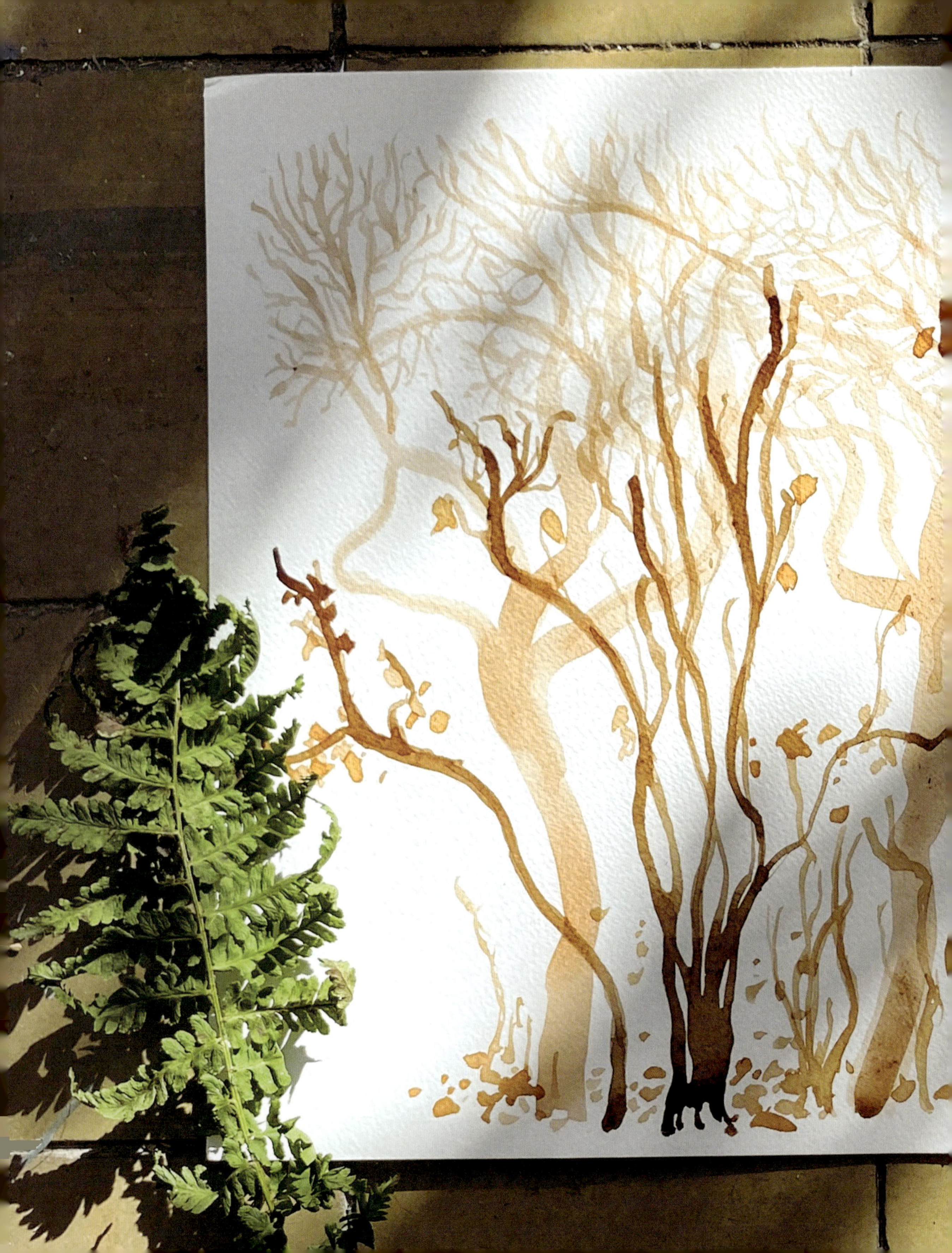

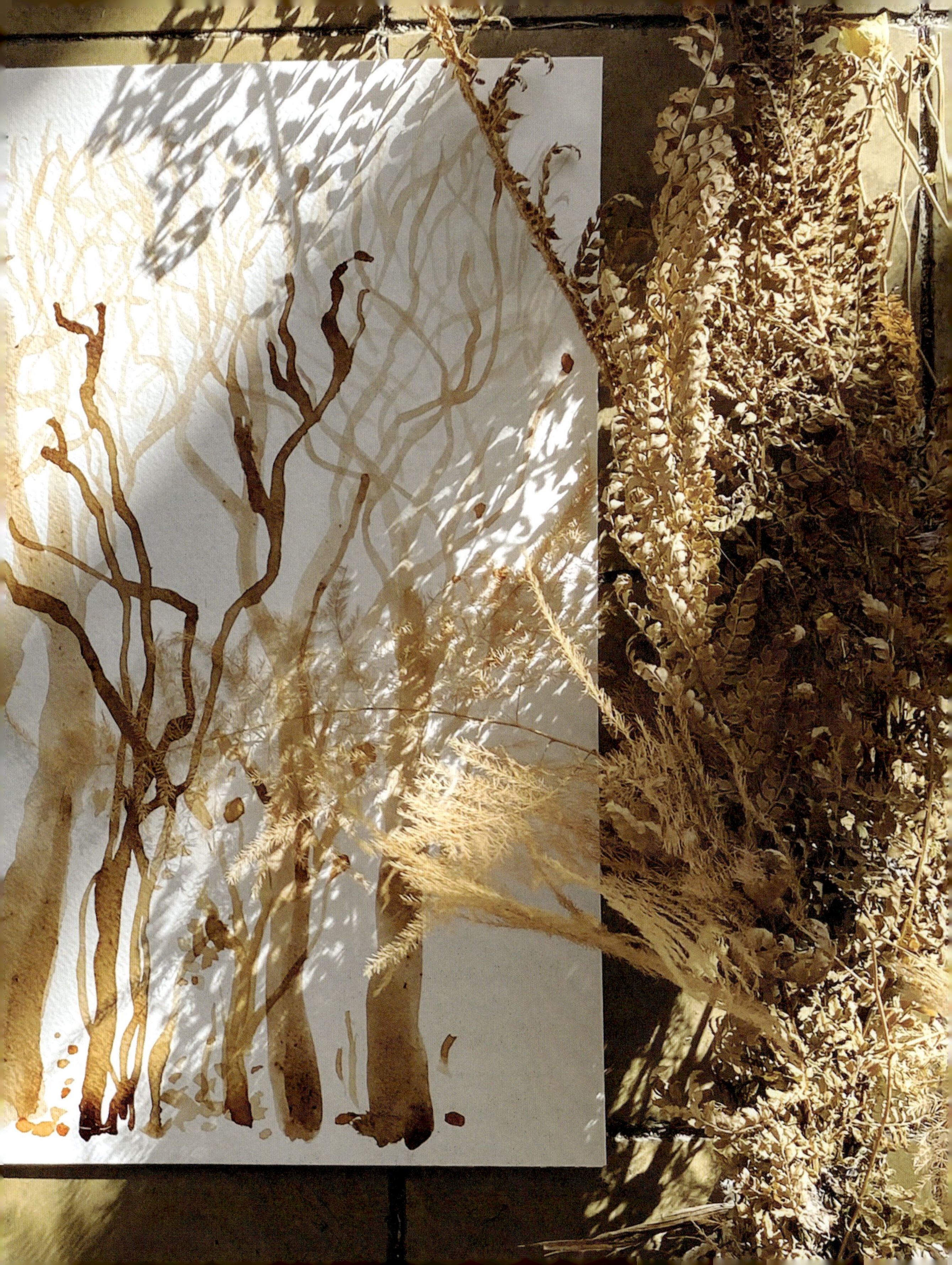

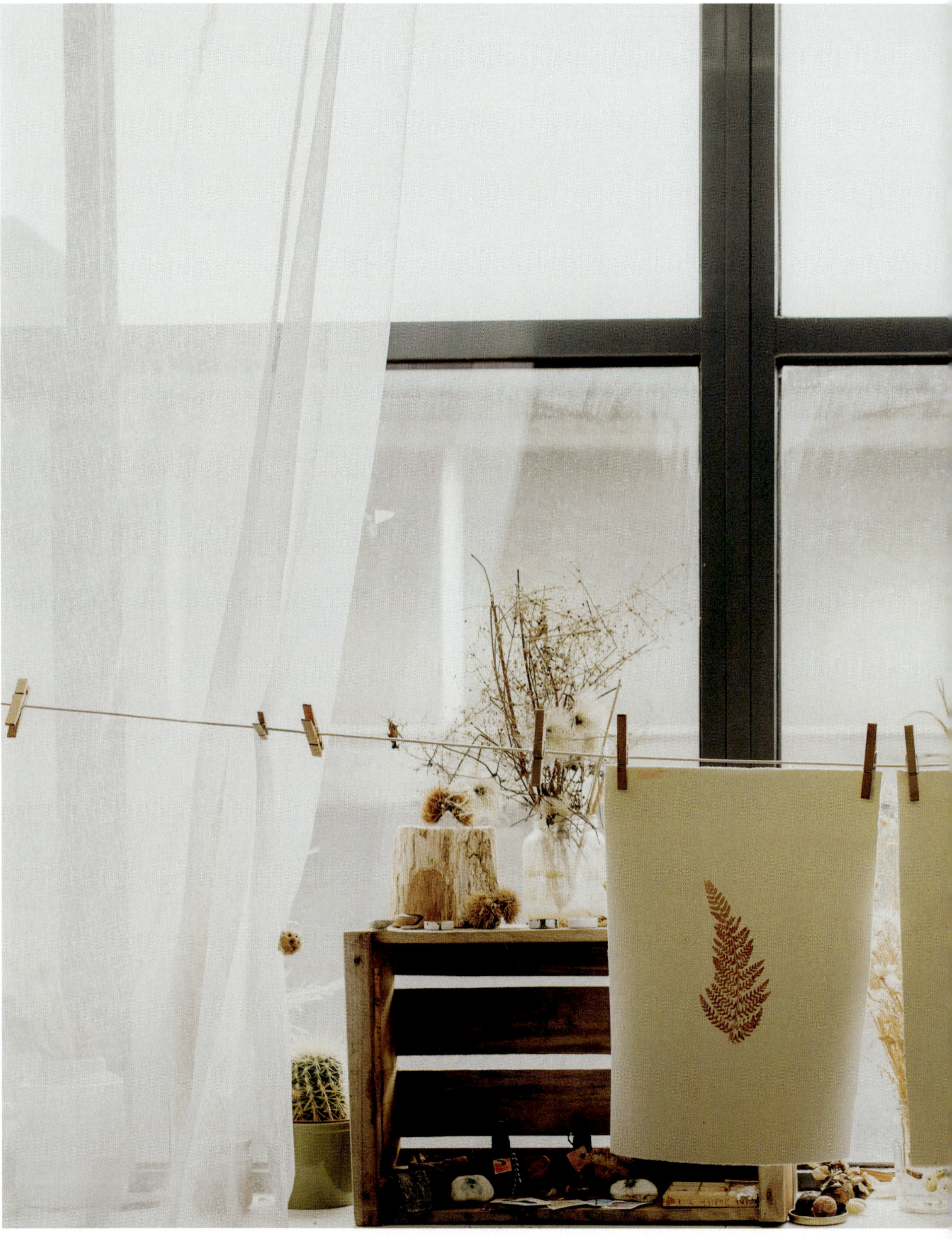

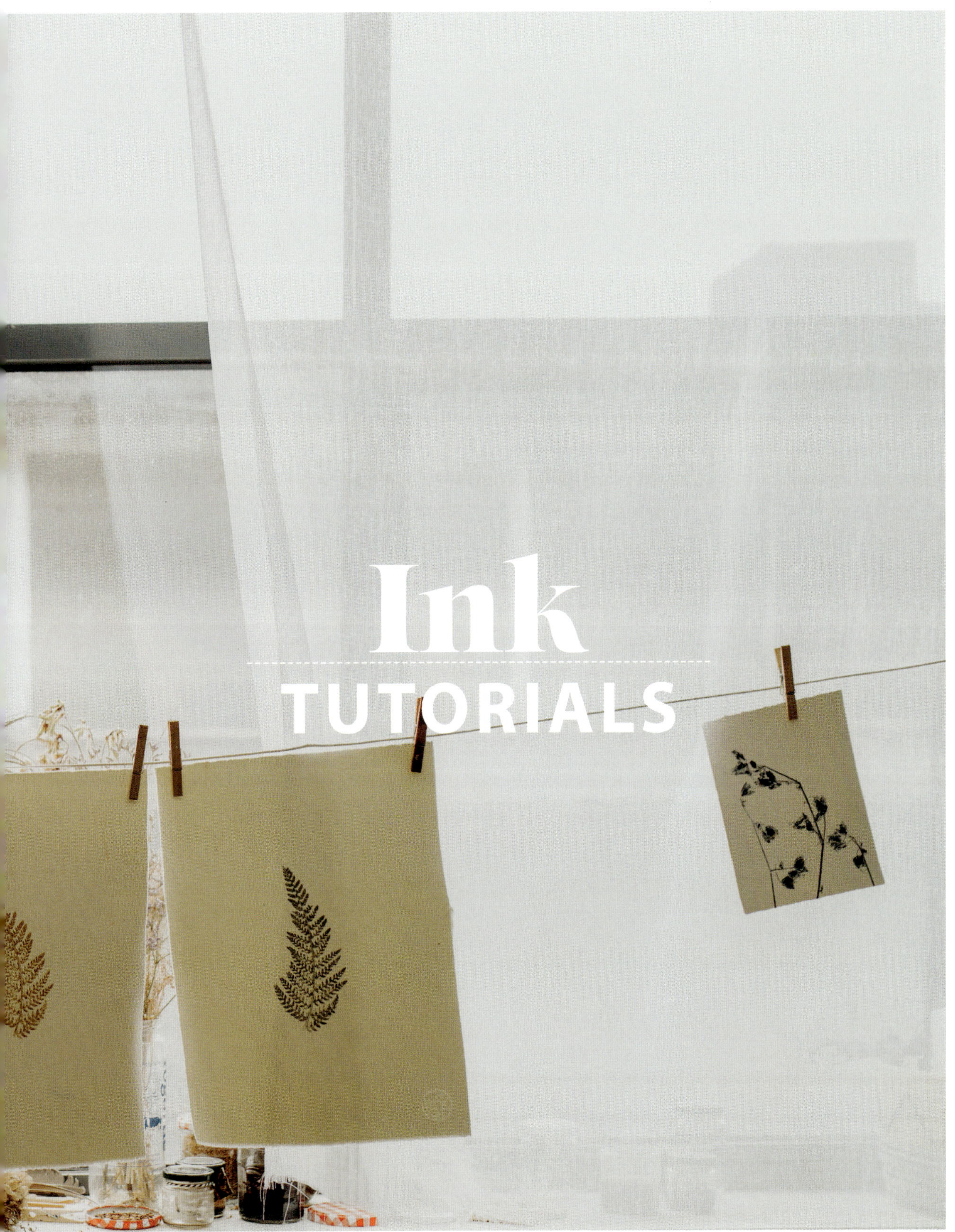

Ink
TUTORIALS

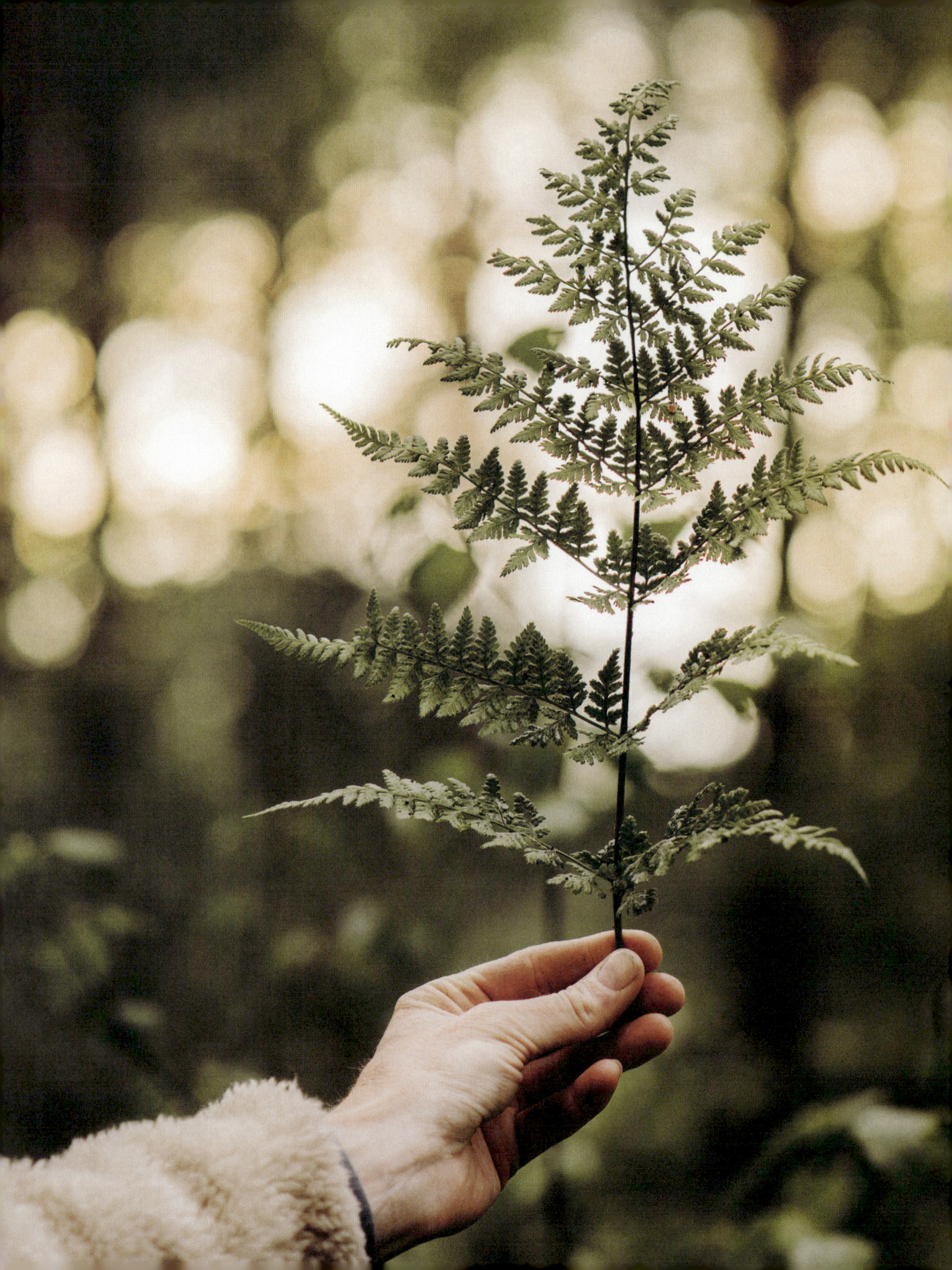

Spring

- BRACKEN
- COW PARSLEY
- GALLNUTS
- DAFFODIL
- TULIP
- BLACK HOLLYHOCK

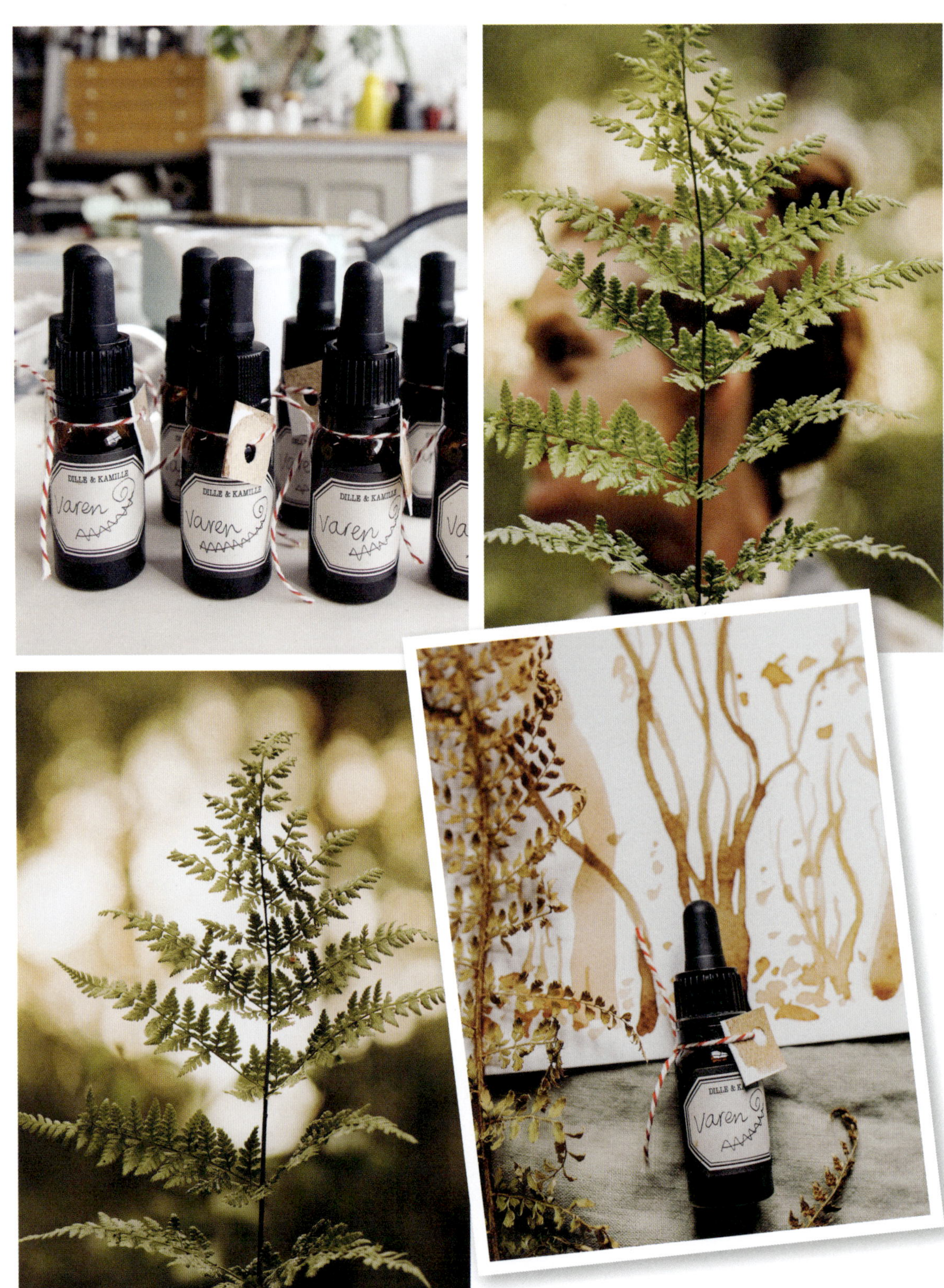

PALE PINK

Bracken

Ink from bracken is lightfast +++

Ferns are prehistoric plants. They have been growing on Earth for a very long time and in large numbers. They can be found throughout the world but prefer to grow in humid areas such as tropical rainforests. In fact, ferns love moisture. In the UK, there are 53 species of fern, of which the imposing bracken (or eagle fern) is both the largest and the most aggressive. It can spread over large areas and quickly propagates through a network of underground creeping rhizomes. The plant can grow up to 3m (10ft) tall. Because bracken spreads and takes up so much space, it also prevents a lot of other plants from accessing the sunlight in summer – a piece of jungle in the woods. The plant dies off in autumn. It decays at a very slow speed, leaving behind a nutrient-poor and – because of its toxicity – poisonous area of soil. Young saplings often fall victim to this poison, and cannot germinate easily in that area. In spring, the plant sprouts up again from the rhizome. Long leaves begin to appear above the ground like the scroll of a violin. Bracken can be found in deciduous and coniferous woods, heathland and on the edges of woods. The most beautiful ink is made using young shoots of bracken. Use the leaves while they are fresh.

Ingredients
- 2 handfuls of bracken leaves
- 1 pinch of potash (optional)

Equipment
- old pan with lid
- sieve and bowl
- coffee filter

METHOD

1. Cut the bracken leaves into very small pieces and put them in a pan.
2. Pour in just enough water to cover the leaves.
3. Place the pan on the heat but turn it down as soon as the water has almost reached boiling point. Make sure it doesn't boil.
4. Place the lid on the pan and leave to steep for 1 hour.
5. Turn off the heat and then leave the pan to stand overnight with the lid on.
6. Strain the bracken mixture through a sieve and collect the liquid in a bowl.
7. Rinse the pan and then pour the liquid back into it through a coffee filter.
8. Gently heat the liquid until it reaches the consistency of syrup; do not allow it to boil. It will be pale pink in colour.
9. Add potash as required to turn the colour brownish-pink.
10. Bottle the ink following the instructions on page 29.

LATIN NAME
Anthriscus sylvestris

YELLOW-GREEN

Cow parsley

Ink from cow parsley is lightfast +++

Cow parsley is found in abundance in the UK, growing plentifully on roadsides, along banks and at the edges of woods. It is an umbellifer, blooming with umbels full of small white flowers between the months of April and June. The stems are hollow and striated. It can be easily identified, with plants reaching up to 1.5m (5ft) in height. With the arrival of those first warmer days in April, cow parsley begins to sprout from the ground. Where previously only grass grew, bunches of cow parsley can suddenly be seen swaying in the wind. It is a sight that always makes me happy! Huge bunches of light green feathered leaves are the perfect complement to the creamy-white clouds of flowers above them.

Cow parsley is edible. Unfortunately, there are a few plants that look the same as cow parsley but that are poisonous, so you have to be certain that you have identified the correct plant. One lookalike is water hemlock, also known as cowbane. Cowbane has a toxic yellow sap, while cow parsley has white sap. Another lookalike is poison hemlock. This can be recognized by its foul smell and the purple spots on the stem. Cow parsley, on the other hand, smells pleasant and herbal.

Ingredients
- 2 handfuls of fresh cow parsley leaves
- 1 pinch of potash (optional)

Equipment
- old pan with lid
- sieve and bowl
- coffee filter

METHOD

1. Cut the cow parsley leaves into very small pieces and put them in a pan.
2. Pour in just enough water to cover the leaves.
3. Place the pan on the heat but turn it down as soon as the water has almost reached boiling point. Make sure it doesn't boil.
4. Place the lid on the pan and leave to steep for 3 hours.
5. Turn off the heat and then leave the pan to stand overnight with the lid on.
6. Strain the cow parsley mixture through a sieve and collect the liquid in a bowl.
7. Rinse the pan and then pour the liquid back into it through a coffee filter.
8. Gently heat the liquid until it reaches the consistency of syrup; it is very important that you do not allow it to boil. It will be yellow-green in colour.
9. Add potash as required to make the colour greener.
10. Bottle the ink following the instructions on page 29.

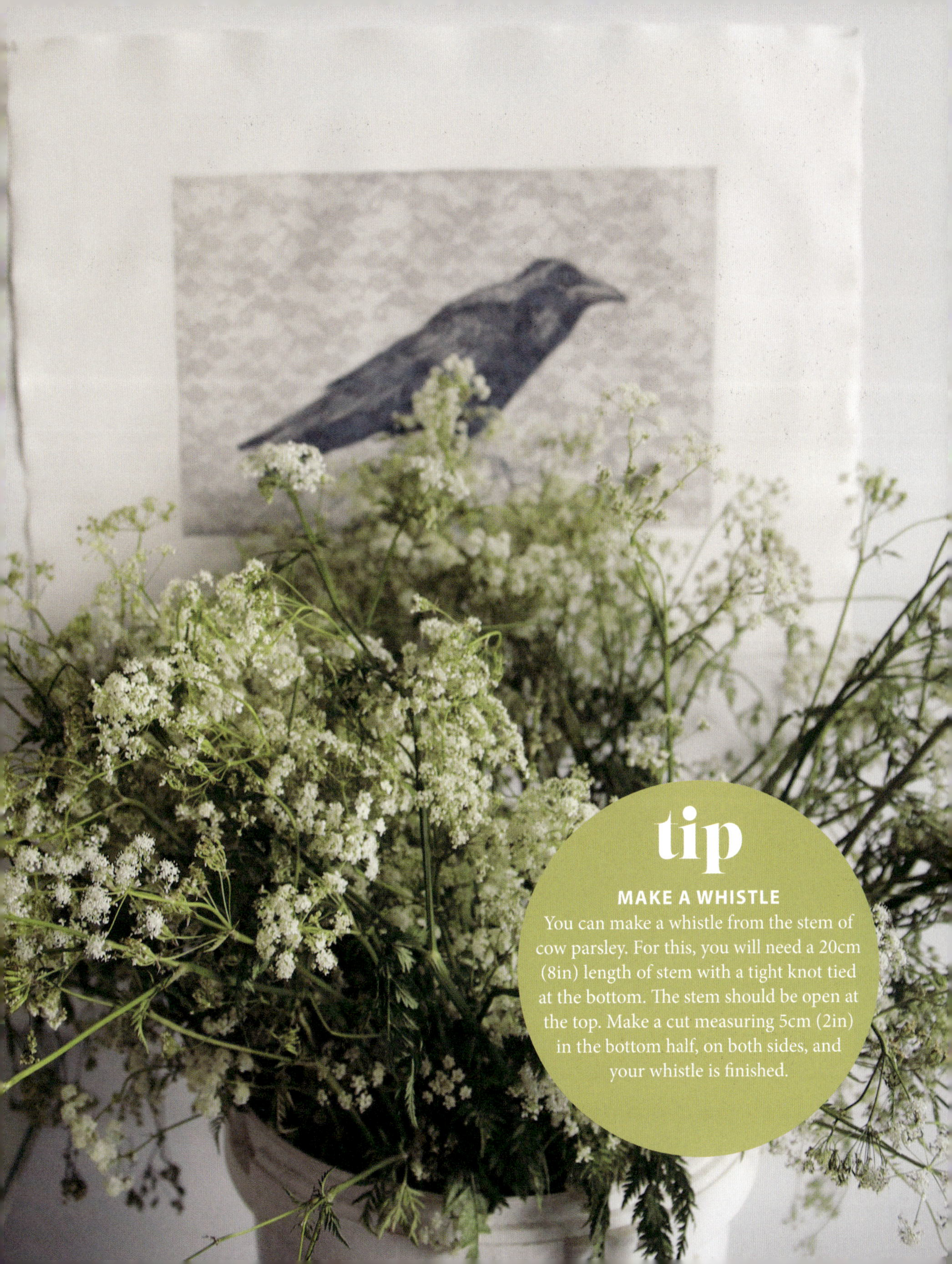

tip

MAKE A WHISTLE

You can make a whistle from the stem of cow parsley. For this, you will need a 20cm (8in) length of stem with a tight knot tied at the bottom. The stem should be open at the top. Make a cut measuring 5cm (2in) in the bottom half, on both sides, and your whistle is finished.

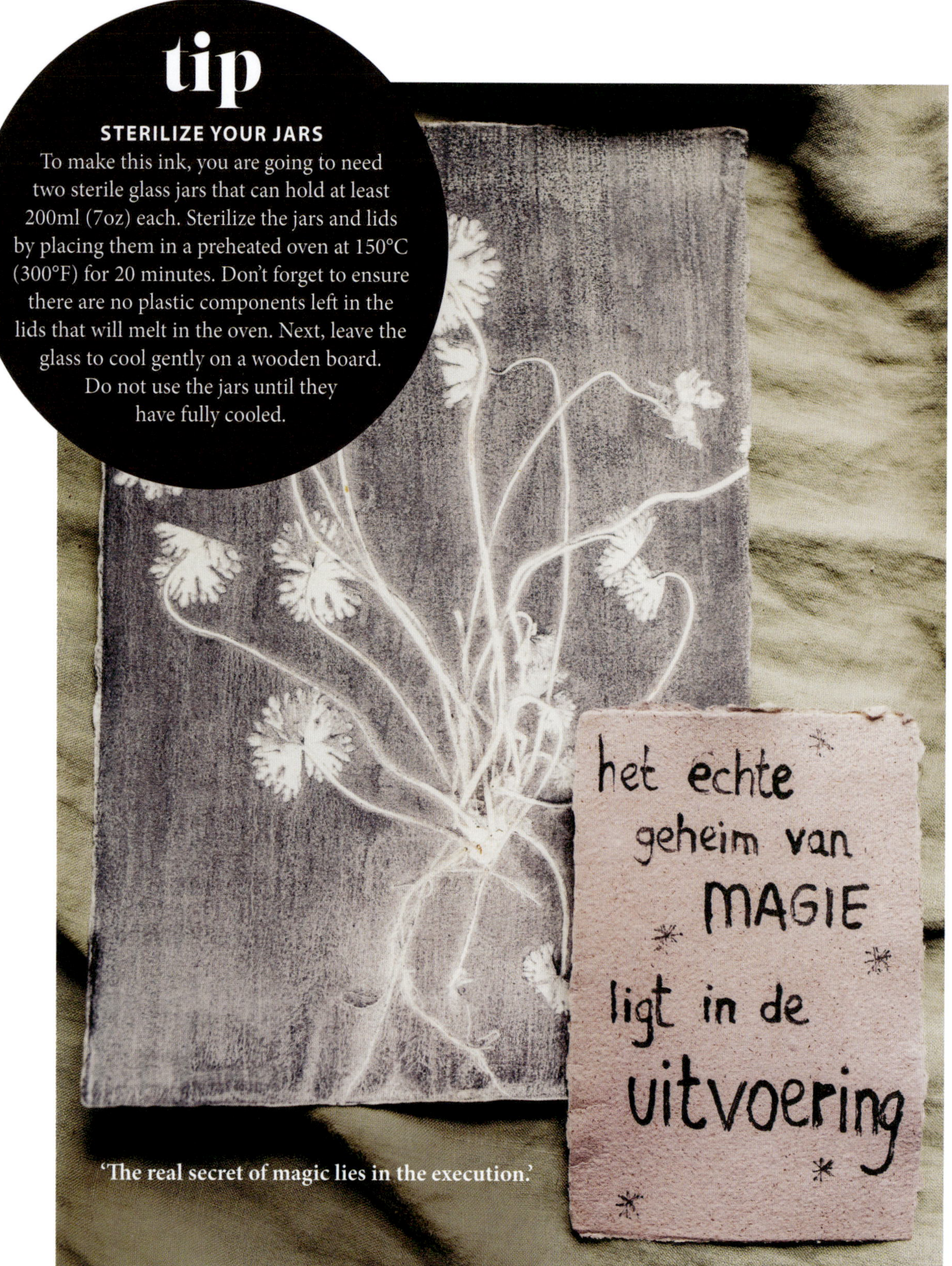

tip

STERILIZE YOUR JARS

To make this ink, you are going to need two sterile glass jars that can hold at least 200ml (7oz) each. Sterilize the jars and lids by placing them in a preheated oven at 150°C (300°F) for 20 minutes. Don't forget to ensure there are no plastic components left in the lids that will melt in the oven. Next, leave the glass to cool gently on a wooden board. Do not use the jars until they have fully cooled.

'The real secret of magic lies in the execution.'

Gallnuts

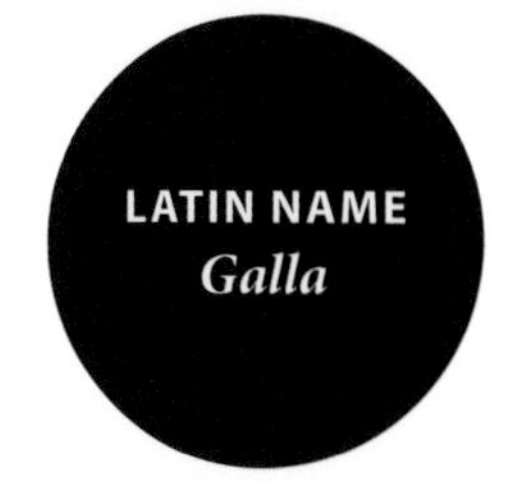

Ink from gallnuts is lightfast ++++

Gallnuts, oak apples and Aleppo oak galls are all names for the same thing. Found in the axils of oak branches, gallnuts grow to 10–20mm (⅜–¾in) in size, are round in shape and have a thick skin. In the summer they are green, before turning brown later in the year. A gall wasp lays eggs in the axils of an oak tree. Because the tree wants to protect itself, it responds by making a gall, inside of which can be found the larva of the gall wasp. In early September, the larva creates a spherical hole through which it crawls out. The gallnut, however, remains attached to the tree. It can be pulled directly off the branch, but it's important to first check whether there is a hole in it. If so, the wasp has flown and the gallnut is ready for use. Gallnuts can also be bought in art supply shops or shops where materials to dye wool are sold.

The beautiful black ink that you can make from gallnuts does have one unfortunate side effect: ink corrosion. Over the years, a combination of moisture, acid and iron will literally burn holes in the paper upon which the ink has been used to write. Fortunately, the inking process takes decades, but do make sure you use good quality, strong paper.

Ingredients
- 7 gallnuts
- ½tsp iron sulphate

Equipment
- tea towel
- hammer
- pestle and mortar or coffee grinder
- coffee filter and two glass jars

METHOD

1. Wrap the gallnuts in a tea towel and smash them into pieces using the hammer.
2. Place the pieces of gallnut in a mortar and grind them (or use a coffee grinder).
3. Put the ground-up gallnuts in a glass jar and pour 150ml (5¼oz) of cold water over them.
4. Put the lid on and leave the jar to stand overnight.
5. Pour the liquefied gallnuts through a coffee filter into a second jar. The liquid should be beige in colour.
6. Grind the iron sulphate to powder in the mortar.
7. Add this powder to the beige liquid and stir it in well.
8. Try the ink on watercolour paper. It will be dark brown to red in colour at first but will slowly darken to an intense black.
9. Bottle the ink following the instructions on page 29.

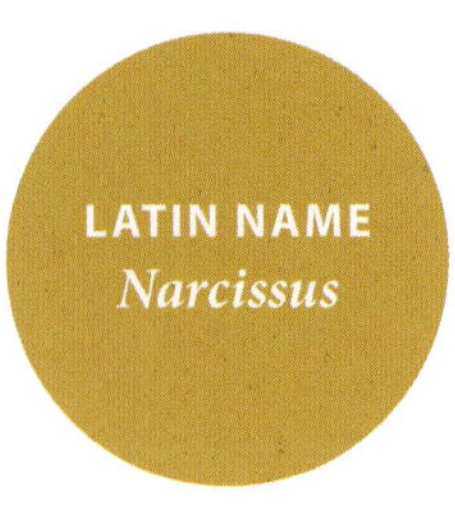

Daffodil

Ink from daffodils is lightfast +++

Narcissus means 'sleep' in Latin, but the daffodil actually heralds the start of spring. These days, daffodils come in all kinds of colours, but the most beautiful ink is made using the bright yellow flowers. Daffodils are really easy to grow in your garden: just leave the bulbs in the ground and more and more daffodils will start to appear. Make sure you plant them in autumn, before the start of overnight frosts. Daffodils don't like waterlogged soils, so don't plant them in clay. It's a good idea to place a handful of sand into the hole before your bulb, as this will allow the water to drain more easily. Daffodils can be poisonous to snails, pets and humans. It's possible to make a warm yellow ink from daffodils in the mortar. Follow the same method as described for sage ink on page 105.

Ingredients
- 2 handfuls of daffodil flowers
- ¼tsp baking soda

Equipment
- newspaper or baking paper
- old pan with lid
- sieve and bowl
- coffee filter

METHOD

1. Place the daffodil flowers on the newspaper to air dry them. This will take a few days. It is also possible to dry them in the oven, which is quicker. Preheat the oven to 50°C (120°F). Place the flowers separated from each other on a sheet of baking paper. Dry them in the oven for 30 minutes. You need to monitor this stage and carefully check the flowers to avoid them burning.

2. Tear the dry daffodils into small pieces and put them in a pan.

3. Pour in just enough water to cover the daffodils.

4. Place the pan on the heat but turn it down as soon as the water has almost reached boiling point. Make sure it doesn't boil.

5. Place the lid on the pan and leave to steep for 1 hour. The liquid will turn a very pale yellow colour.

6. Strain the daffodil mixture through a sieve and collect the liquid in a bowl.

7. Rinse the pan and then pour the liquid back into it through a coffee filter.

8. Gently heat the liquid until it reaches the consistency of syrup; it is very important that you do not allow it to boil.

9. Add the baking soda. The colour then turns an intense, warm yellow.

10. Bottle the ink following the instructions on page 29.

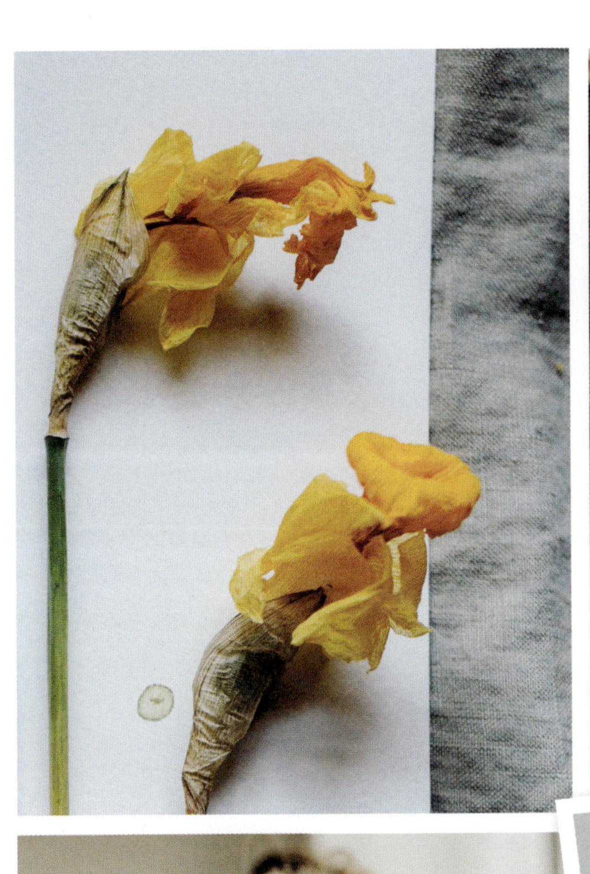

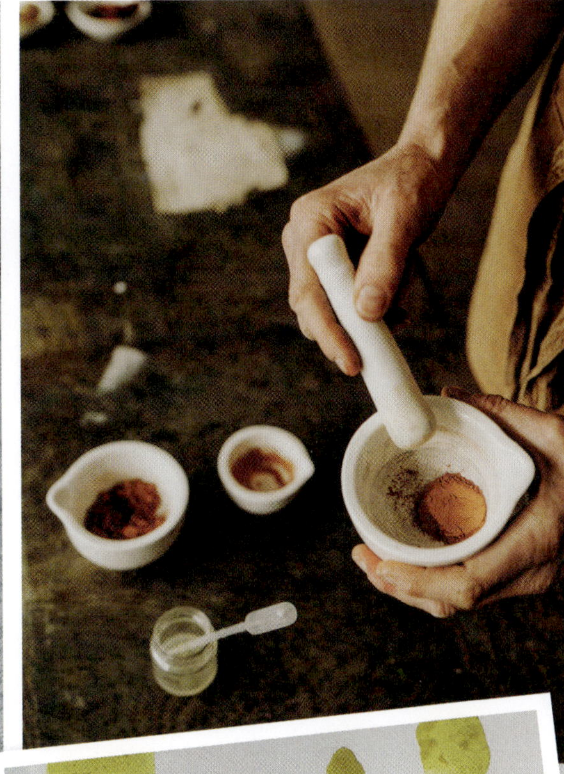

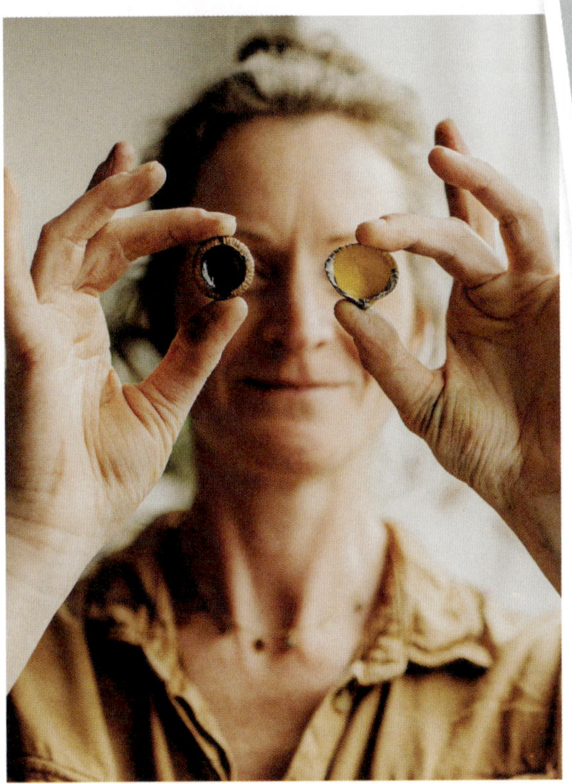

tip

LIKE A SPONGE

You might need to add some extra water after step 4 because dry daffodils tend to soak up the water like a sponge. Check the pan regularly.

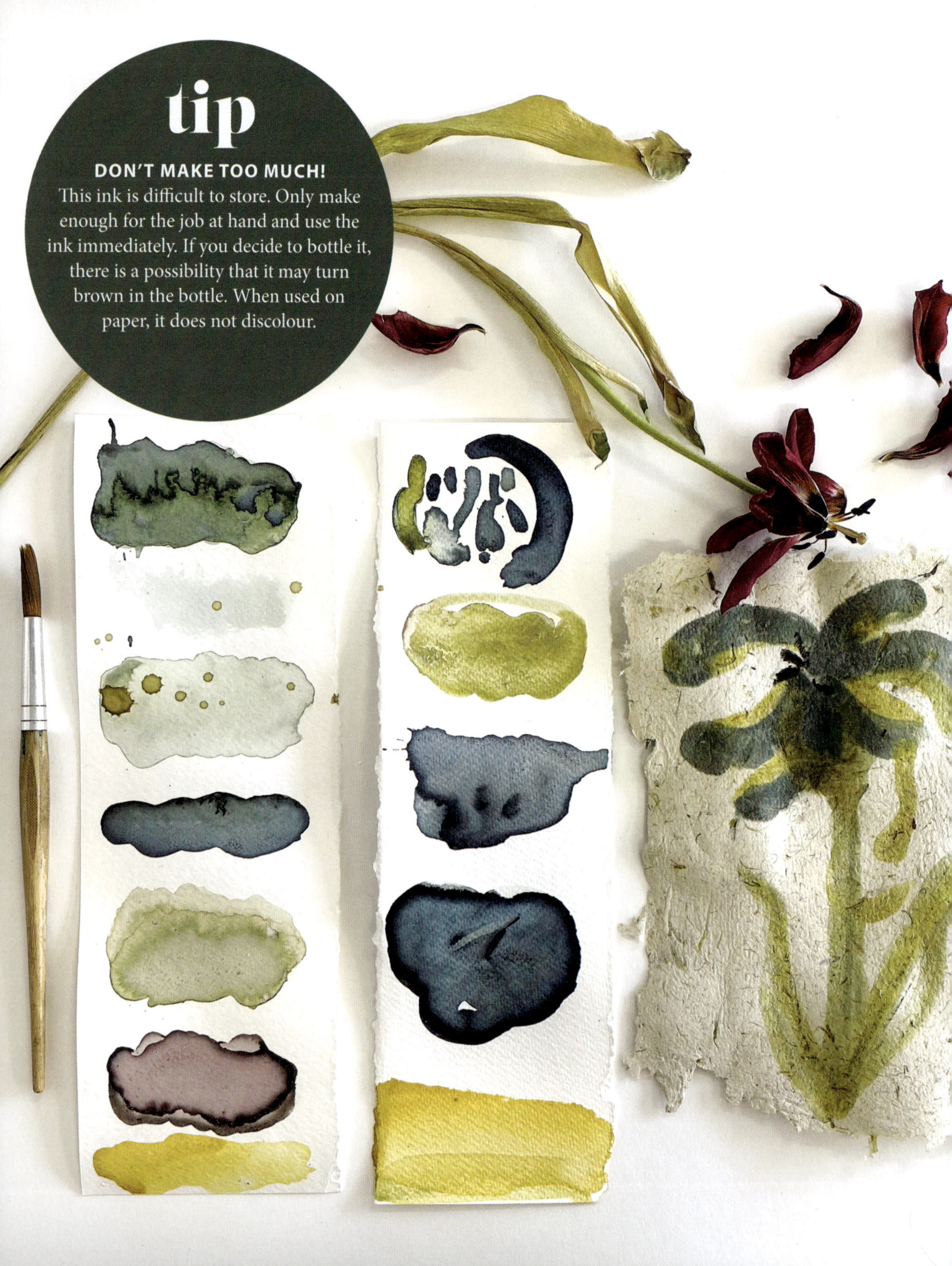

tip
DON'T MAKE TOO MUCH!
This ink is difficult to store. Only make enough for the job at hand and use the ink immediately. If you decide to bottle it, there is a possibility that it may turn brown in the bottle. When used on paper, it does not discolour.

Tulip

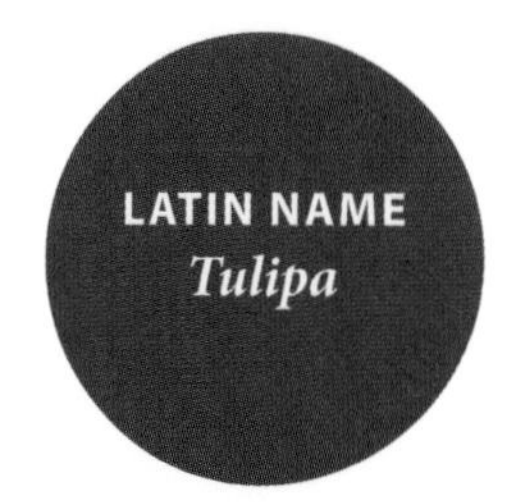

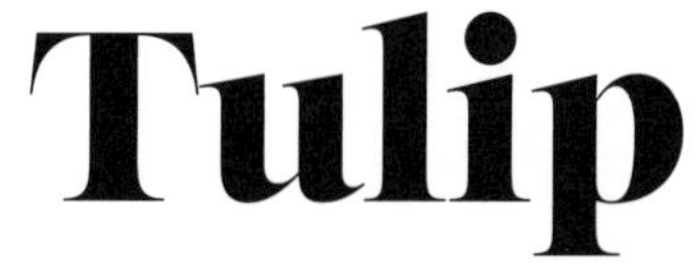

Ink from tulip stamens is lightfast ++

Tulips are native to Kazakhstan in Central Asia, where they suit the cold winters, a long spring season full of cold nights and the dry summers. Tulips need cold weather to grow. In approximately 1500, tulips were introduced to Turkey where the sultan was particularly impressed by the flower, requesting that it be planted in his garden. The tulips attracted lots of visitors and were symbols of wealth and power. Each year when the tulips were in bloom, the sultan would throw a party. To demonstrate his wealth, he wore tulips on his turban. The name 'tulip' is derived from the Persian word *tulipan*, which means turban: this is because of the similarity in shape between a tulip and a turban.

My favourite tulip is definitely the *Tulipa undulatifolia*. It is a large, red tulip with a black heart outlined in yellow and stamens that are purple-black in colour. It really is a garden gem. When the tulips have finished flowering, the leaves will fall off on their own; you can then cut off the bud and harvest the stamen to be used for ink. You can also make ink from the tulip petals by following the recipe for poppies (see page 83). The stem and leaf are left to sit and shrivel up. This is how the tulip stores energy for the following year. By leaving the bulbs in the ground, you will be encouraging a natural, wild garden. The insects will enjoy it too!

Ingredients
- 2½tbsp fresh black tulip stamens
- 1 pinch of washing soda (optional)
- gum arabic

Equipment
- pestle and mortar
- coffee filter
- bowl

METHOD

1. Place the stamens in a mortar.
2. Pour in just enough hot water to cover the stamens. You won't need very much water at all. The water should be just off the boil.
3. Using the pestle, finely grind the stamens. The water will immediately change colour.
4. Keep grinding until the water stops getting any darker. This takes about 1 minute.
5. Pour the stamen mixture through a coffee filter and collect the liquid in a bowl. It will be blue-black in colour.
6. For a moss green colour, add washing soda.
7. Add 5 drops of gum arabic to every 30ml (1oz) of liquid; your ink is then ready to use.

LATIN NAME
Alcea rosea

Black hollyhock

Ink from hollyhocks is lightfast +++ Ink from mallow is lightfast ++

The hollyhock is a member of the malva, or mallow family. Hollyhock is a biennial plant. In the first year, the plant only forms leaves and remains quite small in size. The following year, however, the stem can grow several metres high. The flower buds emerge from the bottom and open one by one. The flower blooms for a few days, then closes and falls to the ground. While in flower, hollyhocks attract lots of insects, especially bumblebees. Hollyhocks come in all sorts of colours: from pale yellow to deep red and from pale pink to black-purple. If you put the different coloured varieties together, you might well get a lovely surprise when a different colour grows the following year. It's almost as if the hollyhocks mingle together to generate a new palette of colours in your garden.

In the past, dark-coloured hollyhocks were used to add colouring to wine and other foods.

Most hollyhocks grow best in poor clay soil but the dark varieties, which in my opinion create the most beautiful ink, grow best in sandy soil. The plants don't have many requirements when it comes to soil, but they do need lots of sunshine. They prefer being in a sheltered spot close to a wall or fence. Alternatively, you could think about digging out a little space around the pavement in front of your house and use it to sow some hollyhock seeds there. That would make a lovely little garden at the front of the house. Dark hollyhocks contain a large quantity of anthocyanin, a dye that was formerly used to add colour to wine and other foods. Because the darker varieties contain a larger amount of this dye, you can use it to make a coloured ink that is intense in colour.

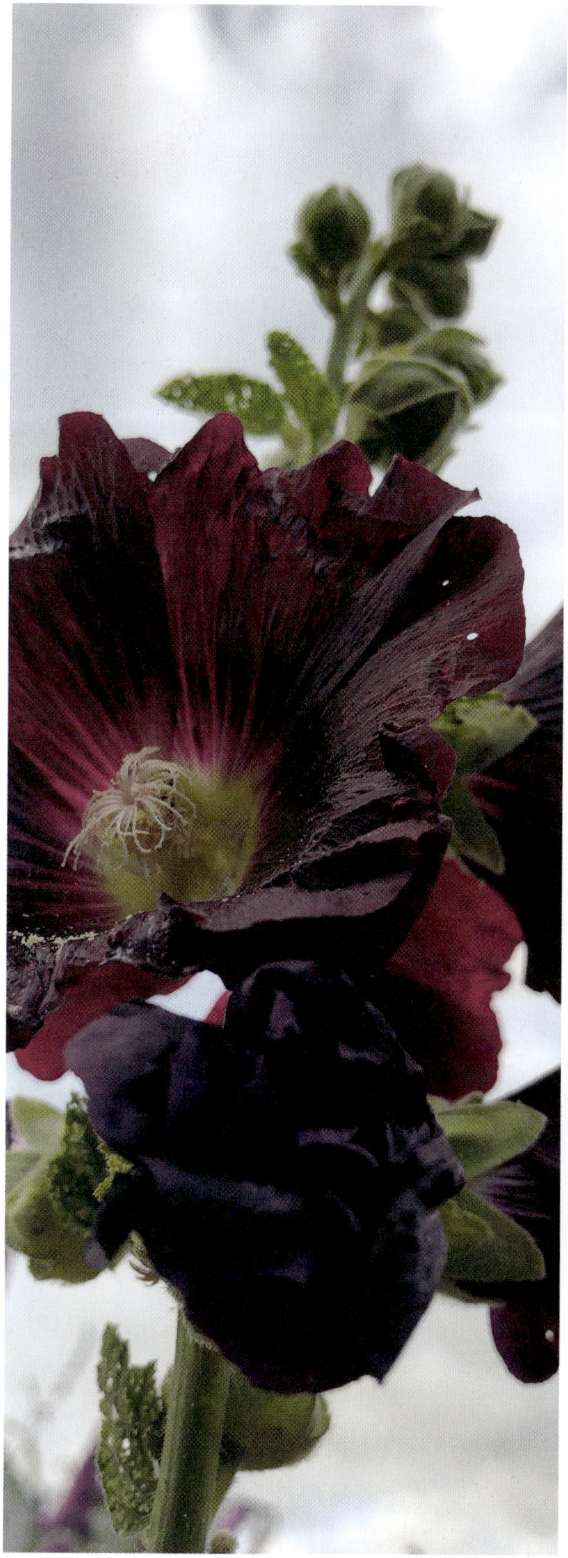

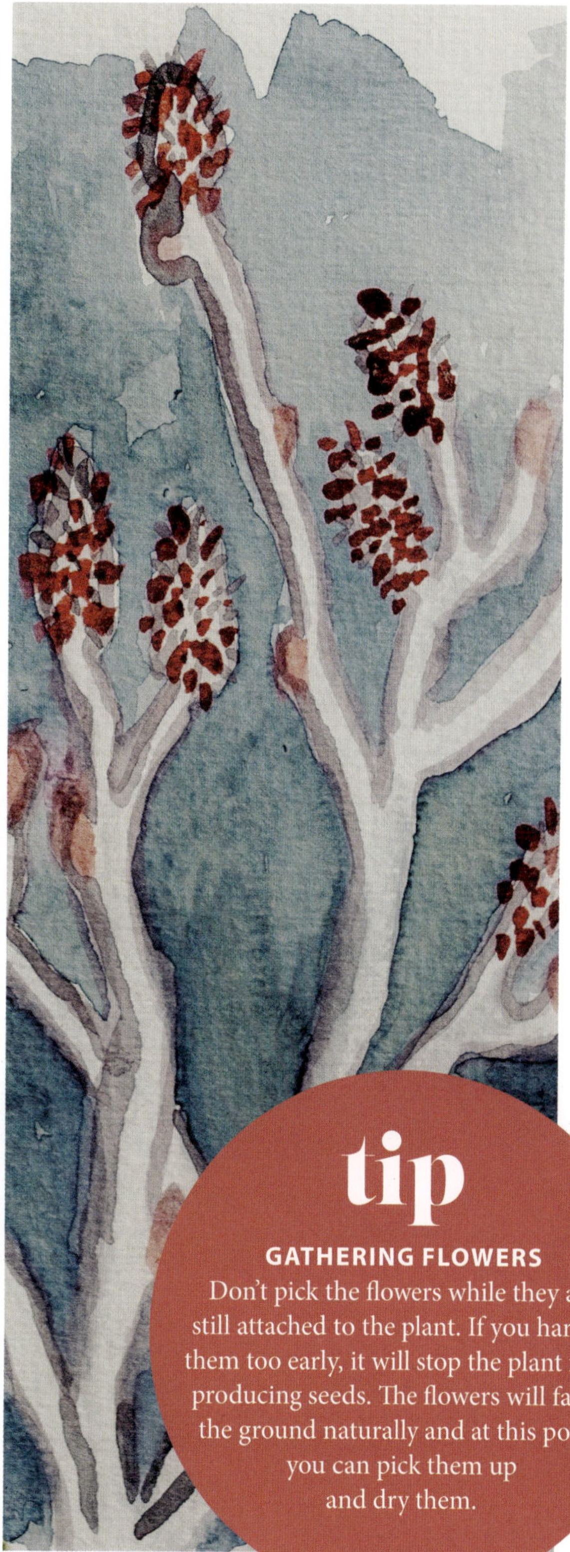

tip

GATHERING FLOWERS

Don't pick the flowers while they are
still attached to the plant. If you harvest
them too early, it will stop the plant from
producing seeds. The flowers will fall to
the ground naturally and at this point,
you can pick them up
and dry them.

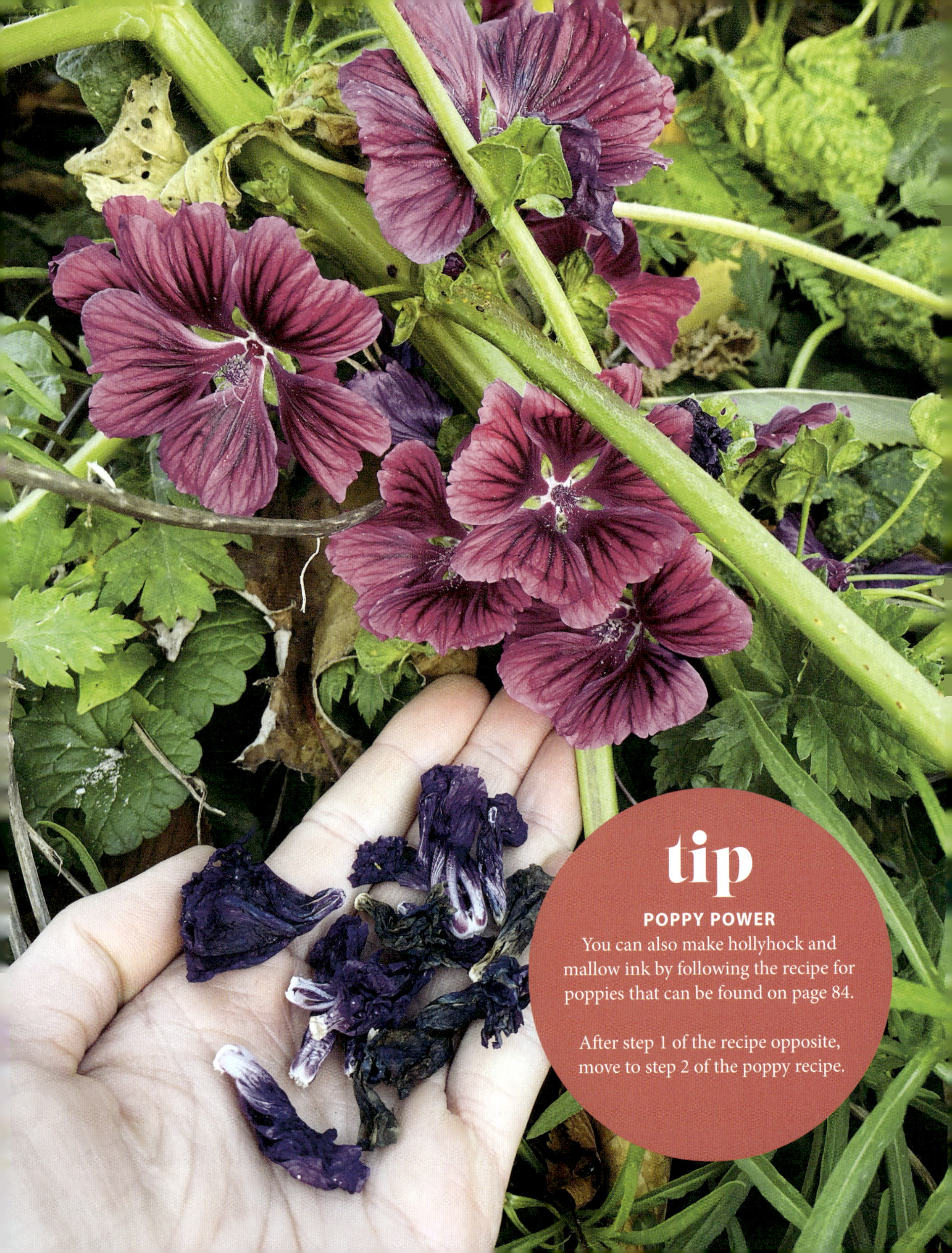

tip

POPPY POWER

You can also make hollyhock and
mallow ink by following the recipe for
poppies that can be found on page 84.

After step 1 of the recipe opposite,
move to step 2 of the poppy recipe.

Black hollyhock

Ingredients
- black hollyhock flowers – as many as you can fit in your mortar
- 1 pinch of washing soda (optional)
- 1 pinch of citric acid or 1 squeeze of lemon juice (optional)

Equipment
- newspaper or baking paper
- pestle and mortar
- coffee filter
- bowl

METHOD

1. Place the hollyhock flowers on the newspaper to air dry them. This will take a few days. It is also possible to dry them in the oven, which is quicker. Preheat the oven to 50°C (120°F). Place the flowers separated from each other on a sheet of baking paper. Dry them in the oven for 30 minutes. You need to monitor this stage and carefully check the flowers to avoid them burning.

2. Cut off the white stamen attachment on the flowers.

3. Crumble the flowers in a mortar. If you have a small mortar, you will need to repeat this process a number of times to make a full bottle of ink.

4. Pour in just enough hot water to cover the crumbled flowers. You won't need very much water at all. The water should be just off the boil.

5. Using the pestle, finely and thoroughly grind the crumbled flowers. The water will immediately change colour.

6. Pour the hollyhock water through a coffee filter and collect it in a bowl. The filtered hollyhock water will be an intense colour.

7. Try the ink on watercolour paper. Black hollyhock will turn blue on paper.

8. For a blue-black colour, add washing soda.

9. For a pink colour, add citric acid or lemon juice.

10. Bottle the ink following the instructions on page 29.

DILLE & KAMILLE
Fluitenkruid
DILLE & KAM
Fluitenkruid
DILLE & KAMILLE
Fluitenkruid
Fluitenb

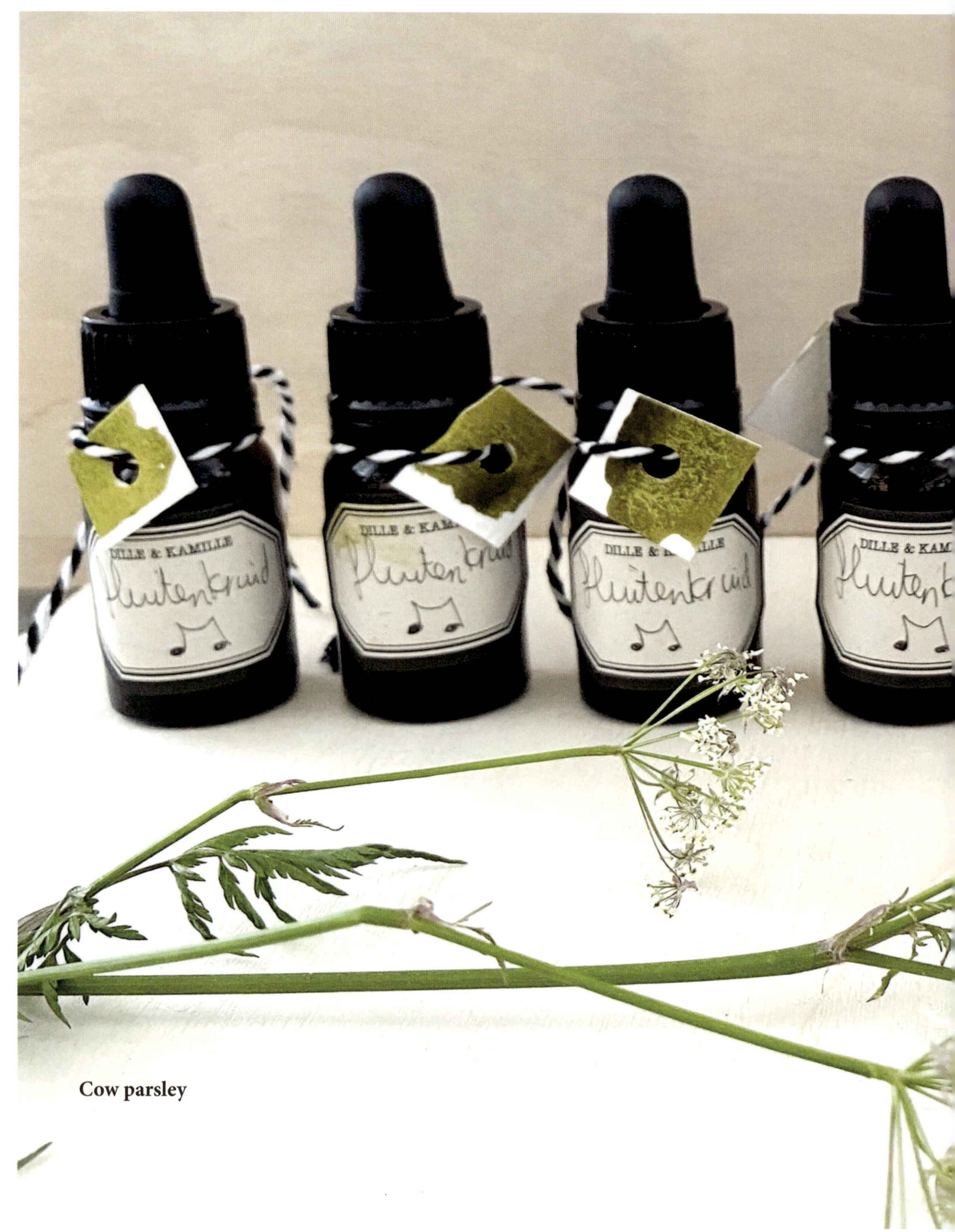

Cow parsley

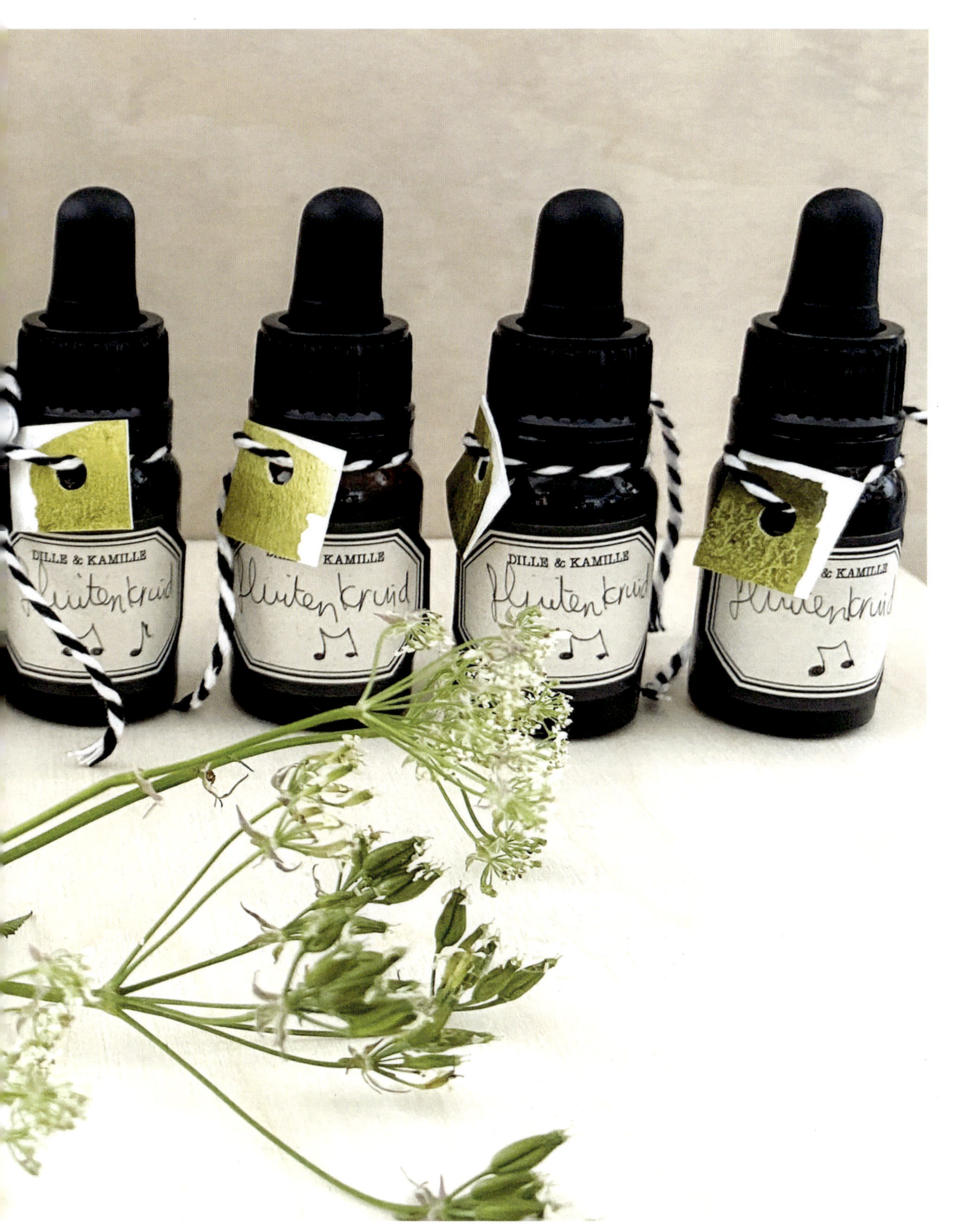

DILLE & KAMILLE
Fluitenkruid
DILLE & KAMILLE
Fluitenkruid
DILLE & KAMILLE
Fluitenkruid
& KAMILLE
Fluitenkruid

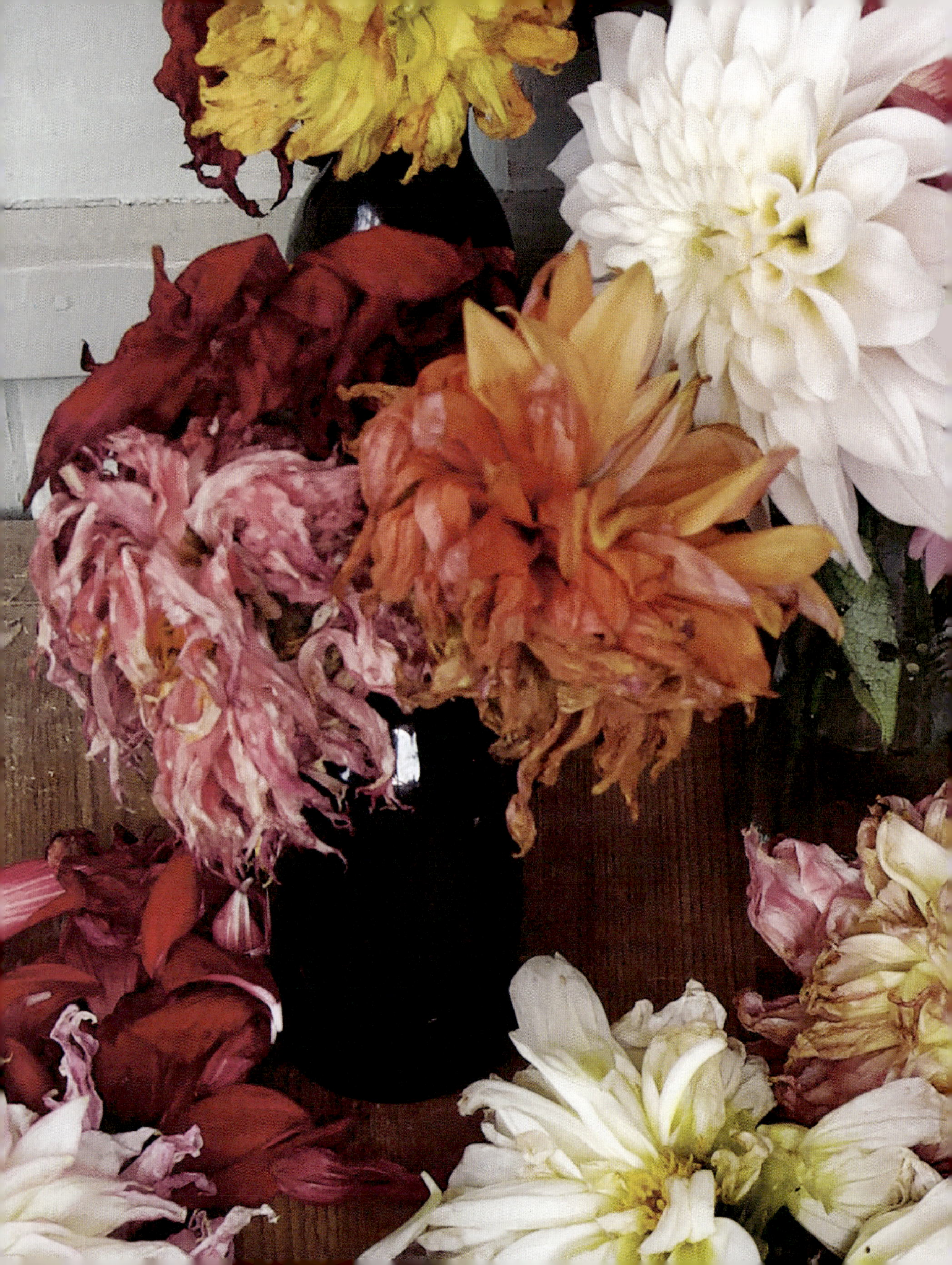

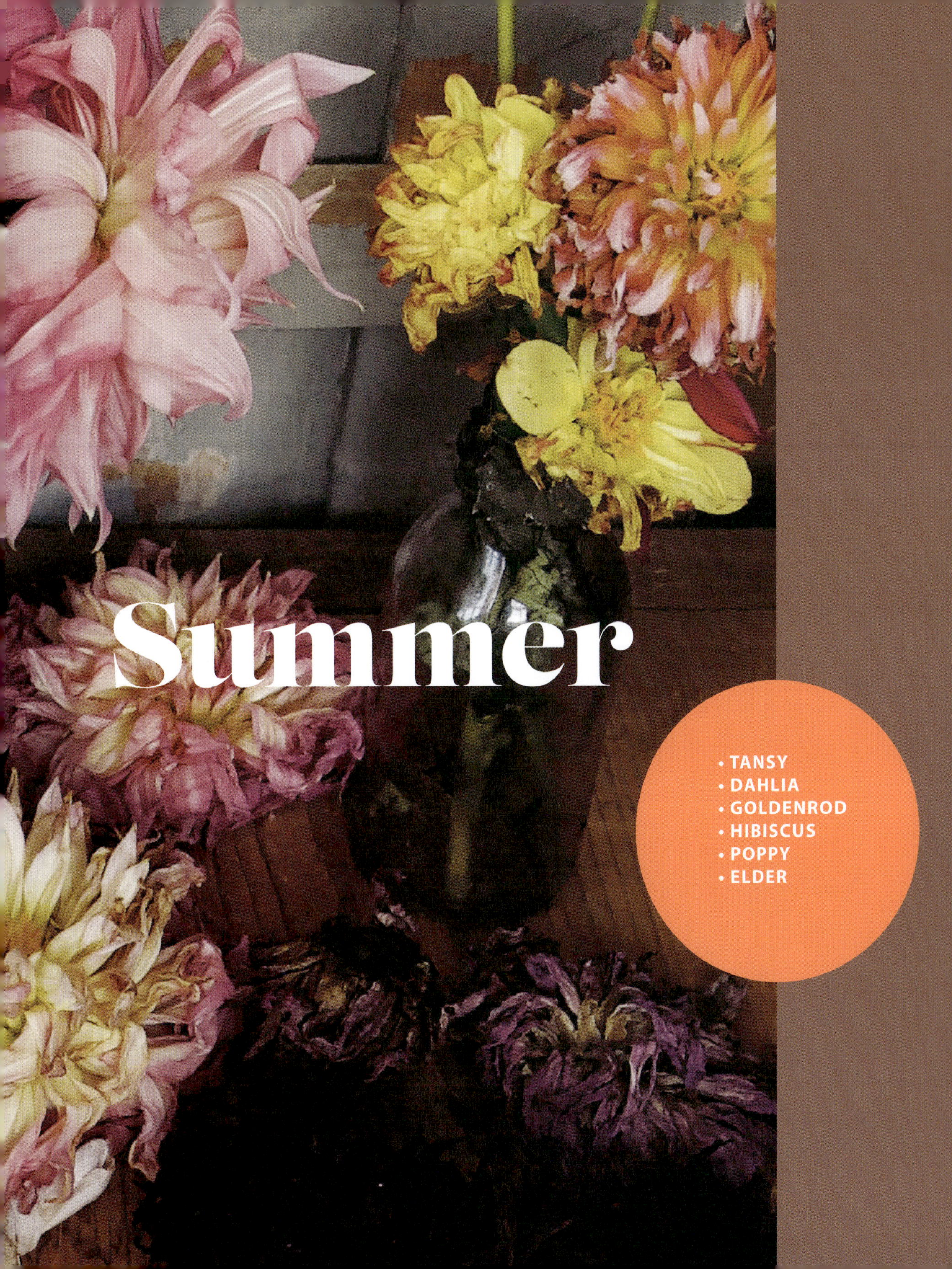

Summer

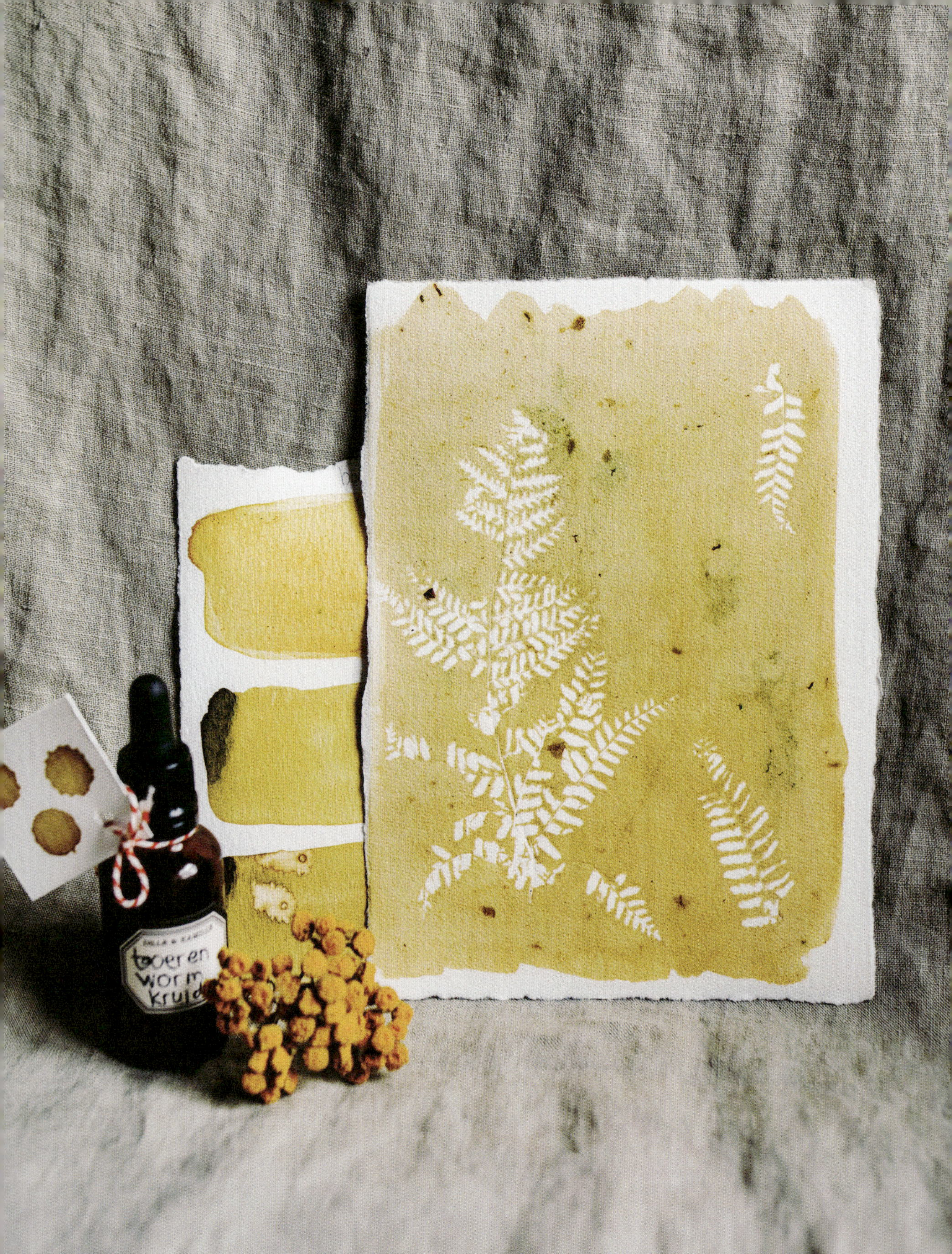
boeren
worm
kruid

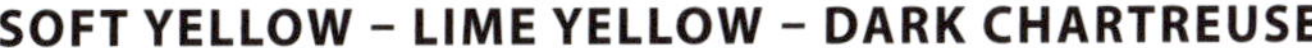

Tansy

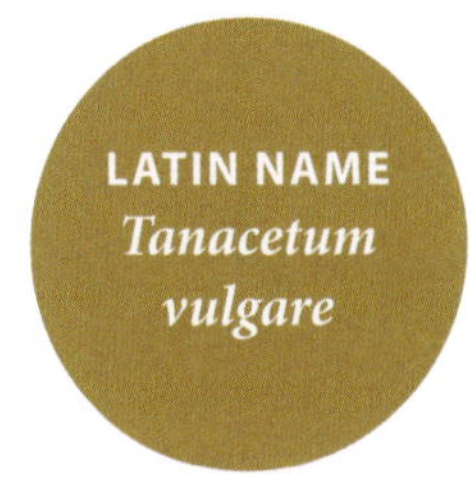

Ink from tansy is lightfast +++

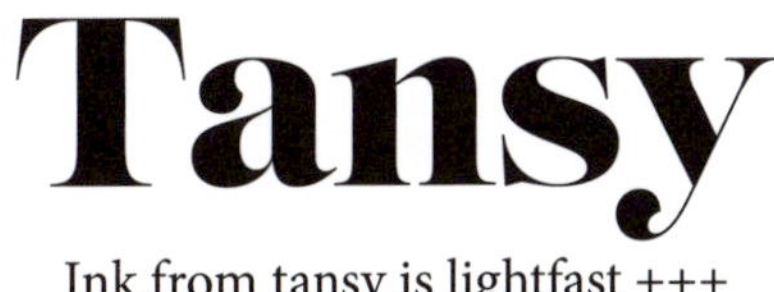

This beautiful flower blooms alongside roadsides from summer into autumn and often for longer. The fact it blooms for so long can be seen in its name: the botanical name *Tanacetum* is derived from the Ancient Greek word *athanasia* meaning 'immortal'. As early as February, the plant starts to emerge above ground level, with pinnate leaves that look like those of a fern. There is a strong smell to the leaf and flower. They smell a little like camphor and even though some people hate it, it's a smell that I love. Tansy has an angular, dark brown stem. The yellow flowers look like small, round, flat cushions. They bloom in dense clusters close together. The plant can reach 1.2m (47¼in) in height. It is what is called a compass plant since the flower heads face south in full sunlight.

Tansy contains the toxic substance thujone, which is also used to make absinthe.

Tansy contains the toxic substance thujone, which has vermifugal properties. Thujone is also used to make absinthe, a green liquor famous for being the addiction of choice for many a hallucinating artist in the late 19th century. Artist Henri de Toulouse-Lautrec was a fan of the drink and created several paintings of absinthe drinkers. Back then, the percentage of thujone found in absinthe was a lot higher than it is now. This is why absinthe was banned for a while, but nowadays, it can be purchased in off-licences.

Tansy

Ingredients
- 1 handful of tansy flowers
- 1 pinch of potash (optional)
- 1 pinch of washing
  soda (optional)

Equipment
- newspaper or baking paper
- old pan with lid
- sieve and bowl
- coffee filter

METHOD

1. Place the flowers on the newspaper to air dry them. This will take a few days. It is also possible to dry them in the oven, which is quicker. Preheat the oven to 50°C (120°F). Place the flowers, separated from each other, on a sheet of baking paper. Dry them in the oven for 30 minutes. You need to monitor this stage and carefully check the flowers to avoid them burning.
2. Break the tansy flowers into very small pieces and put them in a pan.
3. Pour in just enough water to cover the flowers.
4. Place the pan on the heat but turn it down as soon as the water has almost reached boiling point. Make sure it doesn't boil.
5. Place the lid on the pan and leave to steep for 1 hour.
6. Turn off the heat and then leave the pan to stand overnight with the lid on.
7. Strain the tansy mixture through a sieve and collect the liquid in a bowl.
8. Rinse the pan and then pour the liquid back into it through a coffee filter.
9. Gently heat the liquid until it reaches the consistency of syrup; it is very important that you do not allow it to boil.
10. It will be soft yellow in colour. For a dark chartreuse colour, add potash. The more you add, the darker the colour will become.
11. For a lime yellow colour, add washing soda.
12. Bottle the ink following the instructions on page 29.

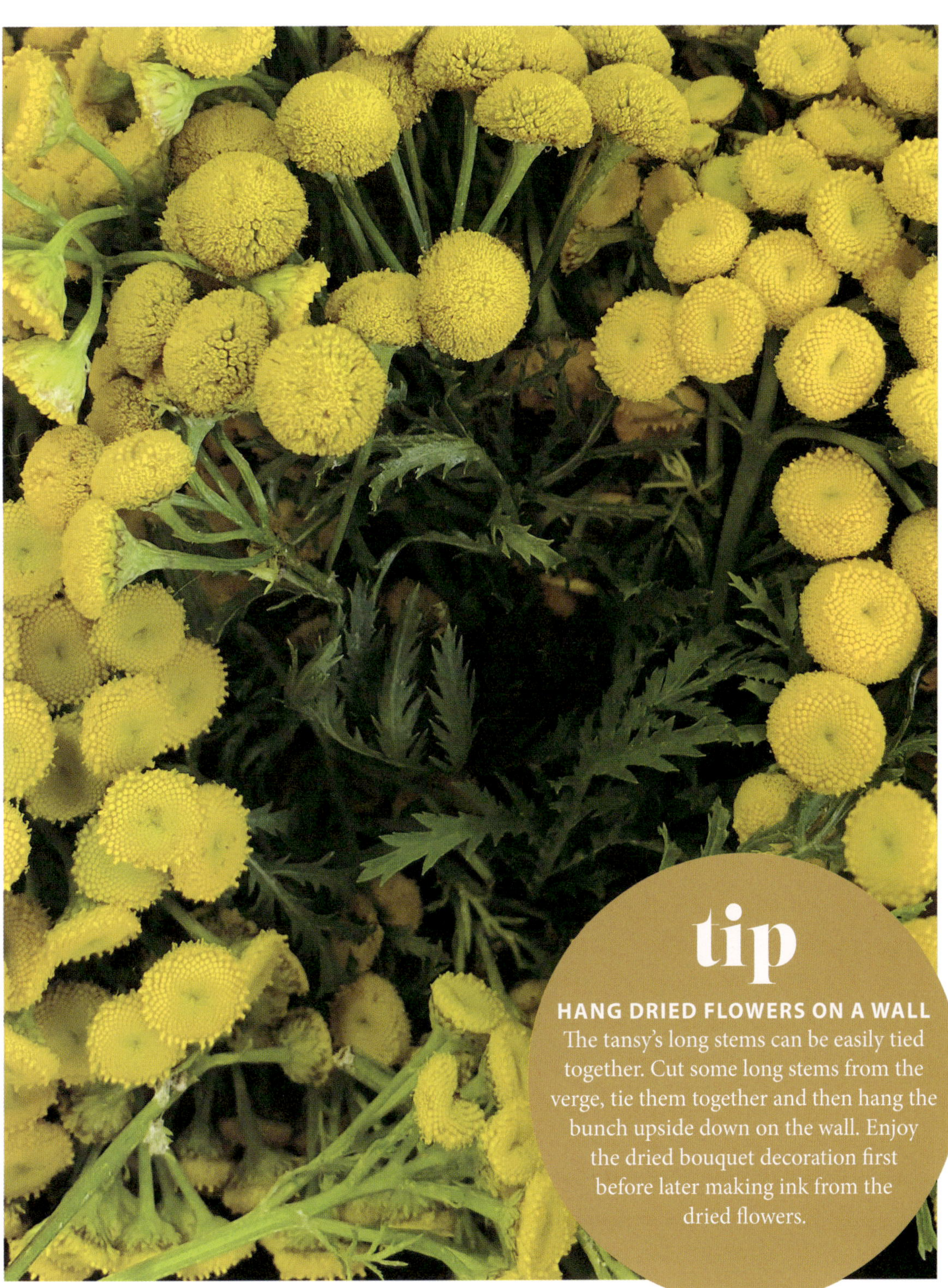

tip

HANG DRIED FLOWERS ON A WALL
The tansy's long stems can be easily tied together. Cut some long stems from the verge, tie them together and then hang the bunch upside down on the wall. Enjoy the dried bouquet decoration first before later making ink from the dried flowers.

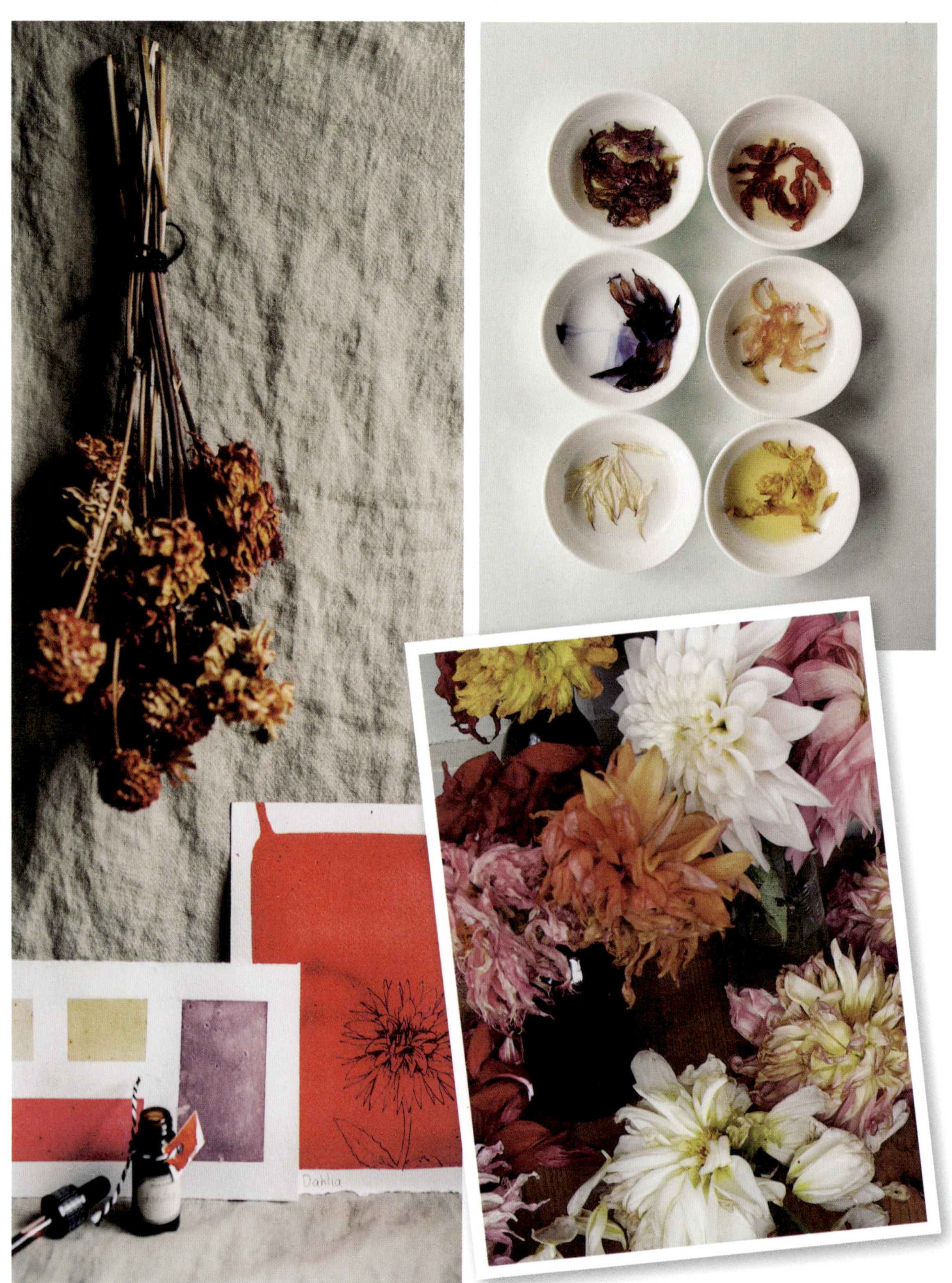
Dahlia

Dahlia

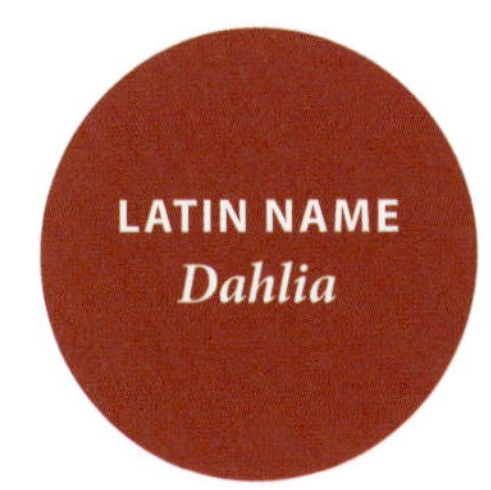

Ink from dahlia is lightfast +++

Dahlias were introduced to Europe in around 1800. Since the plant originated from Mexico, Europeans believed it needed to be grown in the same way as a subtropical plant and kept warm and dry. This caused lots of dahlias to die. It was only later that people realized that the growing conditions for dahlias in Mexico were quite often at an altitude of 1,500m (5,000ft), so they are not subtropical plants at all. There are now more than 20,000 different varieties and they come in all kinds of colours, except for blue and black. Dark dahlias often have names like 'Black Jack', 'Black Barbara' or 'Arabian Night'. However, the flowers are not black but a very dark burgundy colour. To make ink from dahlias, you need dried flowers. It is best to cut them after they have been flowering for a while and still remain beautiful. If you leave them on the plant for any longer, they become sticky. But by cutting them off, you also encourage the plant to start making new flowers again – a win-win situation!

Ingredients
- 6 dark dahlia flowers
- ½tsp citric acid (optional)
- ½tsp potash (optional)

Equipment
- newspaper or baking paper
- old pan with lid
- sieve and bowl
- coffee filter

METHOD

1. Place the flowers on the newspaper to air dry them. This will take a few days. It is also possible to dry them in the oven. Preheat the oven to 50°C (120°F). Place them separated from each other on a sheet of baking paper. Dry them in the oven for 30 minutes. Monitor this carefully to avoid them burning.
2. Pull them apart and put them in a pan.
3. Pour in just enough water to cover the shreds of flowers.
4. Place the pan on the heat but turn it down as soon as the water has almost reached boiling point. Make sure it doesn't boil. The water will immediately take on colour.
5. Place the lid on the pan and leave to steep for 1 hour.
6. Turn off the heat and then leave the pan to stand overnight with the lid on.
7. Strain the dahlia mixture through a sieve and collect the liquid in a bowl.
8. Rinse the pan and then pour the liquid back into it through a coffee filter.
9. Gently heat the liquid until it reaches the consistency of syrup; do not allow it to boil.
10. Try the ink on watercolour paper. The colour should develop once it is applied to the paper. What initially looks brown in colour will turn a beautiful shade of purple after 15 minutes.
11. For a deep red colour, add citric acid.
12. For a light green colour, add potash.
13. Bottle the ink following the instructions on page 29.

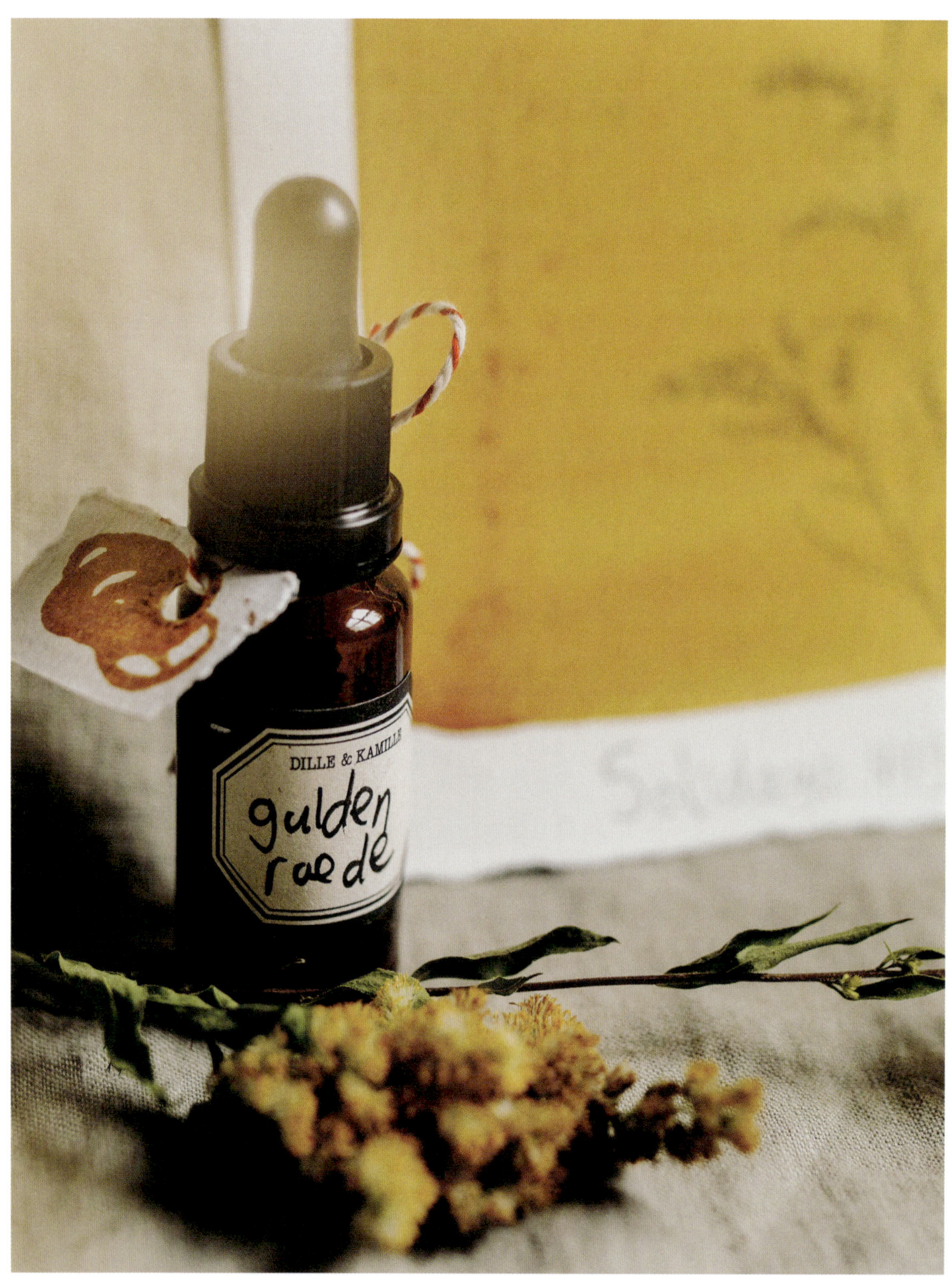

DILLE & KAMILLE
gulden
roede

Goldenrod

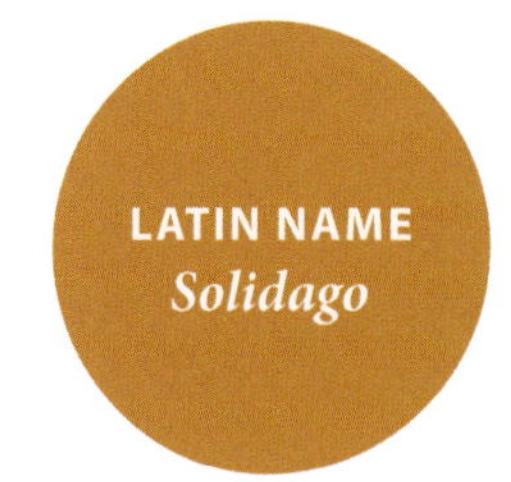

Ink from goldenrods is lightfast ++++

Goldenrod: such a beautiful name for a beautiful plant. The scientific name, *Solidago*, comes from the Latin word *solidare*, which means 'cure' or 'heal'. There are in fact lots of different species of goldenrod, but the true goldenrod is a perennial plant that can grow to heights of up to 1m (3¼ft). From July to October it blooms a beautiful yellow colour, the flowers coming together in panicles that look like feathered plumes. Goldenrods like the sunshine or semi-shaded plots that have dry, sandy soil. They can be found growing on fallow land or on the edges of deciduous woods. Unfortunately, it is now rare to find true goldenrod and it has been added to the Red List of threatened plants. This means you cannot pick it in the wild.

> **Unfortunately, it is now rare to find true goldenrod and it has been added to the Red List of threatened plants. This means you cannot pick it in the wild.**

Canadian goldenrod, *Solidago canadensis*, is a species that you do see increasingly often. The true goldenrod plant is not an invasive species, but the Canadian goldenrod is. It spreads by sending out long-reaching rhizomes under the ground and is difficult to control. Even a small piece of root can actually grow back to form a new plant. This species can be found on wasteland, on the verges of roads and alongside railway tracks: Canadian goldenrod flowers with panicles full of yellow flowers. The green leaves are elongated, pointed and serrated. Because it looks so marvellously decorative, people like to use it in floral arrangements. Once the goldenrod has finished flowering, the yellow flowers will turn fluffy and a light beige to pale yellow in colour. They look lovely in your garden. If you prune the plant when it is flowering, you can tie the stems together and dry them by hanging them upside down. The flowers will stay yellow for a while.

Goldenrod

<table>
<tr><td>

Ingredients
- 2 handfuls of goldenrod flowers
- 1 pinch of potash (optional)
- 1 pinch of washing
  soda (optional)

</td><td>

Equipment
- newspaper or baking paper
- old pan with lid
- sieve and bowl
- coffee filter

</td></tr>
</table>

METHOD

1. Place the flowers on the newspaper to air dry them. This will take a few days. It is also possible to dry them in the oven, which is quicker. Preheat the oven to 50°C (120°F). Place the flowers separated from each other on a sheet of baking paper. Dry them in the oven for 30 minutes. You need to monitor this stage and carefully check the flowers to avoid them burning.
2. Break the goldenrod flowers into very small pieces and put them in a pan.
3. Pour in just enough water to cover the flowers.
4. Place the pan on the heat but turn it down as soon as the water has almost reached boiling point. Do not allow it to boil.
5. Place the lid on the pan and leave to steep for 1 hour.
6. Turn off the heat and then leave the pan to stand overnight with the lid on.
7. Strain the goldenrod mixture through a sieve and collect the liquid in a bowl.
8. Rinse the pan and then pour the liquid back into it through a coffee filter.
9. Gently heat the liquid until it reaches the consistency of syrup; it is very important that you do not allow it to boil. It will be pale golden yellow in colour.
10. For a chartreuse colour, add potash. The more you add, the darker the colour will become.
11. For a warm yellow colour, add washing soda.
12. Bottle the ink following the instructions on page 29.

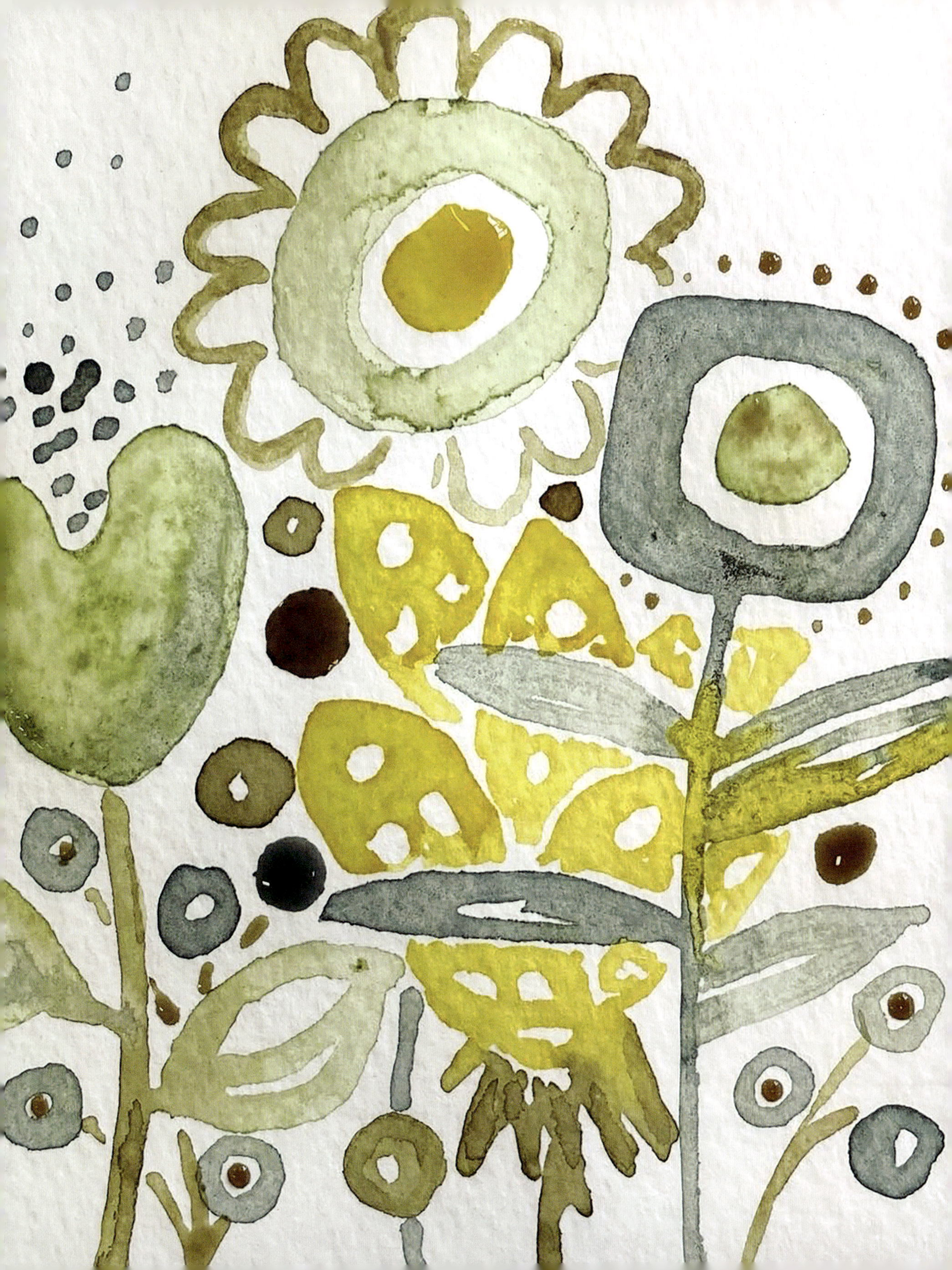

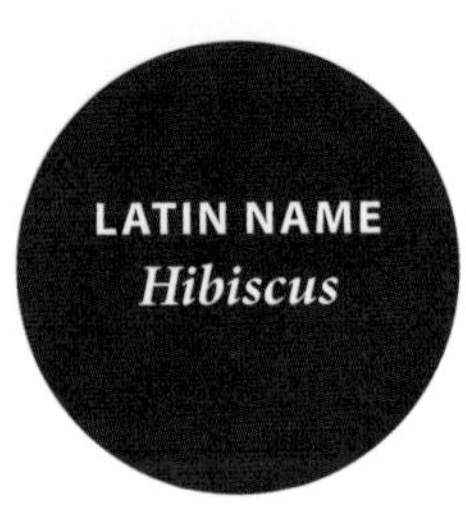

RED – PURPLE – VIOLET

Hibiscus

Ink from hibiscus is lightfast +++

Hibiscus is a member of the rich family of *Malvaceae* (the mallow family, which also includes hollyhocks and mallow). It is native to the Mediterranean and (sub)tropical regions. Hibiscus comes in many species, sizes and colours. All of the flowers are large, brightly coloured and shaped like a trumpet. It is a favourite plant for gardens. In the UK, *Hibiscus syriacus*, also known as common hibiscus, grows well. This hibiscus can be positioned in both semi-shaded areas and full sunlight and is hardy. It blooms with white, red, blue or purple flowers and has apple-green oval leaves. The flowering period for hibiscus is from August to October. The flowers are edible and look beautiful when used as a garnish on salad. The recipe below uses red hibiscus flowers.

Ingredients
- 1 handful of red hibiscus flowers
- 1 pinch of citric acid (optional)
- 1 pinch of washing soda (optional)

Equipment
- newspaper or baking paper
- old pan with lid
- sieve and bowl
- coffee filter

METHOD

1. Place the flowers on the newspaper to air dry them. This will take a few days. It is also possible to dry them in the oven, which is quicker. Preheat the oven to 50°C (120°F). Place the flowers away from each other on a sheet of baking paper. Dry them in the oven for 30 minutes. You need to monitor this stage and carefully check the flowers to avoid them burning.
2. Break the hibiscus flowers into very small pieces and put them in a pan.
3. Pour in just enough water to cover the flowers.
4. Place the pan on the heat but turn it down as soon as the water has almost reached boiling point. Make sure it doesn't boil.
5. Place the lid on the pan and leave to steep for 1 hour.
6. Turn off the heat and then leave the pan to stand overnight with the lid on.
7. Strain the hibiscus mixture through a sieve and collect the liquid in a bowl.
8. Rinse the pan and then pour the liquid back into it through a coffee filter.
9. Gently heat the liquid until it reaches the consistency of syrup; it is very important that you do not allow it to boil. It will be bright red in colour.
10. Try the ink on watercolour paper. The bright red colour will slowly take on a purple hue.
11. For a red colour, add citric acid.
12. For a violet colour, add washing soda.
13. Bottle the ink following the instructions on page 29.

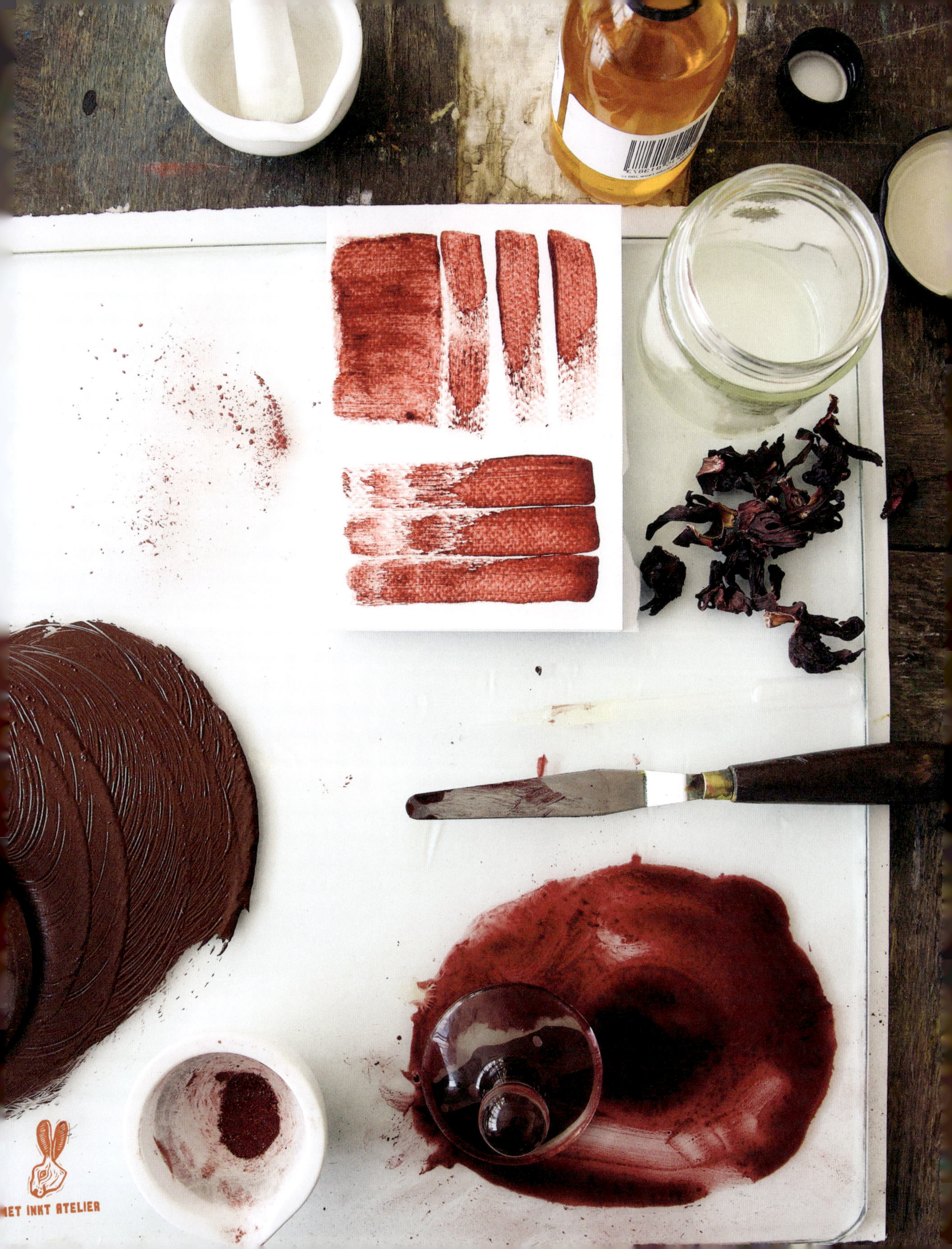
HET INKT ATELIER

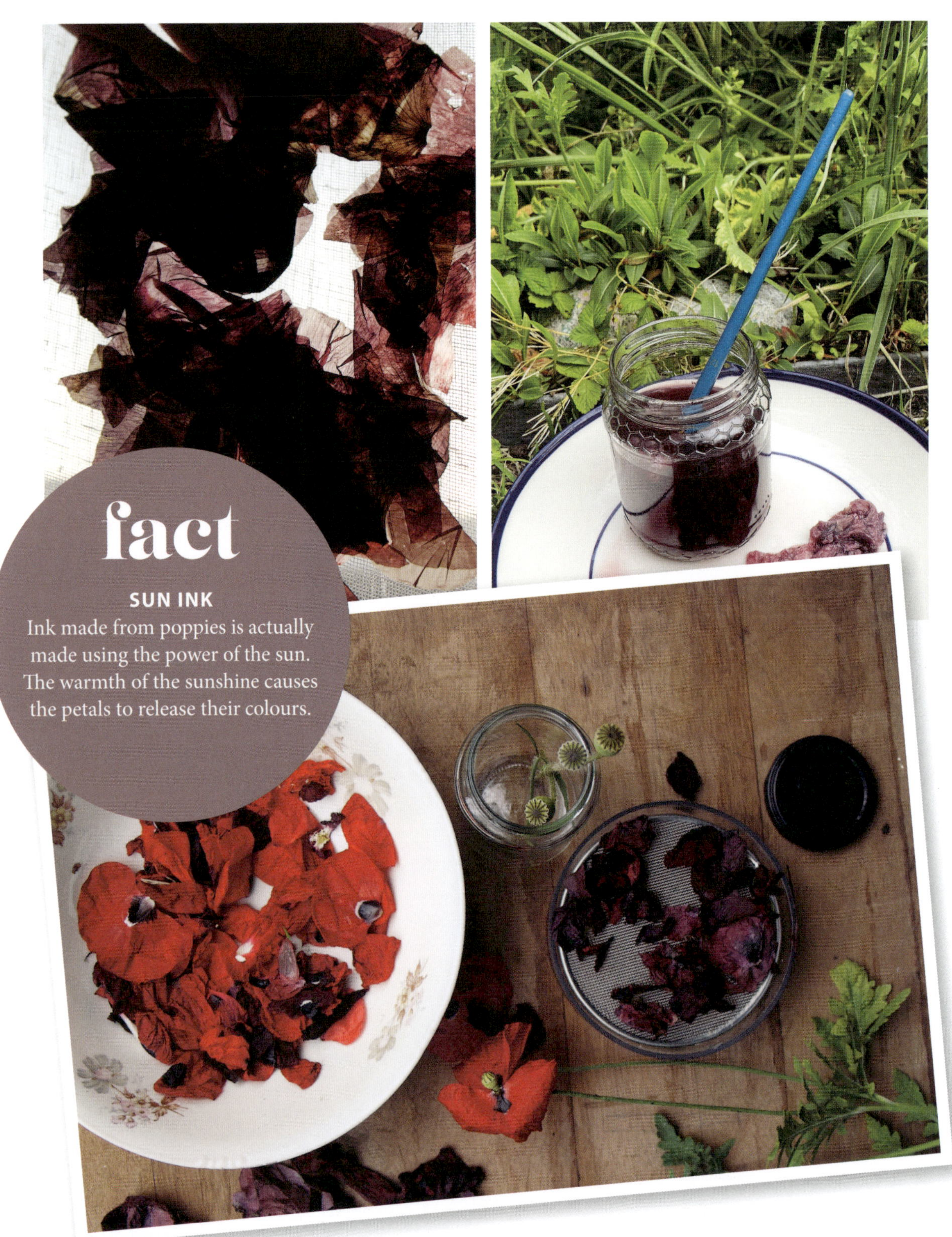

fact

SUN INK
Ink made from poppies is actually
made using the power of the sun.
The warmth of the sunshine causes
the petals to release their colours.

Poppy

Ink from poppies is lightfast ++

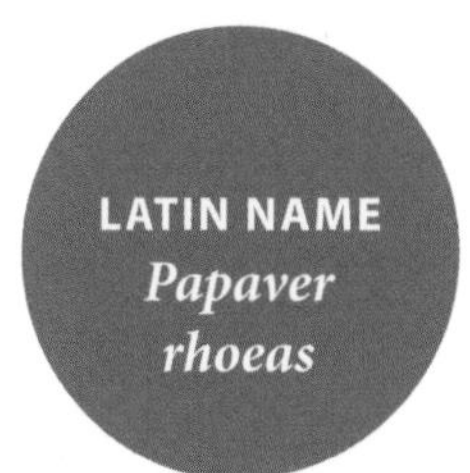

Poppy seeds can remain in the ground for up to 50 years. Poppies germinate in light, so the seeds have to be exposed to sunlight to successfully germinate. When numerous trenches were dug during the First World War and shells smashed into the land, forming craters, poppy seeds came to the surface and created fields full of poppies. In the UK, Canada, Belgium and France, people celebrate a day of remembrance each year, when a poppy symbolizes the blood that flowed during the war. The Latin name *Papaver* is believed to be derived from the Celtic word *papa*, which means 'porridge'. This refers to the Celtic custom of adding poppy juice to porridge to help crying babies go to sleep.

Poppies are annual plants. They have hairy stems and soft hairy green leaves. They flower from May to August in all different shades of red, from bright red to pale pink. It's possible to tell when a flower will open because the drooping flower bud will stand straight and open up in the morning. A poppy flower will often fall off in the evening, leaving a characteristic seed pod that can be used as a stamp.

People celebrate a day of remembrance each year, when a poppy symbolizes the blood that flowed during the war.

The seeds of *Papaver somniferum*, the opium poppy, are sometimes called maw seed as well as poppy seed: these small blue-black balls are used in baking on bread and cakes. This type of poppy has been cultivated for its seeds since the Stone Age, and they also produce a nice oil when pressed. The first pressing results in edible oil, which is similar to sunflower oil. The second pressing is used in the soap and paint industry because it is quick to dry and colourless. Using the red dye extracted from the flowers, it is easy to make red vinegar. Infuse white table vinegar with red poppy petals, leave them for one week and the result will be beautifully coloured vinegar. It would look great in a pretty bottle on your dining table. Red ink can be made just as easily as this red vinegar.

Poppy

METHOD

1. Place the poppy petals on the newspaper to air dry them. This will take a few days. It is also possible to dry them in the oven, which is quicker. Preheat the oven to 50°C (120°F). Place the petals separated from each other on a sheet of baking paper. Dry them in the oven for 30 minutes. You need to monitor this stage and carefully check the petals to avoid them burning.

2. Fill a jar with poppy petals. Make sure that the jar is as full as possible.

3. Pour nearly boiling water over the poppy petals and fill the jar fully so that no air remains in it.

4. Tighten the lid on the jar and place the jar in the sun. The heat from the sun will loosen the dye, which will take about 1 week.

5. Strain the poppy leaves from the liquid and collect the liquid in a pan. It will be bright red.

6. Heat the red liquid very gently until it reaches the same thickness as syrup; it should not exceed 70°C (160°F), otherwise the colour will turn brown.

7. For a pink colour, add citric acid.

8. For an indigo colour, add washing soda.

9. Bottle the ink following the instructions on page 29.

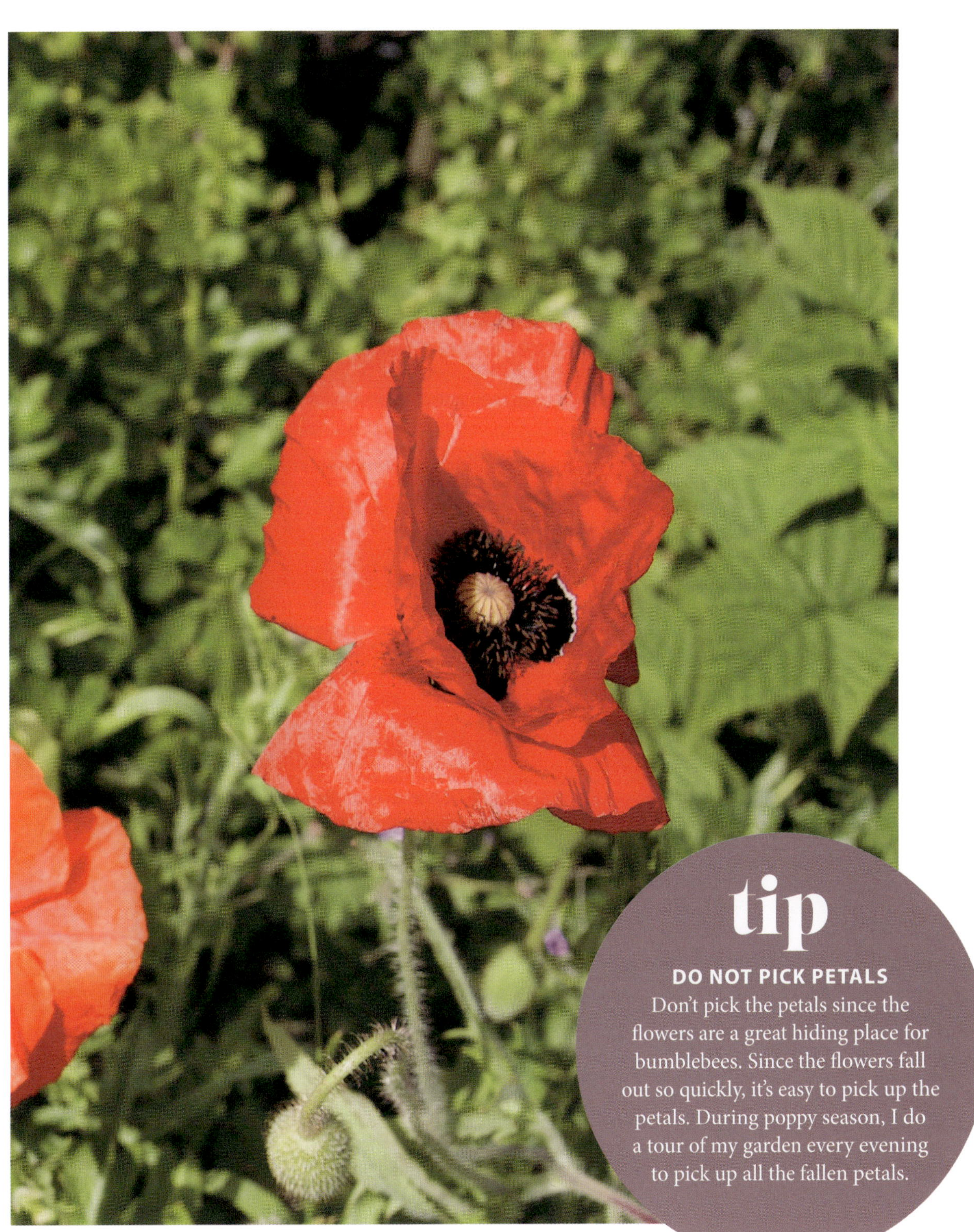

tip

DO NOT PICK PETALS
Don't pick the petals since the
flowers are a great hiding place for
bumblebees. Since the flowers fall
out so quickly, it's easy to pick up the
petals. During poppy season, I do
a tour of my garden every evening
to pick up all the fallen petals.

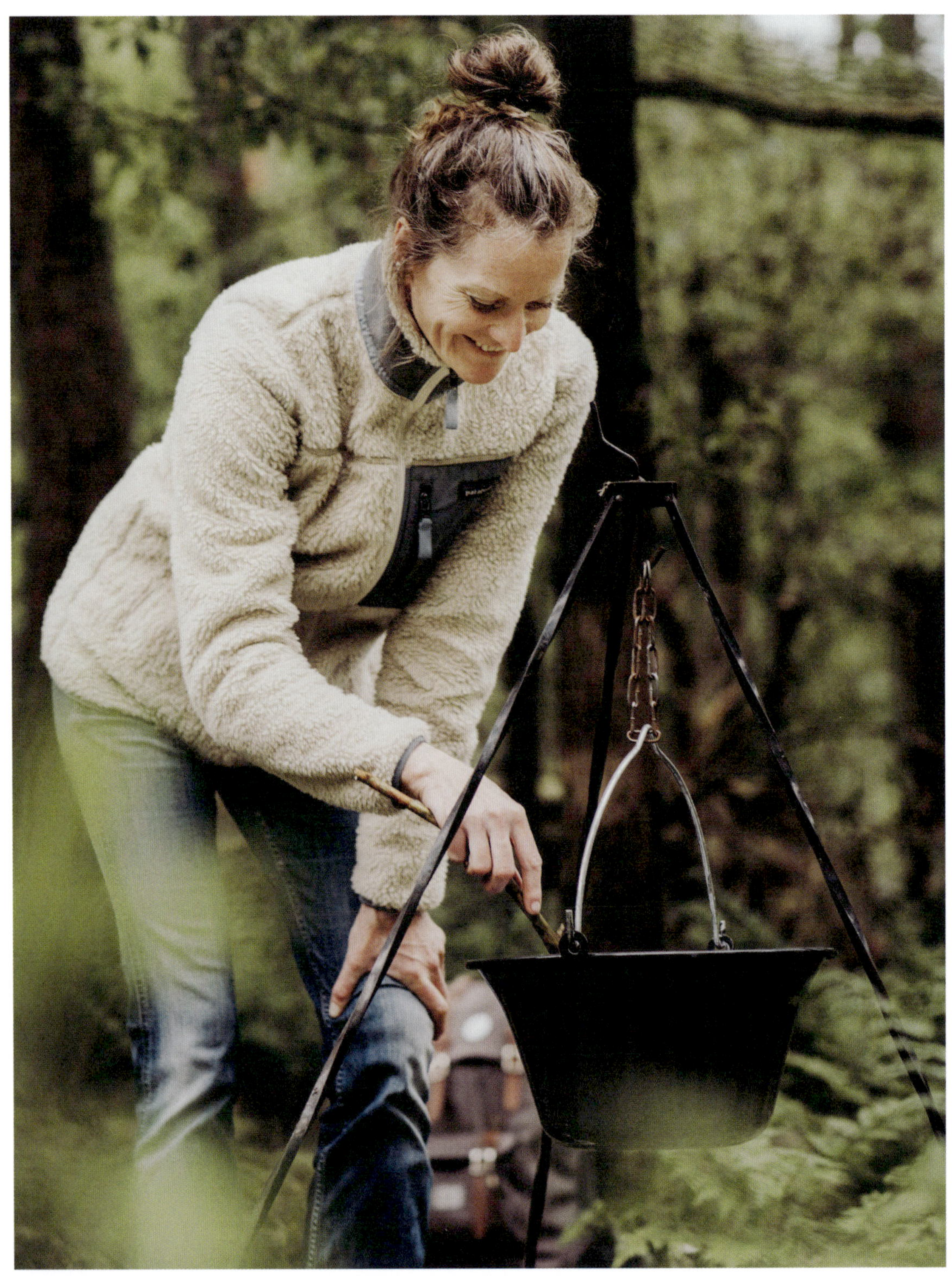

Elder – 1

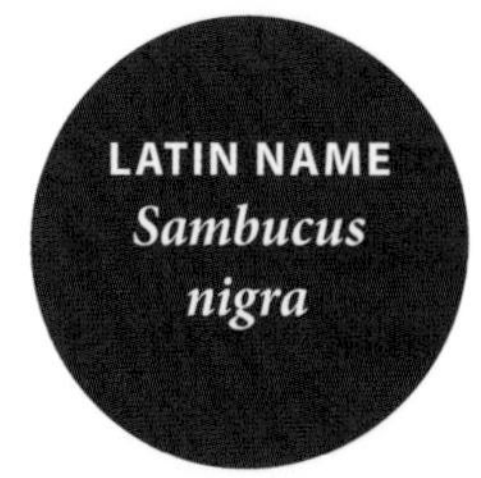

Ink from elder is lightfast +++

The common elder is a shrub that grows to 5m (16½ft) in height. You can use the leaves and berries of the elder for ink. The flower heads and berries can also be used for cooking: make delicious syrup using the flower heads or dip them in a fluffy batter and fry them so they turn crispy. The berries can be used to make jam, juice or syrup. Be careful, though, because raw berries are not edible. You need to boil them first as otherwise they are mildly toxic and can cause diarrhoea and vomiting. Lots of legends and stories are centred on the elder. For instance, people on farms used to plant elder underneath their kitchen window to ward off evil spirits. Judas is said to have hanged himself from an elder tree and the wood of the cross that bore Jesus is also believed to have been made from elder. Different countries and cultures also know the story of the Elder Mother. She was seen as a protector of elder and you needed to ask her permission if you wanted to pick berries or cut wood. Today, those who have read the 'Harry Potter' books are sure to be aware of the magical powers of elder. Harry's final wand is made from elder, which has the ability to make him invincible. I am so very happy with our large elder in the garden because it is such a generous plant. It grows at the speed of light and you can use everything from it. The elder is found in lots of different places in nature. It is quite often planted in parks. It is also commonly found in deciduous woods and on dunes.

Ingredients
- 1 handful of elderberries

Equipment
- old pan
- potato masher
- sieve and bowl
- coffee filter

METHOD

1. Put the elderberries in a pan.
2. Pour in just enough water to cover the berries.
3. Place the pan on the heat but turn it down as soon as the water has almost reached boiling point. Make sure it doesn't boil.
4. Simmer for 1 hour.
5. Using a potato masher, mash the berries into a puree. The water will turn purple.
6. Strain the elderberry mixture through a sieve and collect the liquid in a bowl.
7. Rinse the pan and then pour the liquid back into it through a coffee filter.
8. Gently heat the liquid until it reaches the consistency of syrup; it is very important that you do not allow it to boil.
9. Bottle the ink following the instructions on page 29.

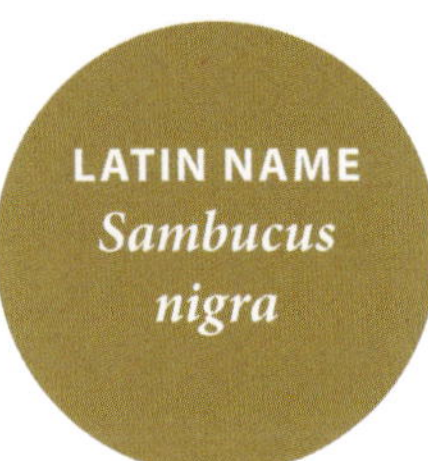

Elder – 2

Ink from elder is lightfast +++

Ingredients
- 2 handfuls of elder leaves

Equipment
- newspaper or baking paper
- old pan with lid
- sieve and bowl
- coffee filter

METHOD

1. Place the elder leaves on the newspaper to air dry them. This will take a few days. It is also possible to dry them in the oven, which is quicker. Preheat the oven to 50°C (120°F). Place the leaves separated from each other on a sheet of baking paper. Dry them in the oven for 30 minutes. You need to monitor this stage and carefully check the leaves to avoid them burning.
2. Break the elder leaves into small pieces and put them in a pan.
3. Pour in just enough water to cover the leaves.
4. Place the pan on the heat but turn it down as soon as the water has almost reached boiling point. Ensure it doesn't boil.
5. Place the lid on the pan and leave to simmer for 3 hours.
6. Turn off the heat and then leave the pan to stand overnight with the lid on.
7. Strain the elder leaf mixture through a sieve and collect the liquid in a bowl.
8. Rinse the pan and then pour the liquid back into it through a coffee filter.
9. Gently heat the liquid until it reaches the consistency of syrup; it is very important that you do not allow it to boil.
10. Bottle the ink following the instructions on page 29.

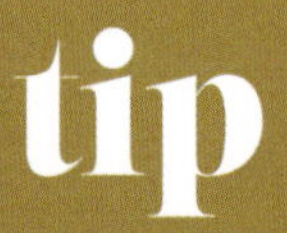

tip

PARTY IN A GLASS

Put some elderflowers in a nice champagne coupe and pour prosecco, cava or another sparkling dry wine over it. The elderflower aroma released by the bubbles is simply delicious combined with the wine!

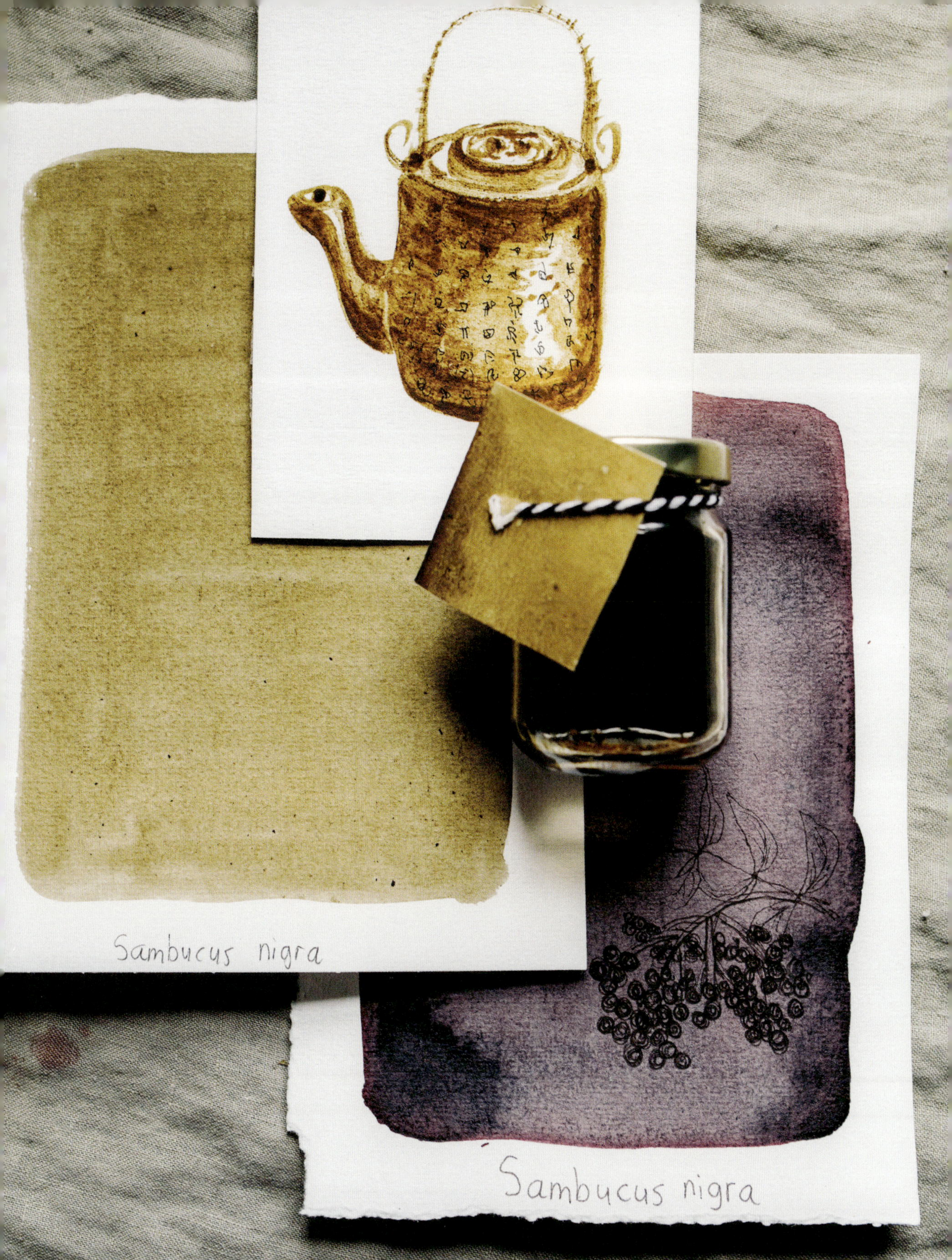
Sambucus nigra
Sambucus nigra

The colours from the garden

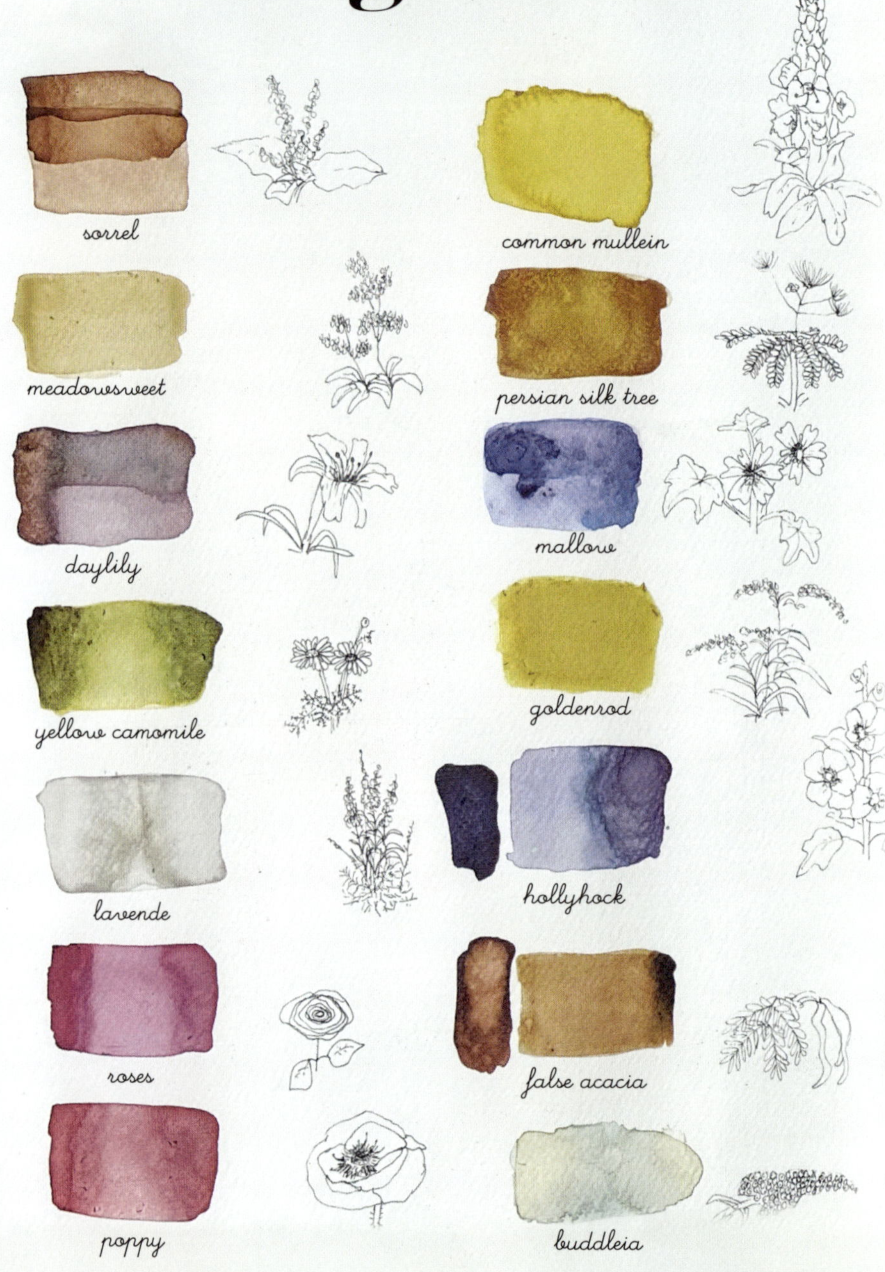

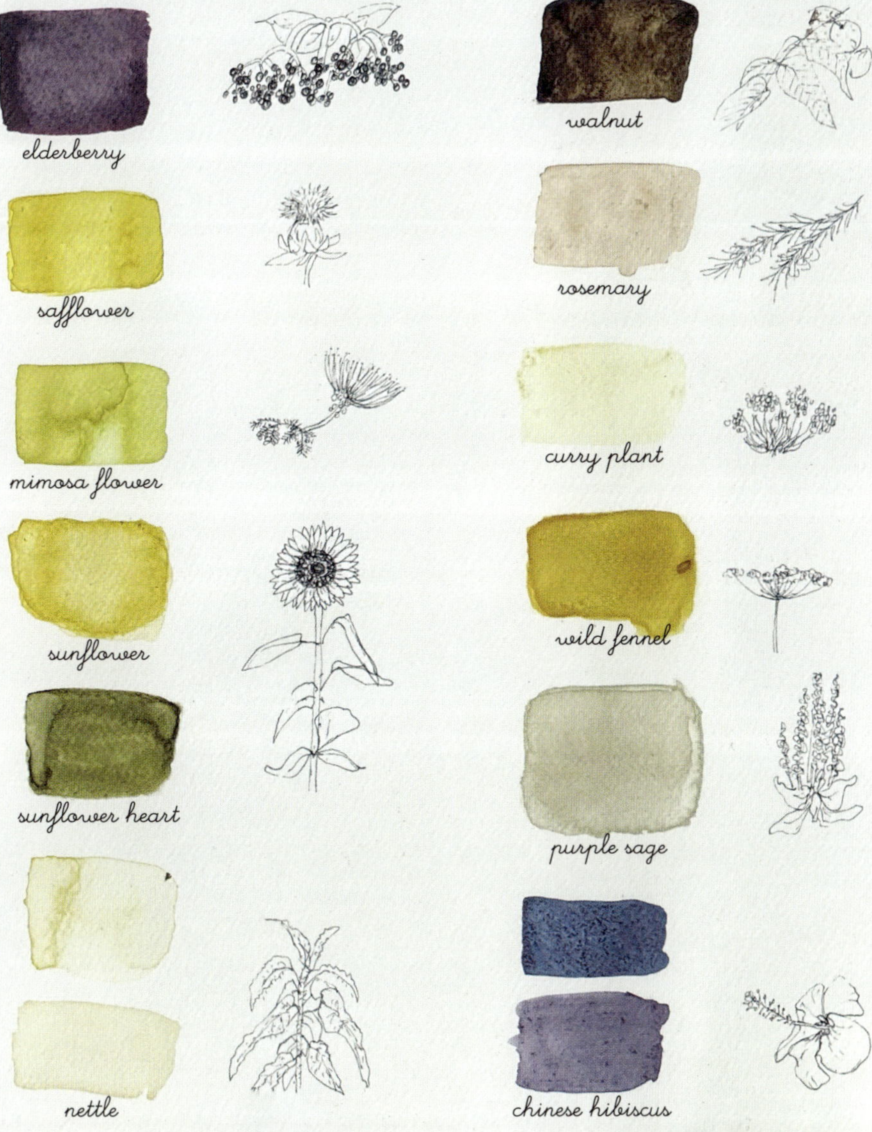
elderberry
safflower
mimosa flower
sunflower
sunflower heart
nettle
walnut
rosemary
curry plant
wild fennel
purple sage
chinese hibiscus

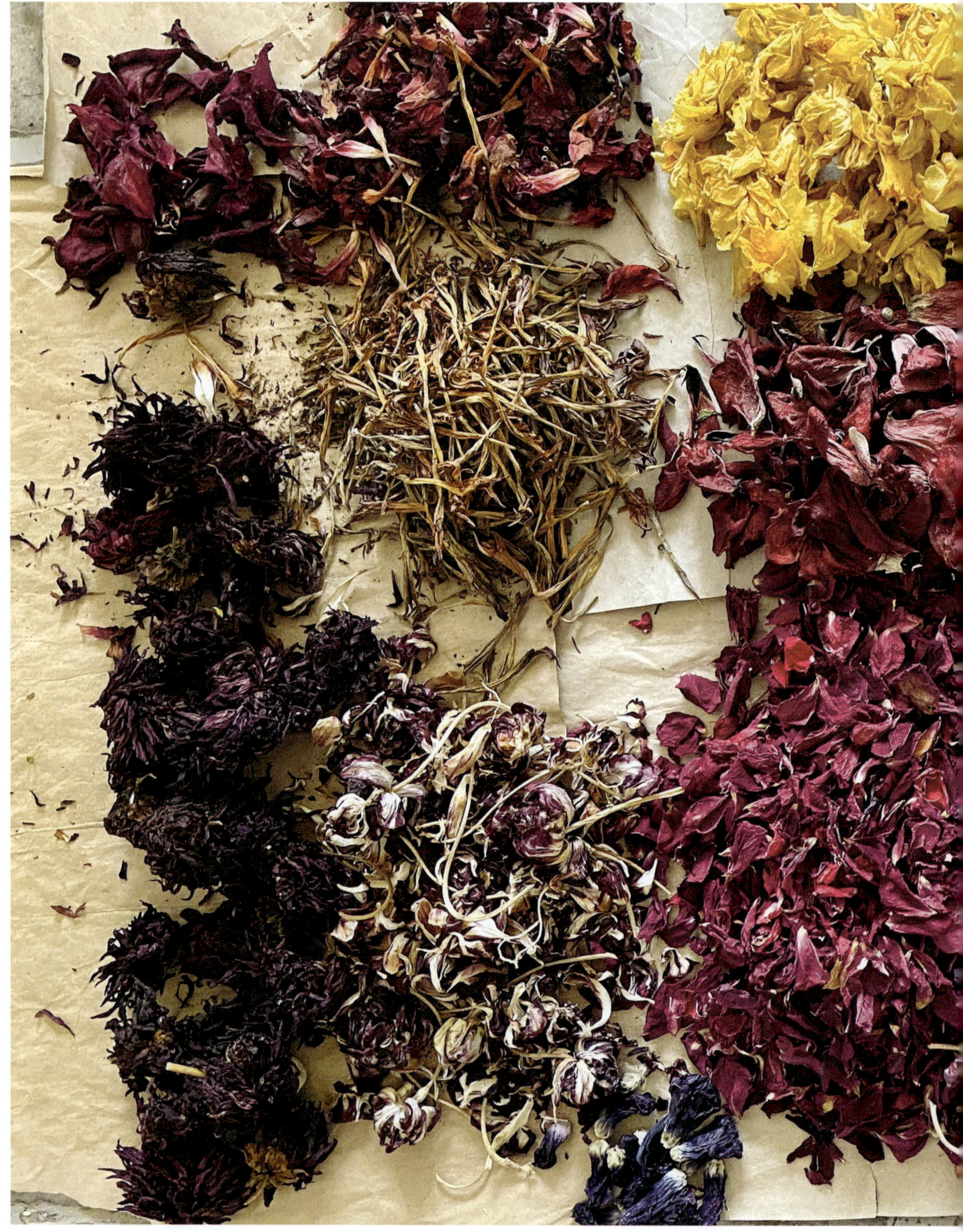

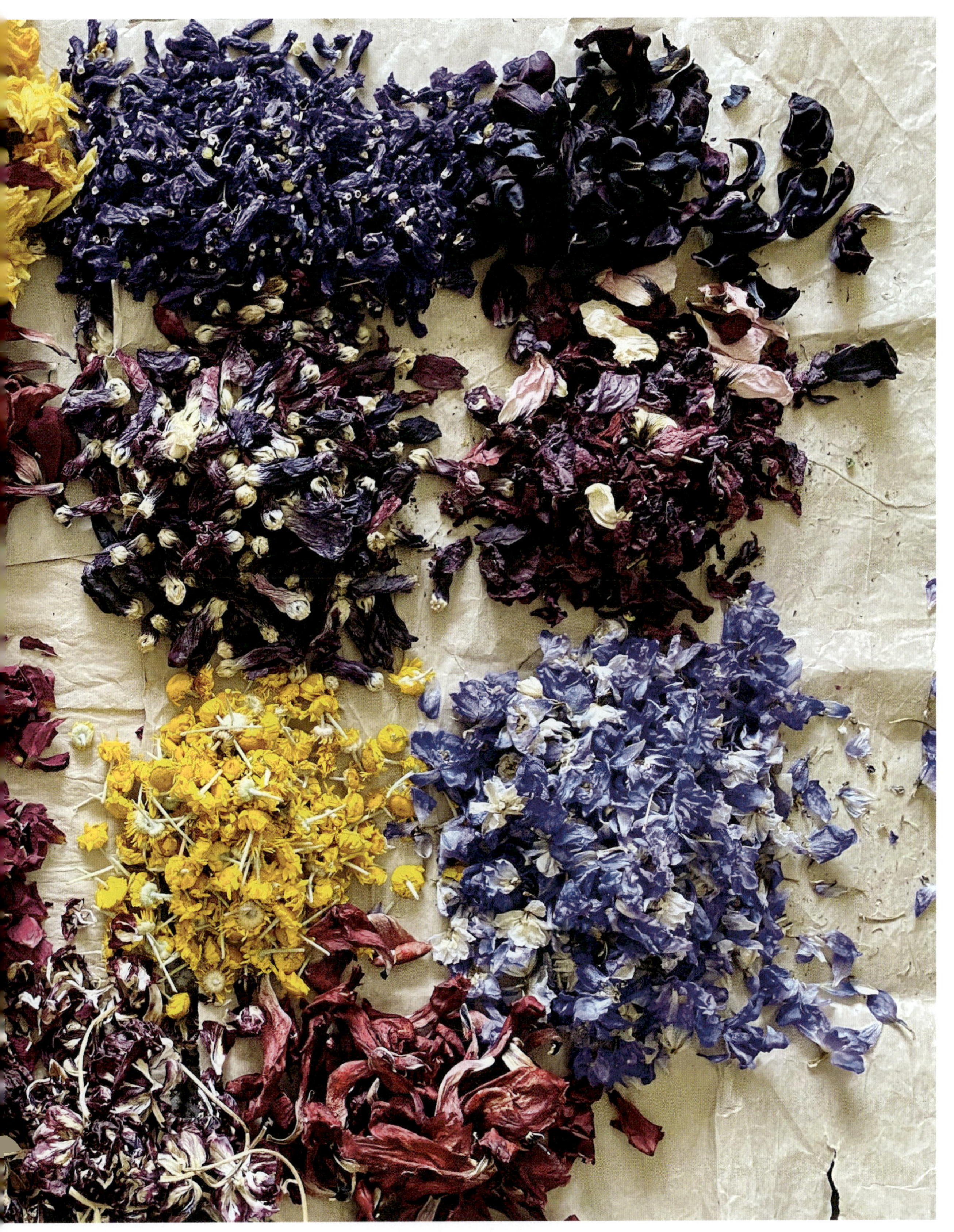

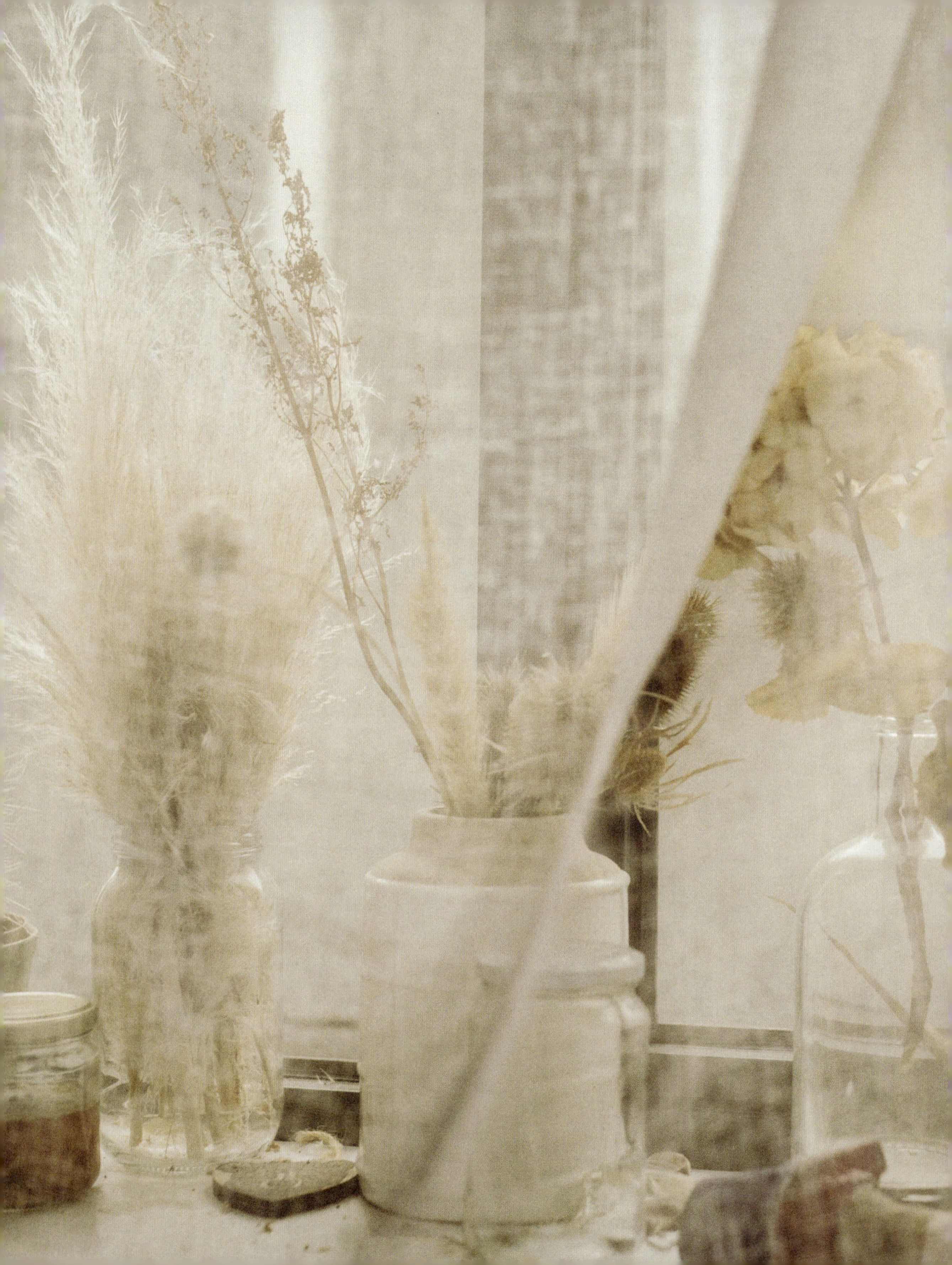

Autumn

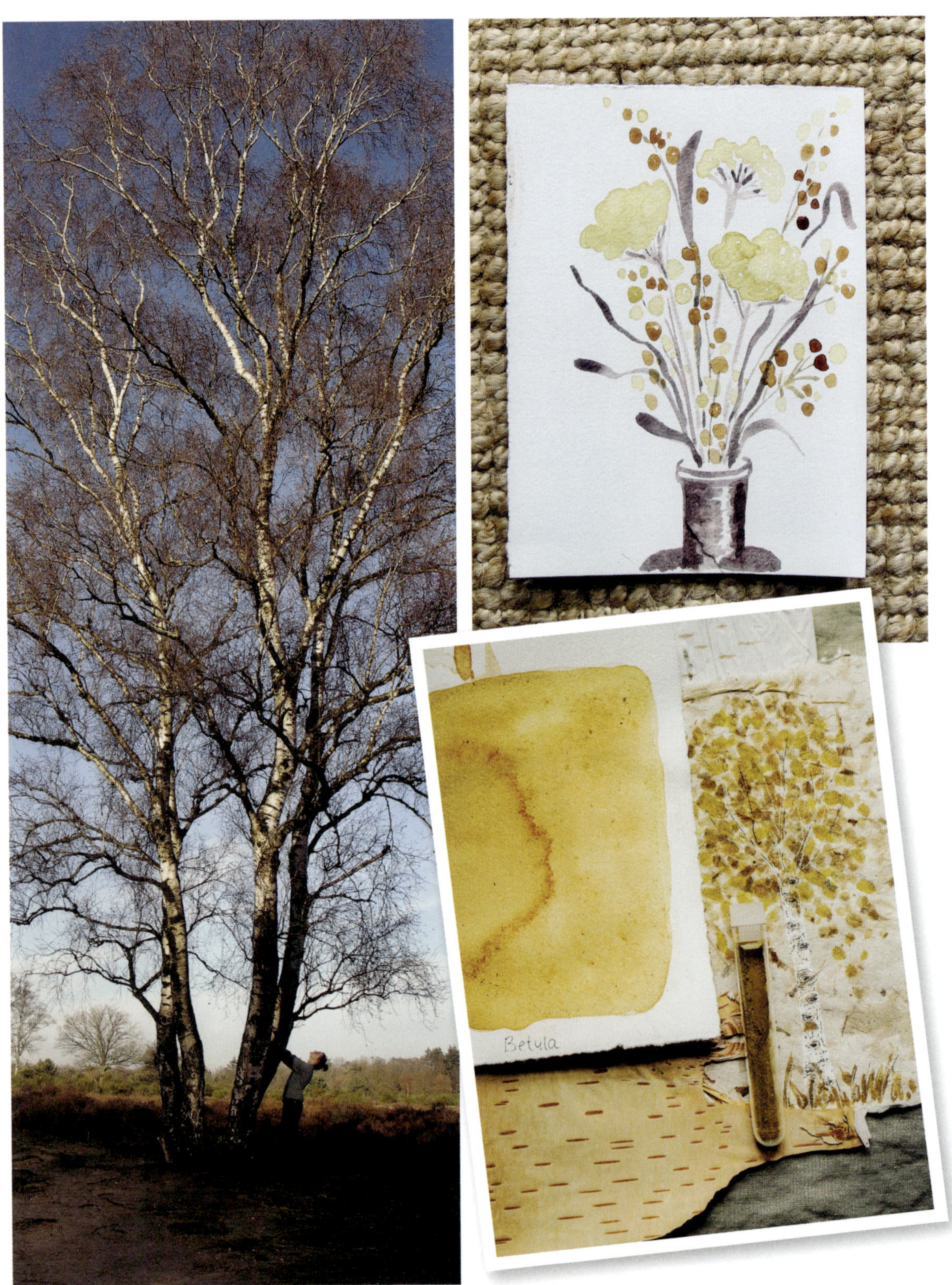

Betula

Birch

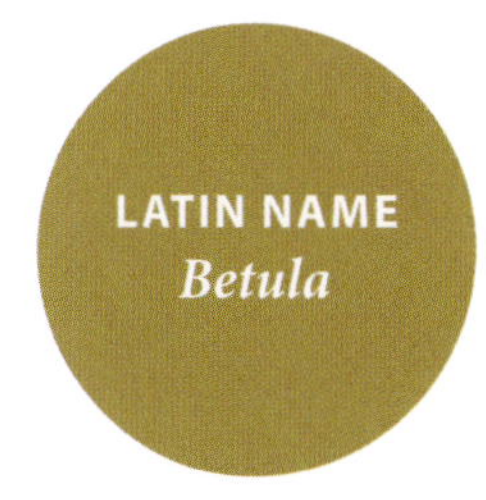

Ink from birch is lightfast +++

I think the birch is a beautiful tree. It has a white, flaky bark that reminds me of paper. Sometimes when I look at it, I can almost imagine there are eyes painted on the bark and the tree is looking at me. It's one of my favourite trees, partly because it is such a lot of fun to draw. Birch is a pioneer tree. On brackish soils where nothing else has yet grown, it will be the first to gain a foothold. Because the seeds are so very light they are easily carried by the wind, allowing the trees to spread lightning-fast. You can find birch trees in almost all deciduous and coniferous woods and heathlands. Birch contains both carotene and xanthophyll; these are the substances that provide the yellow-orange colour in autumn. Once the level of chlorophyll falls, this colour begins to emerge – and that is why using birch leaves can result in a yellow dye.

Ingredients
- 4 handfuls of birch leaves
- ¼tsp washing soda

Equipment
- newspaper or baking paper
- old pan with lid
- sieve and bowl
- coffee filter

METHOD

1. Place the birch leaves on the newspaper to air dry them. This will take a few days. It is also possible to dry them in the oven, which is quicker. Preheat the oven to 50°C (120°F). Place the leaves separated from each other on a sheet of baking paper. Dry them in the oven for 30 minutes. You need to monitor this stage and carefully check the leaves to avoid them burning.

2. Break the birch leaves into small pieces and put them in a pan.

3. Pour in just enough water to cover the pieces of leaves.

4. Place the pan on the heat but turn it down as soon as the water has almost reached boiling point. Make sure it doesn't boil.

5. Place the lid on the pan and leave to steep for 4 hours.

6. Turn off the heat and then leave the pan to stand overnight with the lid on.

7. Strain the birch mixture through a sieve and collect the liquid in a bowl.

8. Rinse the pan and then pour the liquid back into it through a coffee filter.

9. Gently heat the liquid until it reaches the consistency of syrup; it is very important that you do not allow it to boil.

10. Add washing soda.

11. Try the ink on watercolour paper.

12. The colour should be a warm yellow.

13. Bottle the ink following the instructions on page 29.

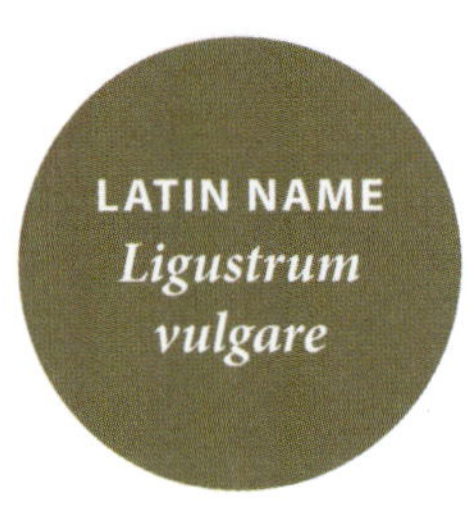

GREEN-GREY – BURGUNDY – BLUE-GREY

Privet

Ink from privet is lightfast +++

Wild privet is an evergreen shrub that flowers beautifully, showcasing large white panicles of flowers. Its flowering period is from May to July. It has sweet-smelling flowers and attracts numerous bees, bumblebees, beetles and butterflies. These are great for pollination. After it has flowered, clusters of black berries grow on the plant in August and September. The berries will remain on the plant until February or until the birds eat them! Birds love the berries, but they can be highly toxic if ingested by humans. In fact, the entire plant is toxic to us, but it does no harm if it comes into contact with your skin.

The leaves are dark green in colour, elongated and leathery and are attached to the branch by a short stalk. You will often find privet planted as a hedge. It grows quickly but it is easy to keep in shape as it responds well to pruning, which means you can soon enjoy a full hedge again after you have pruned it back. Privet hedges are a great place for birds to build a nest, so avoid pruning privet between March and June. In nature, wild privet grows in dunes, along rivers, in deciduous woods and on heathland.

Ingredients
- 1 handful of privet berries
- ¼tsp citric acid (optional)
- ¼tsp alum (optional)

Equipment
- old pan
- hand-held blender
- sieve and bowl
- coffee filter

METHOD

1. Put the privet berries in a pan.
2. Pour in just enough water to cover the berries.
3. Place the pan on the heat but turn it down as soon as the water has almost reached boiling point. Make sure it doesn't boil.
4. Simmer for 1 hour.
5. Using a hand blender, puree the berries into a pulp. The water will turn a reddish-purple colour.
6. Strain the privet berry mixture through a sieve and collect the liquid in a bowl.
7. Rinse the pan and then pour the liquid back into it through a coffee filter.
8. Gently heat the liquid until it reaches the consistency of syrup; do not allow it to boil.
9. Try the ink on watercolour paper. The colour of the liquid is red-purple and it will slowly take on a green-grey hue.
10. For a burgundy colour, add citric acid.
11. For a blue-grey colour, add some alum.
12. Bottle the ink following the instructions on page 29.

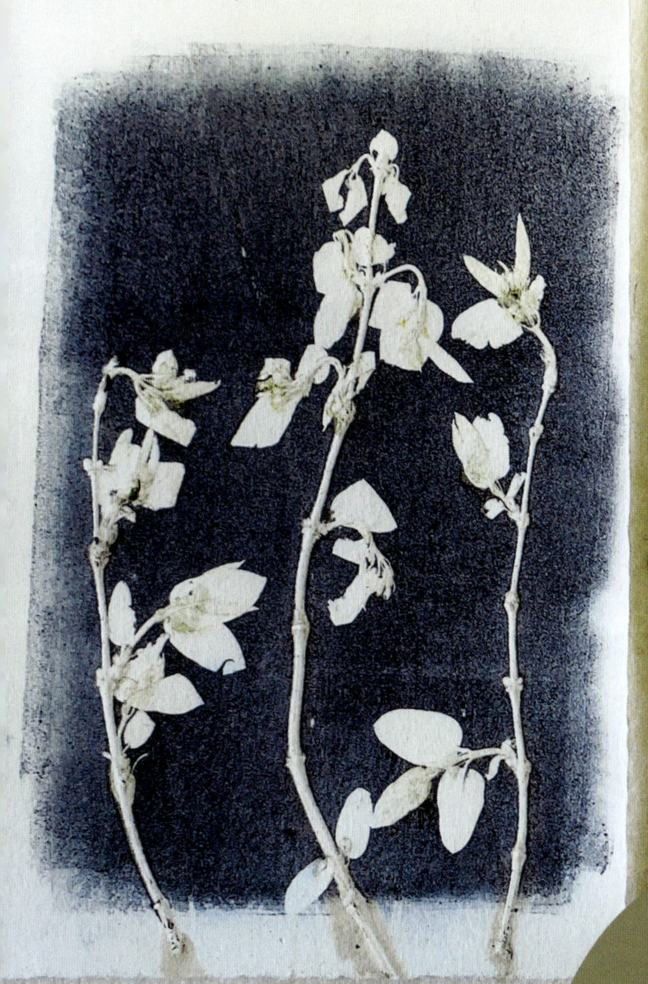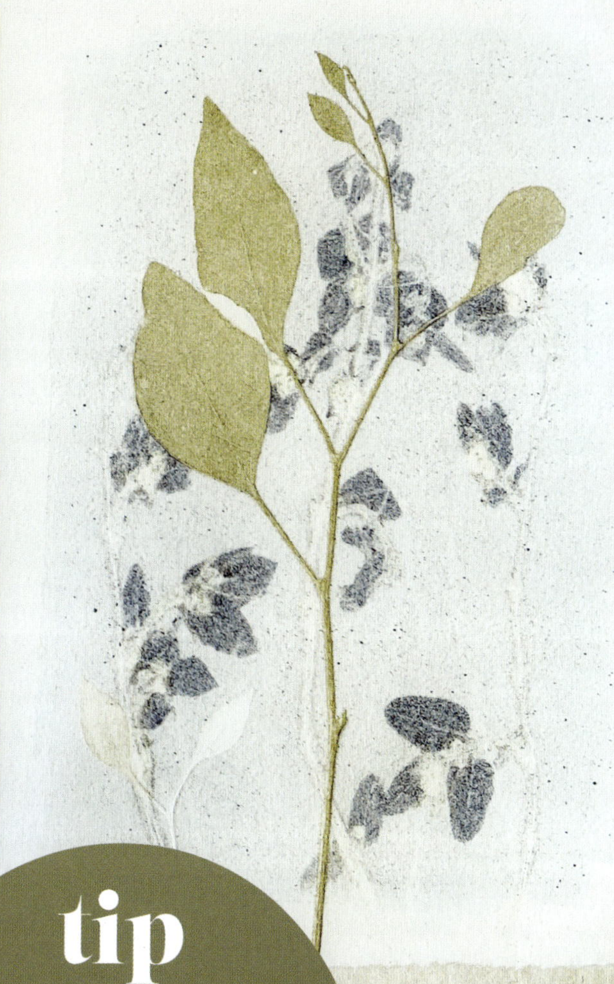

tip

BE CAREFUL!

Take care when working with this ink.
Wash your hands immediately after
handling the berries. The ink remains
toxic even after bottling, so take care
when working with it and keep it
out of the reach of children
and pets.

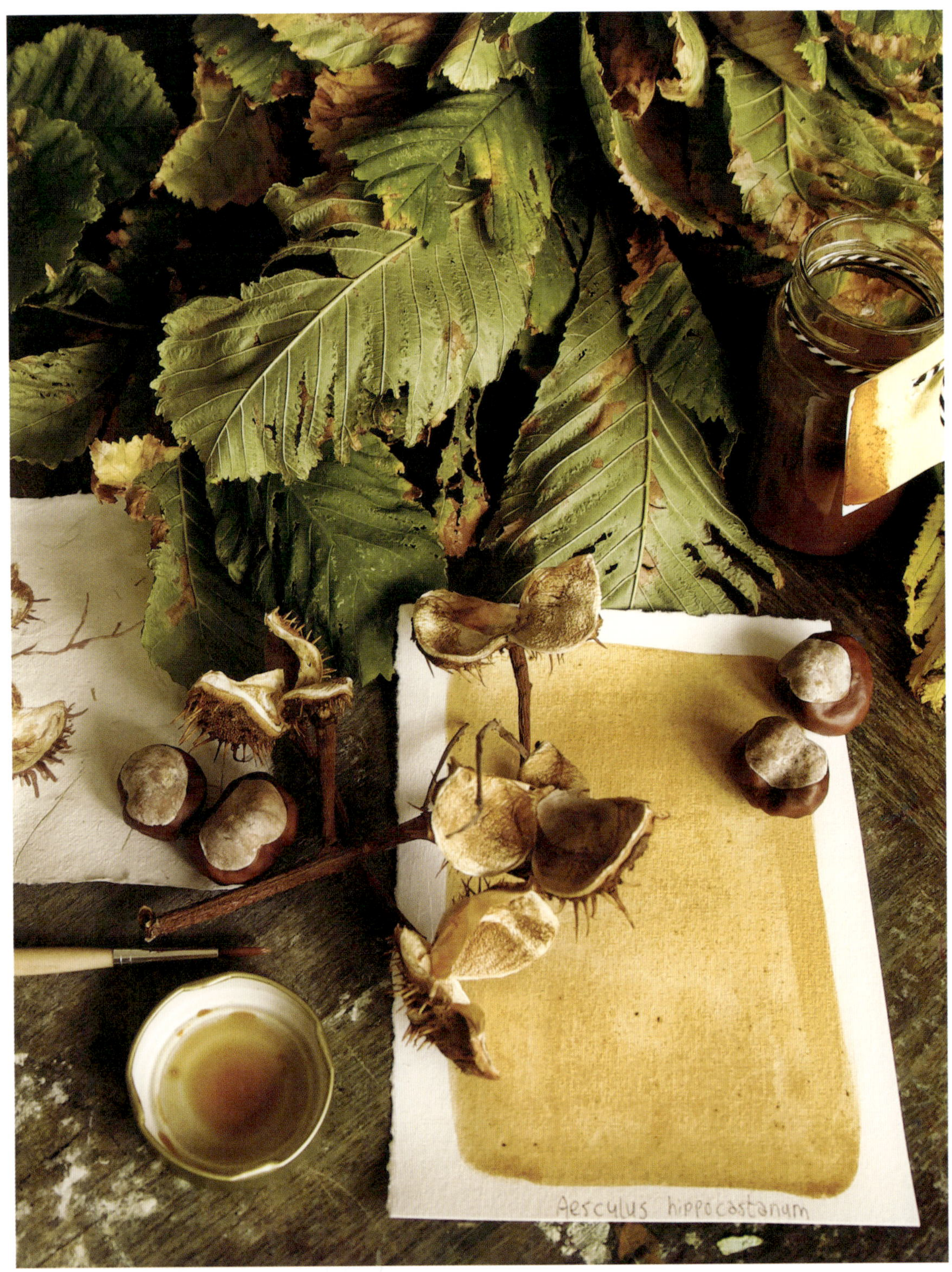

Aesculus hippocastanum

Horse chestnut

Ink from horse chestnut is lightfast +++

There are different varieties of chestnut tree. The most common ones are the white and red horse chestnut tree and the sweet chestnut tree. The first two species are related to each other and form part of the soapberry family, whereas the latter is related to the beech. They have the same name because the seeds look similar. To make this ink, use the leaves of the white horse chestnut tree. When this species is in bloom, it has large clusters of white flowers with yellow tips that turn a red-orange colour once they have been pollinated. Bumblebees particularly like the nectar they can get from chestnut flowers. Incidentally, you can also use the flowers to make an ink that has a warm orange hue. In the UK, white horse chestnut trees are frequently planted along avenues and streets. You can see some beautiful old specimens close to castles and churches, as well as in the wild. They prefer to grow in clay or loamy soils. The leaves are divided into five to seven partial leaves and take the shape of a hand. As long as the tree has room to grow, it is able to reach a height of 20m (66½ft). In autumn, the green coloured chlorophyll starts to disappear from the leaves and yellow, orange and red pigments become more visible.

Ingredients
- 6 large horse chestnut leaves without stalks
- ¼tsp potash

Equipment
- newspaper or baking paper
- old pan with lid
- sieve and bowl
- coffee filter

METHOD

1. Place the leaves on the newspaper to air dry them. This will take a few days. It is also possible to dry them in the oven, which is quicker. Preheat the oven to 50°C (120°F). Place the leaves separated from each other on a sheet of baking paper. Dry them in the oven for 30 minutes. You need to monitor this stage carefully to avoid them burning.
2. Shred the leaves into pieces and add to the pan.
3. Pour in just enough water to cover the leaves.
4. Place the pan on the heat but turn it down as soon as the water has almost reached boiling point. Do not allow it to boil.
5. Place the lid on the pan and leave to steep for 1 hour.
6. Turn off the heat and then leave the pan to stand overnight with the lid on.
7. Strain the chestnut mixture through a sieve and collect the liquid in a bowl.
8. Rinse the pan and then pour the liquid back into it through a coffee filter.
9. Gently heat the liquid until it reaches the consistency of syrup; do not allow it to boil.
10. Add potash. It will be warm ochre in colour.
11. Bottle the ink following the instructions on page 29.

BRIGHT ORANGE – BLUE

Saffron crocus

Ink from saffron crocus is lightfast +++

Can you grow saffron in the UK? Well, yes, you can. Most crocuses bloom in spring, but the saffron crocus blooms in autumn. Plant the bulbs in June in a sunny spot. Around October, as the nights begin to get colder, the crocuses start to poke their heads above the ground. Once the flowers open, you need to harvest them because they wilt very quickly. Carefully pick the flower and remove the saffron stamen using tweezers. Lay out the saffron stamens to dry on kitchen paper. If you store your harvested saffron in a sealed container, it will keep for up to three years. In order to help saffron crocus bulbs overwinter well in the ground, cover them with a layer of organic material. This will allow you to harvest them again the following year. If this all sounds like too much hassle, you can also use saffron that you've bought from a shop. However, you can't then make blue ink from the purple petals; the recipe for this can be found on page 65 – it is the same as for hollyhocks. You can also make ink using the common crocus. Separate the yellow stamen from the purple crocus and leave both of them to dry. The stamens will make yellow ink and the purple crocus will make blue. You can see the recipe for this below.

Ingredients
- stamens from saffron crocus
- gum arabic
- cloves

Equipment
- kitchen paper
- pestle and mortar
- coffee filter
- bowl

METHOD

1. Dry the saffron stamen. Put a piece of kitchen paper in a bowl and carefully place the saffron threads on the paper. They will take 2 days to dry. It is also possible to dry them in the oven, which is quicker. Preheat the oven to 50°C (120°F). Place the saffron stamens separated from each other on a sheet of baking paper. Dry them in the oven for 30 minutes. Carefully check the stamens to avoid them burning.

2. Place the saffron stamens in a mortar.

3. Pour in just enough hot water to cover the saffron stamens. You won't need very much at all. The water should be just off the boil.

4. Using the pestle, grind the saffron stamens in the water until they resemble pulp. The colour should be immediately released and should be an orange shade.

5. Keep grinding the stamens until the orange colour remains constant. This will take about 1 minute.

6. Pour the saffron stamen water through a coffee filter and collect it in a bowl.

7. Add 5 drops of gum arabic and a clove to every 30ml (1oz) of liquid; your ink is then ready to use.

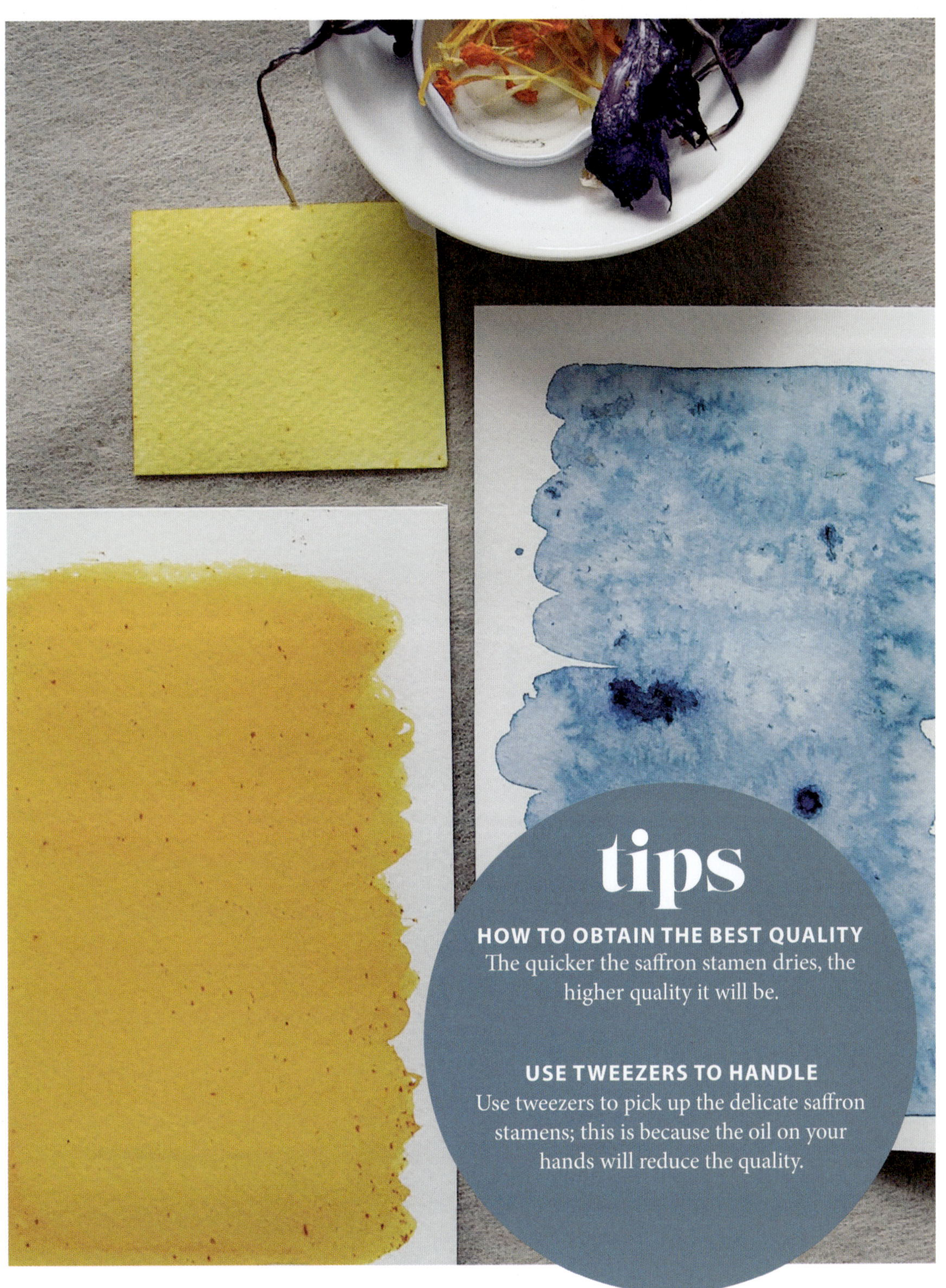

tips

HOW TO OBTAIN THE BEST QUALITY
The quicker the saffron stamen dries, the
higher quality it will be.

USE TWEEZERS TO HANDLE
Use tweezers to pick up the delicate saffron
stamens; this is because the oil on your
hands will reduce the quality.

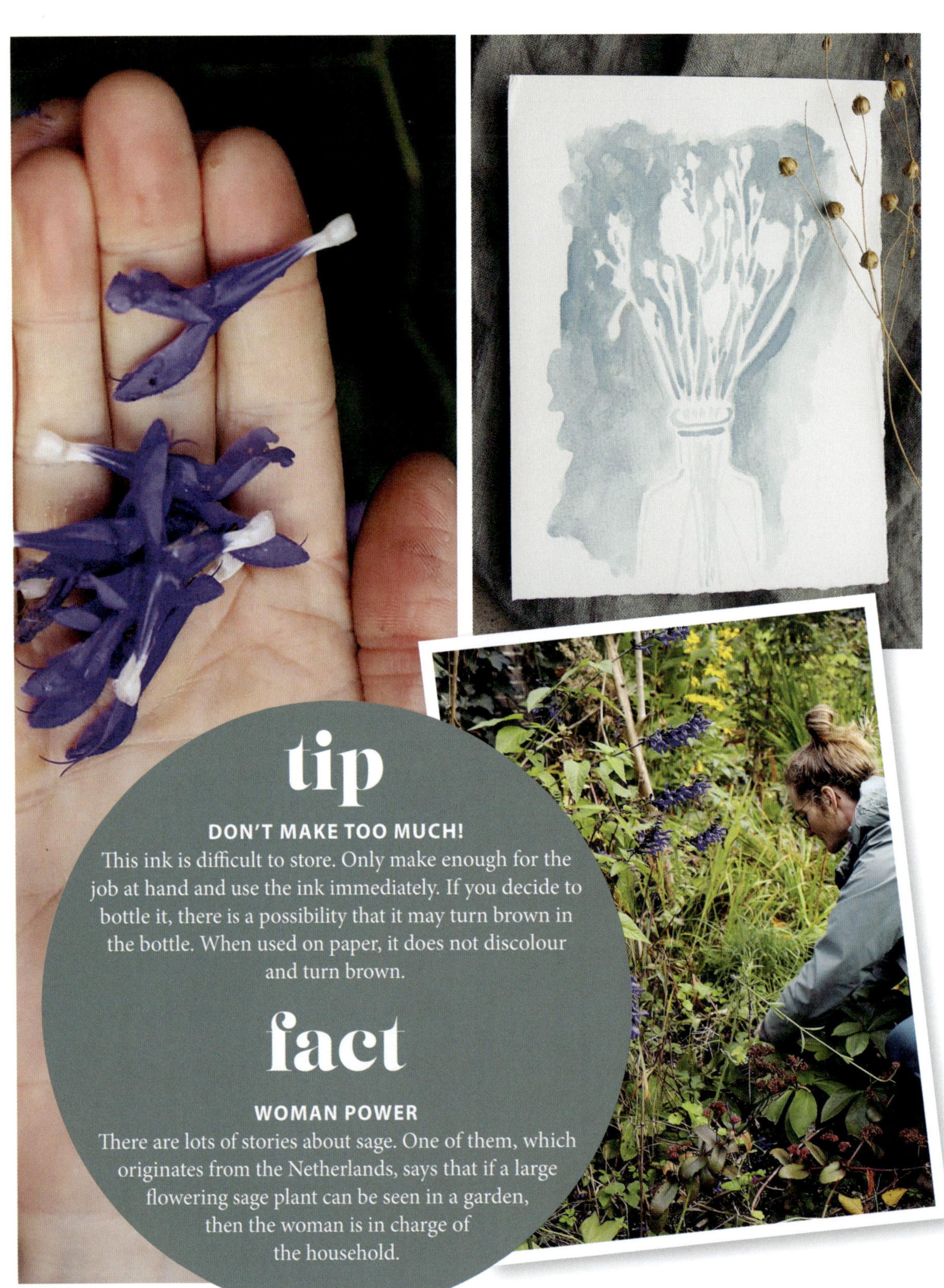

tip

DON'T MAKE TOO MUCH!

This ink is difficult to store. Only make enough for the job at hand and use the ink immediately. If you decide to bottle it, there is a possibility that it may turn brown in the bottle. When used on paper, it does not discolour and turn brown.

fact

WOMAN POWER

There are lots of stories about sage. One of them, which originates from the Netherlands, says that if a large flowering sage plant can be seen in a garden, then the woman is in charge of the household.

Sage

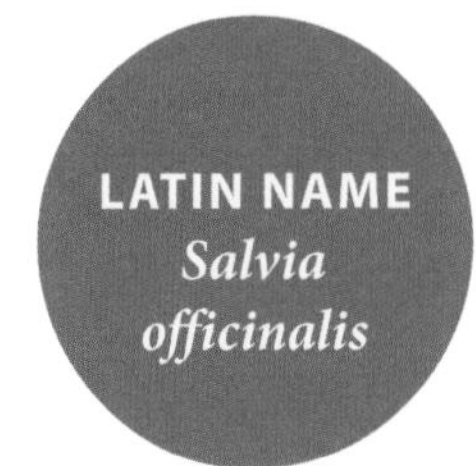

Ink from sage is lightfast ++

The name *Salvia* comes from the Latin *salvare*, which means 'to heal'. The word *officinalis* after a plant name indicates the medicinal effect of the plant; it literally means 'from the apothecary's workshop'. Common sage has been used for thousands of years both for medicine and as a culinary herb. The Greeks and Romans believed that this herb could cure all ailments, a so-called panacea. In the Middle Ages, sage was even believed to have magical properties. It was commonly used as a remedy to assist with a plethora of complaints and ailments, from coughs and insect bites to gum problems and infertility. Sage has not only been used for centuries in Europe; it has also been known to the indigenous population of North America for a very long time. The sage is burned and used to ward off evil spirits using a 'smudge stick'. You can make these yourself. Sage flowers come in shades of pink, white, blue and purple. The most beautiful ink is made using *Salvia patens*: a species of salvia, it has large dark blue flowers that come into bloom from August and remain until the first overnight frost. It grows up to 70cm (27½in) in height and prefers sunny spots with dry, nutrient-poor soil.

Ingredients	Equipment
• sage flowers	• newspaper or baking paper
• washing soda (optional)	• pestle and mortar
• gum arabic	• coffee filter
	• bowl

METHOD

1. Place the flowers on the newspaper to air dry them. This will take a few days. It is also possible to dry them in the oven, which is quicker. Preheat the oven to 50°C (120°F). Place the flowers separated from each other on a sheet of baking paper. Dry them in the oven for 30 minutes. You need to monitor this stage carefully to avoid them burning.

2. Crush the flowers in a mortar.

3. Pour in just enough hot water to cover the crushed flowers. You won't need very much. The water should be just off the boil.

4. Using the pestle, grind the shredded flowers in the water until they resemble pulp. The colour should be immediately released and should be a light blue shade.

5. Keep grinding the flowers until the colour remains constant. This takes about 1 minute.

6. Pour the sage water through a coffee filter and collect it in a bowl.

7. For a mint green colour, add a pinch of washing soda for every 30ml (1oz) of liquid.

8. Add 5 drops of gum arabic to every 30ml (1oz) of liquid; your ink is then ready to use.

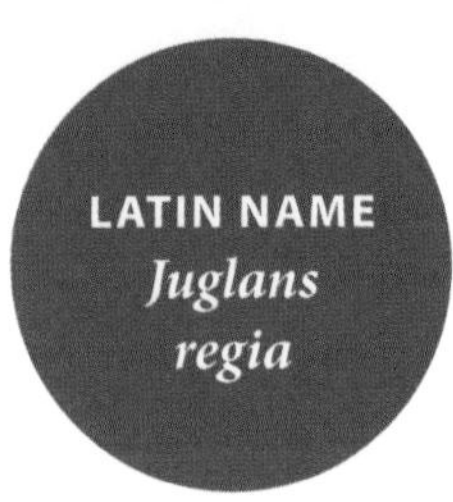

BROWN-BLACK

Walnut

Ink from walnut is lightfast ++++

A walnut tree can reach heights of 30m (98½ft) and have a leaf crown that stretches over 20m (65½ft) in diameter. 'Walnut' is not really a good name for it, because the fruit from a walnut tree is not a nut at all, but a stone fruit. The fruit is protected by a green husk, under which is another hard shell that you have to crack open when you want to eat the walnut. The husk is green with a white inside. This gradually turns black as a result of oxidation. Walnuts are commonly found in Europe but are actually native to Asia. In the UK, walnut trees can be found planted far and wide in gardens and parks. The husks should be picked in autumn, when the walnuts have fallen to the ground. In fact, September and October are the perfect months for collecting walnuts and you'll find that the husks break open by themselves. Walnuts and their husks can be collected for ink making, as well as to dye hair. Just like gallnut ink, walnut ink is a historical ink. People have used it for writing since the Middle Ages.

Ingredients
- 1 handful of black walnut husks
- 1 pinch of iron sulphate (optional)

Equipment
- old pan with lid
- sieve and bowl
- coffee filter

METHOD

1. Break the walnut husks into small pieces and put them in a pan.
2. Pour in just enough water to cover them.
3. Place the pan on the heat but make sure to turn it down as soon as the water has almost reached boiling point. Do not allow it to boil.
4. Place the lid on the pan and leave it to stand for as long as possible – at least 4 hours. The longer you leave the mixture on the heat, the darker the colour will become.
5. Turn off the heat and then leave the pan to stand overnight with the lid on.
6. Strain the walnut mixture through a sieve and collect the liquid in a bowl.
7. Rinse the pan and then pour the liquid back into it through a coffee filter.
8. Gently heat the liquid until it reaches the consistency of syrup; it is very important that you do not allow it to boil.
9. Try the ink on watercolour paper. The colour should be dark brown, but if you want an even darker colour, you can add iron sulphate. The colour will then turn a shade of brown-black.
10. Bottle the ink following the instructions on page 29.

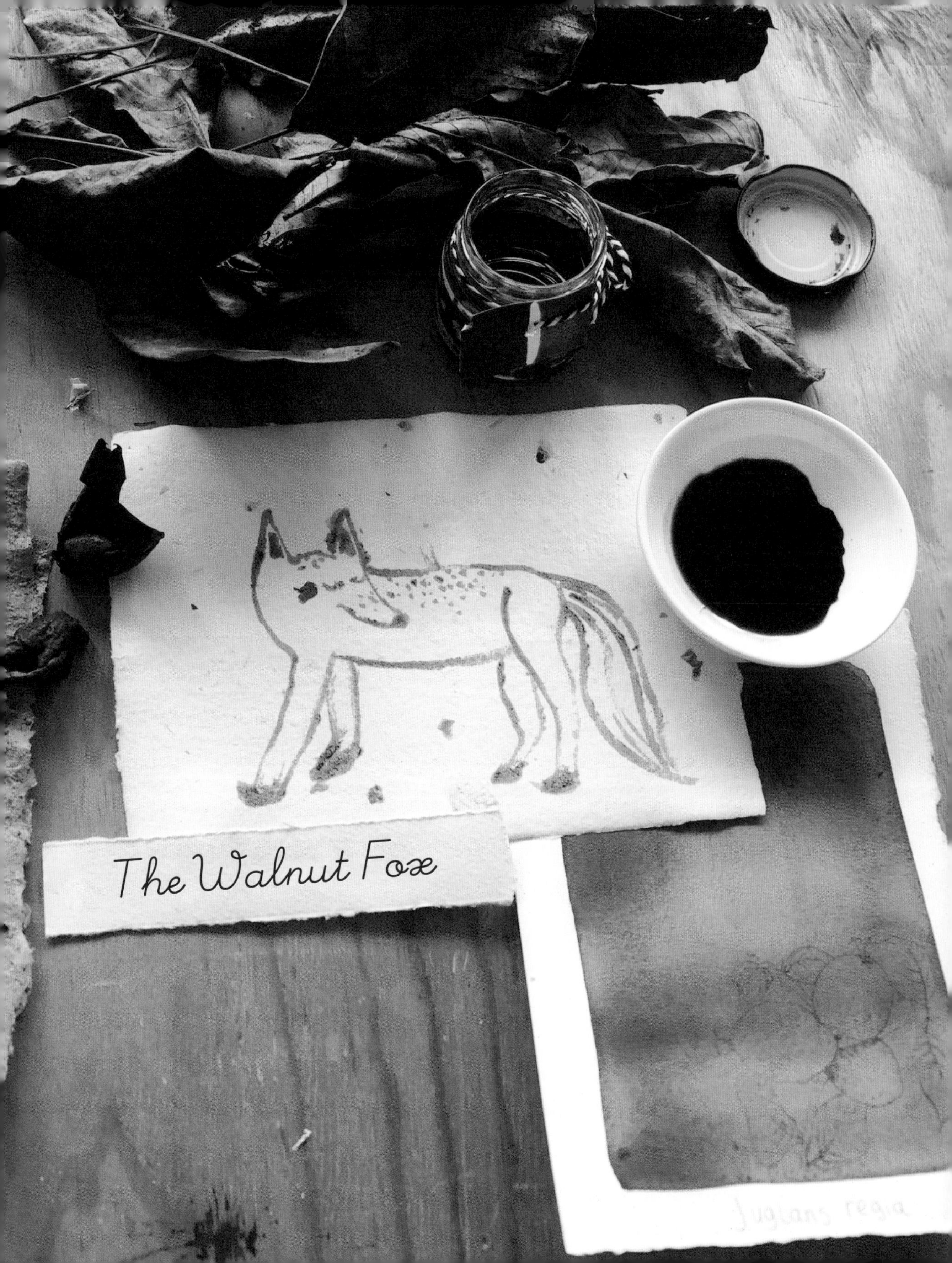
The Walnut Fox
Juglans regia

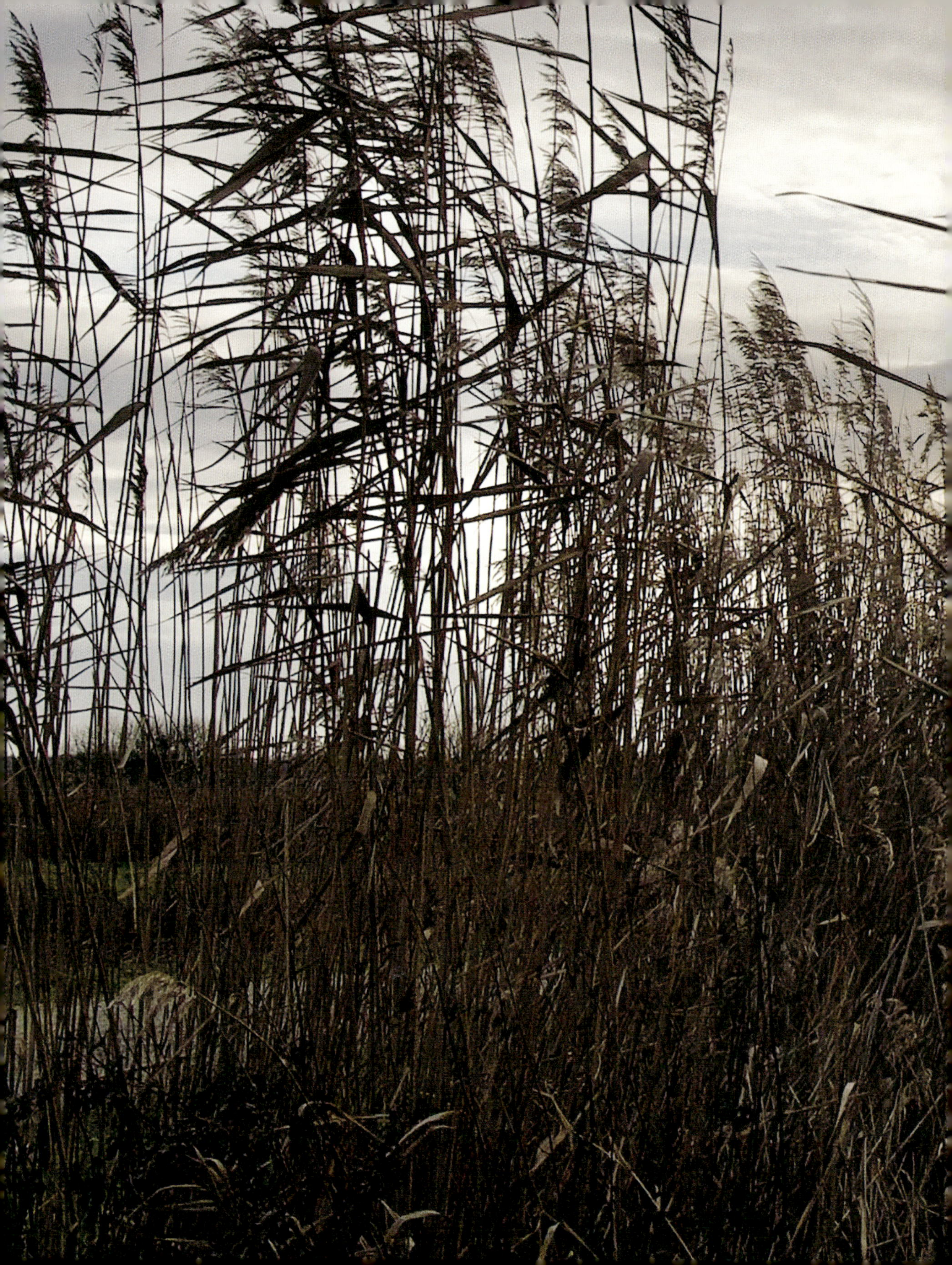

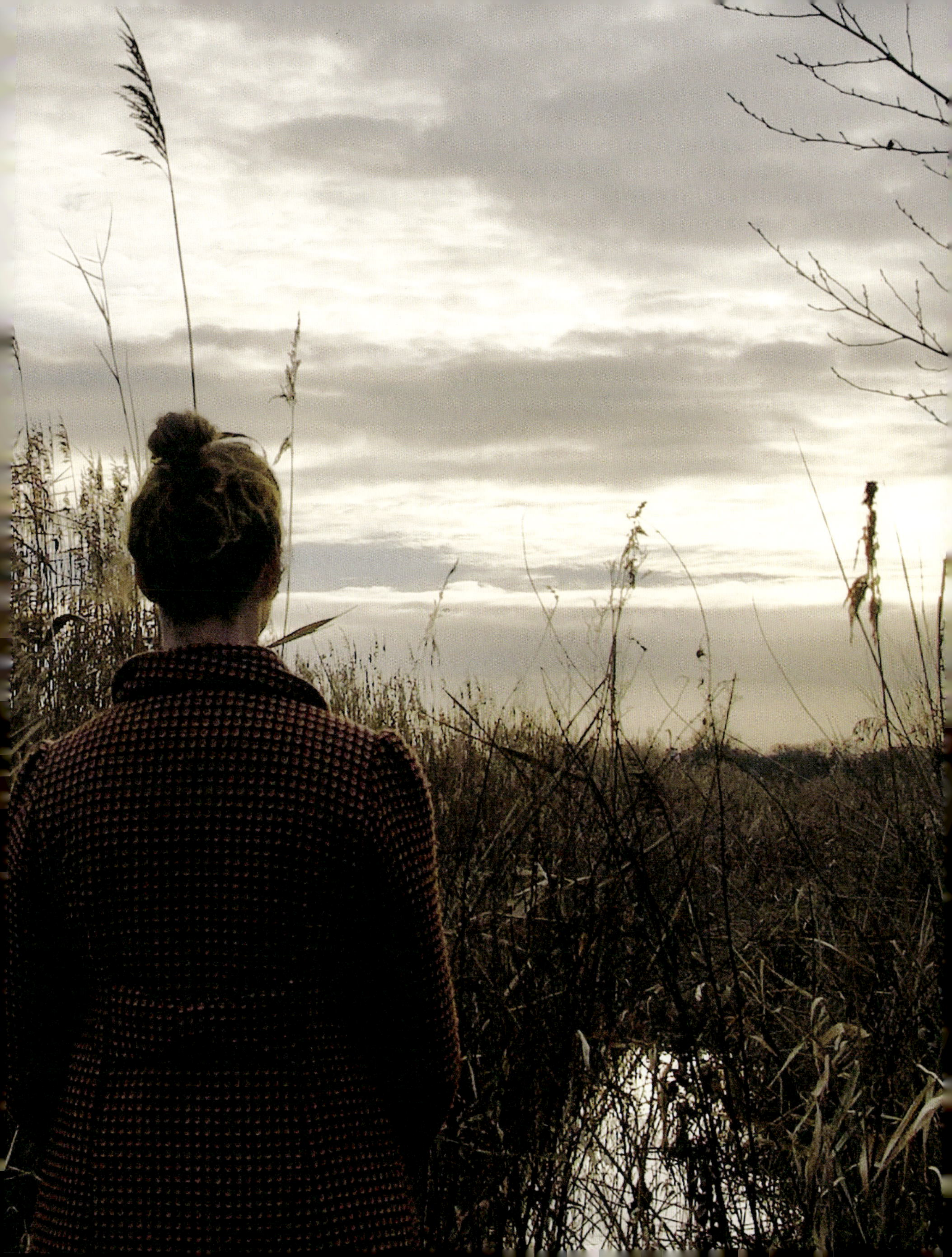

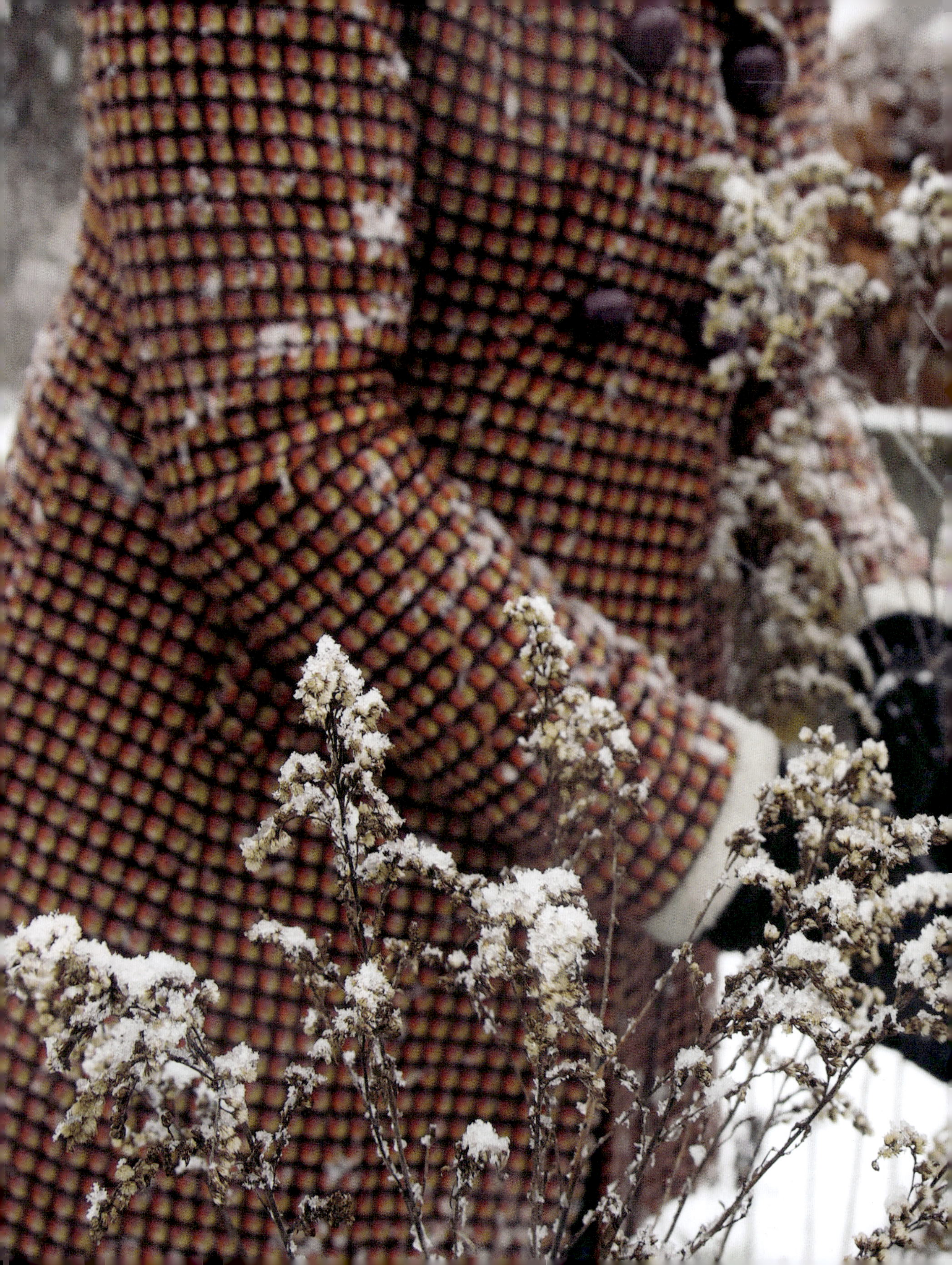

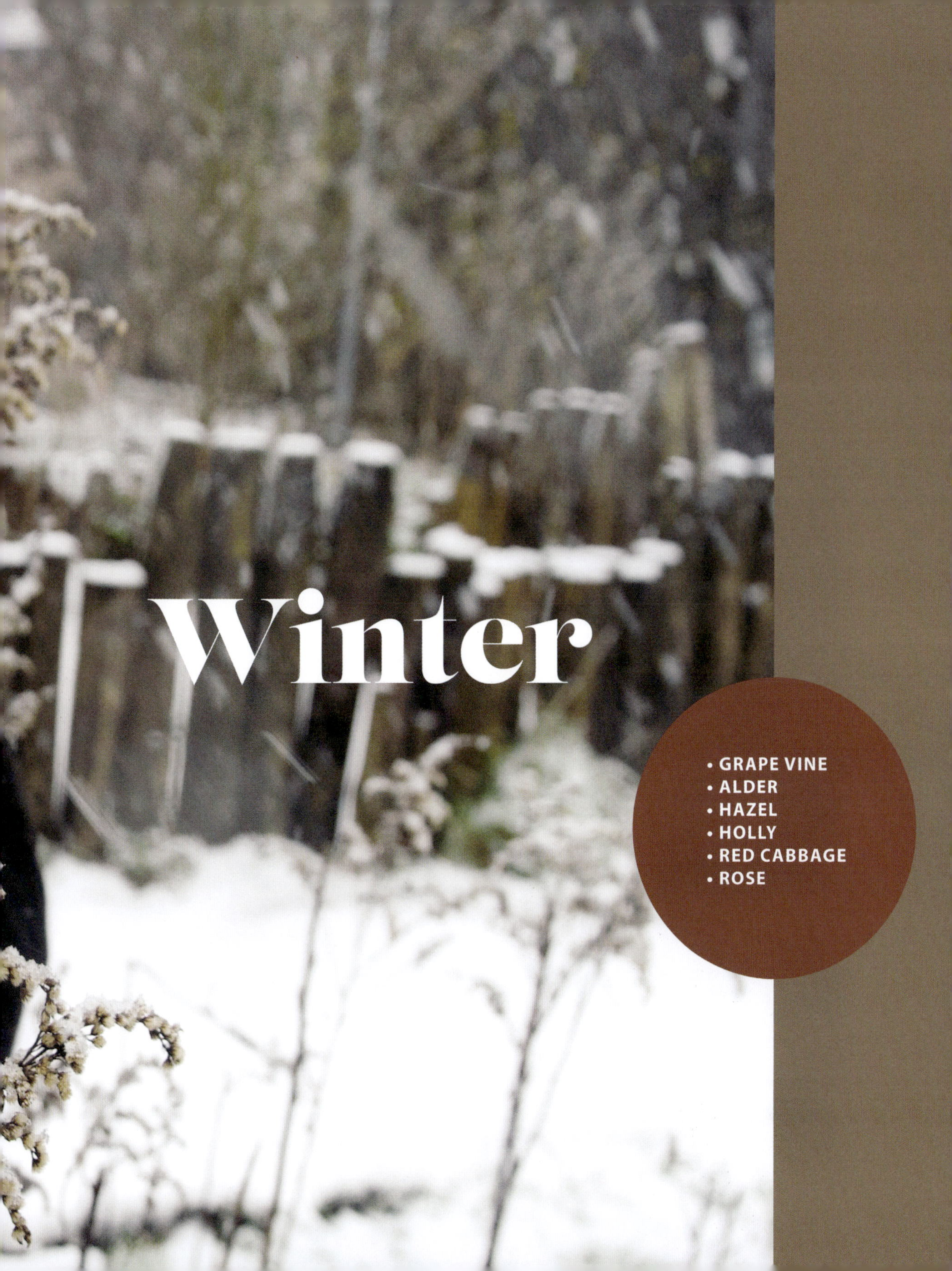

Winter

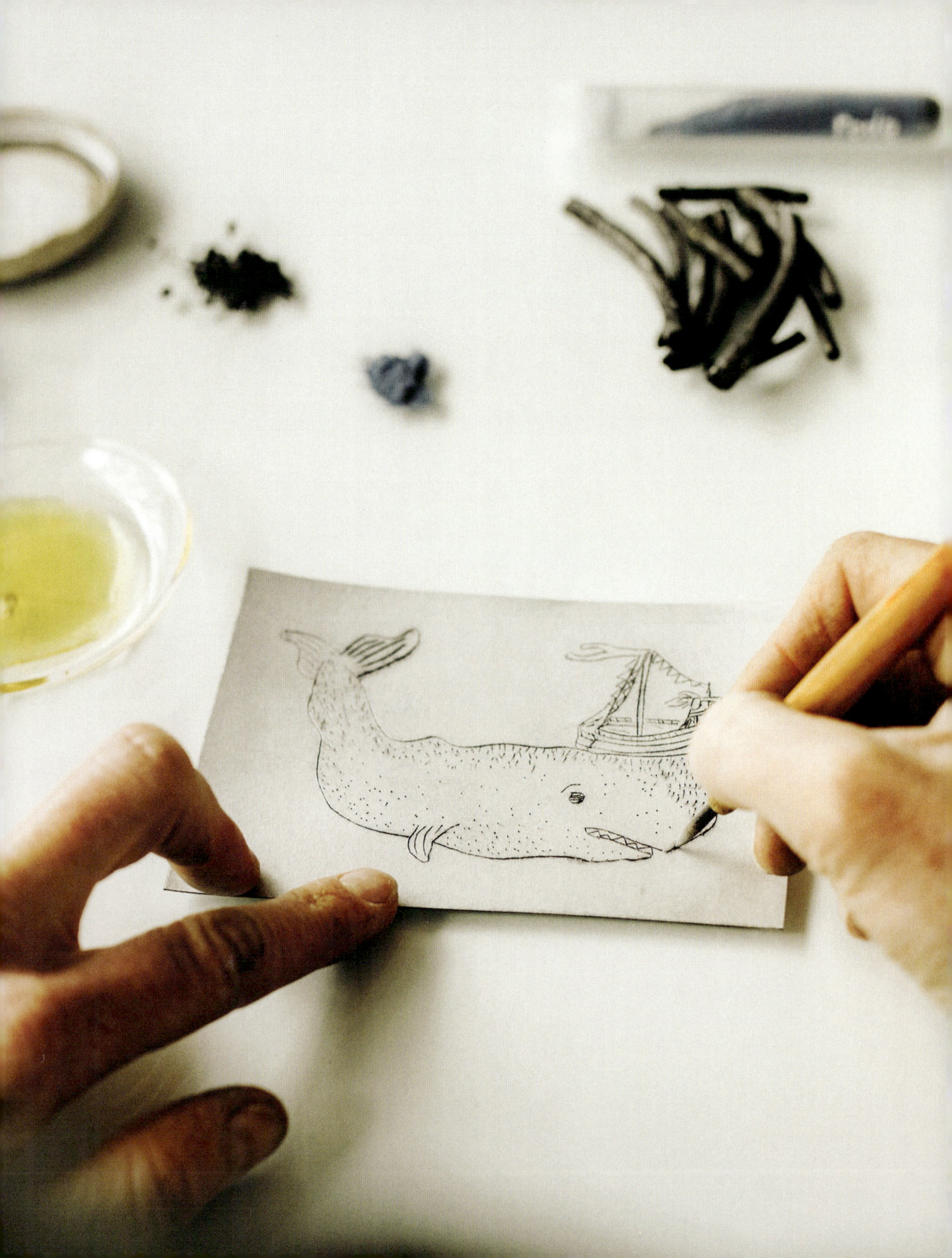

Grape vine

Ink from grape vines is lightfast ++++

LATIN NAME
Vitis vinifera

Are you the proud owner of a grape vine in your garden? If so, you'll know that grape vines need to be heavily pruned each year since it is pruning that really gives the grape vines their lovely dark colour. This recipe can be used to make charcoal for drawing, as well as for making ink or paint. Place the pruned wood in a metal can in the fire. Neatly place the twigs side-by-side and try to fill the can as full as possible as this will stop the twigs from warping. Since the wood is not directly exposed to the flames, it will not burn. However, the heat does cause them to char, which is exactly what is intended. There needs to be a hole in the lid of the can in order to allow the hot gases to escape.

Ink can be made from various types of wood. My favourites are grape vines and willow. This is because the inside of the wood is not as compact as in other species. In fact, grape vine and willow are quite soft, which means they char evenly, and you end up with charcoal that turns into a really nice powder. This is why it's important for the wood to have a soft core. This charcoal ink is the same as the ink made by the Chinese and Egyptians in 2500BC. They bound the ink with bone glue and then pressed it to form rods. The ink rods were then rubbed with water onto an ink stone to produce liquid ink. For this recipe, we use gum arabic as a binder. Make the ink using four to five sticks of charcoal and then keep the rest or use it for drawing. Once charred, grape vines will shrink to about a quarter of their size.

Grape vine

Ingredients
- grape-vine branches (the quantity depends on the size of your metal can)
- gum arabic (the quantity depends on how thick you want to make the ink)

Equipment
- hammer and nail
- metal can with lid
- pruning shears
- iron wire
- wood (for making a fire)
- fire bowl
- firelighters
- tongs
- matches
- pestle and mortar or coffee grinder
- sterile glass jar

METHOD

1. Using the hammer and nail, make a small hole in the lid of the metal can; the hot air will escape through this later.
2. Use the pruning shears to cut the grape vine branches to the size of the metal can.
3. Remove the bark from the grape vine branches.
4. Stuff the can with the branches so it is as full as possible.
5. Put the lid on the can and wrap the iron wire around it to prevent the can from opening when it is placed in the fire.
6. Stack the logs in a fire bowl, place the firelighters on top and then light them. Place the can in the flames for at least 1 hour.
7. Use the tongs to carefully remove the can from the fire and leave it to cool down completely.
8. Open the can and remove the charcoal sticks. You can use the sticks to draw with, but to make ink, move on to the next step.
9. Break the charcoal sticks into small pieces and grind them into a very fine powder using a mortar or grind them in a coffee grinder.
10. Mix drops of gum arabic into the charcoal powder. By adding a little gum, you will get the consistency of paint. The more gum you add, the thinner the ink becomes.
11. Try out the ink or paint on watercolour paper. The colour will be an intense black.
12. Store the ink in a sterile jar.

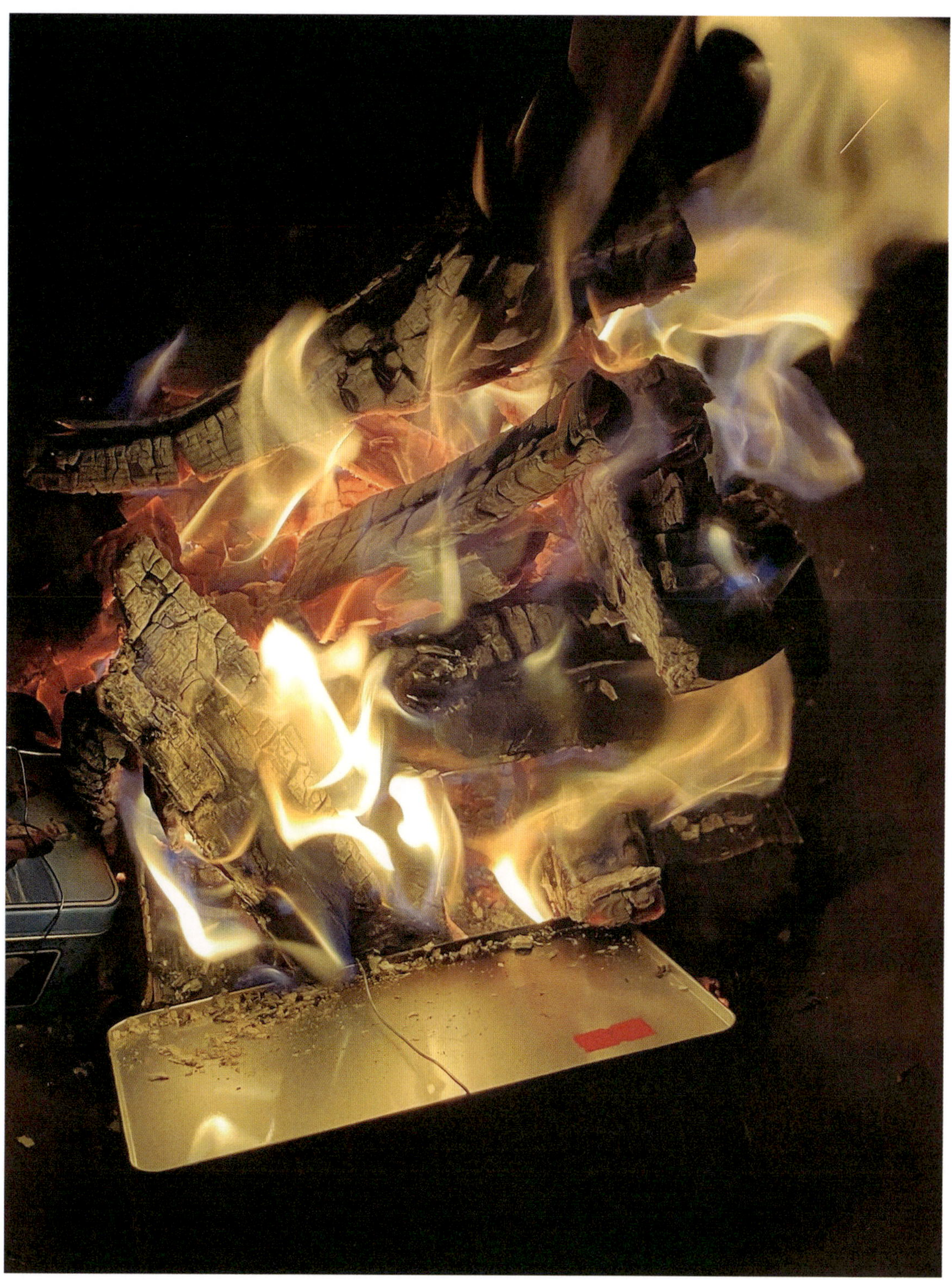

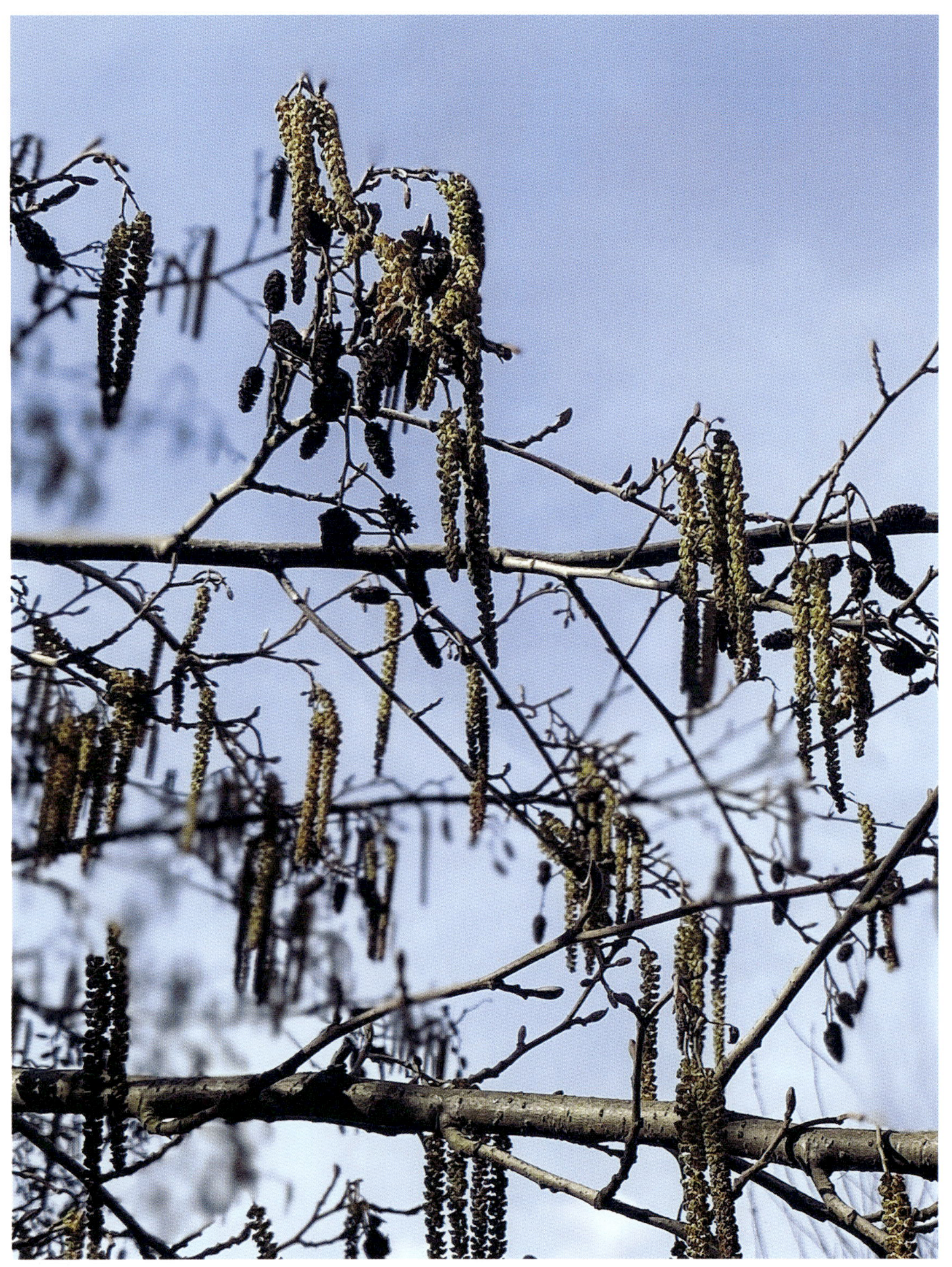

Alder

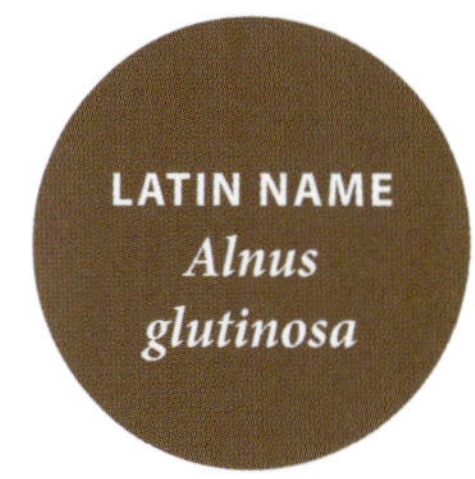

Ink from alder is lightfast +++

The hazel (see page 118) is the first tree to bloom each year, closely followed by black alder, which flowers from February onwards. As is the case with hazel trees, the male and female flowers of the alder also bloom on the same tree. But unlike hazel, they flower at the same time. Black alder therefore self-pollinates. The male catkins are initially a shade of purple, but they transform to yellow and red when maturing. They grow to about 8cm (3in) in length, although the female ones are much smaller and darker. They sit next to each other at the very end of the branches. Once the female flowers are fertilized, they grow into green cone-shaped fruits, which become woody later in the year. Known as alder cones, they are similar to small pinecones and contain the alder seeds. The alder cones will remain on the tree for up to a year and a half. I really love the fact that you find both of these flowers on one tree. I also like the young leaves that grow on an alder. They are jagged, red in colour and have strong striations. Alder loves being in wet ground. It can be found along the edges of water, on the banks of streams and ditches, and in marshland. It can grow to as high as 24m (78¾ft). It has a dark green to black-brown trunk with deep grooves. It is found throughout Europe, except in Scandinavia.

Ingredients
- 2 handfuls of alder cones
- ¼tsp potash

Equipment
- old pan with lid
- sieve and bowl
- coffee filter

METHOD

1. Put the alder cones in a pan.
2. Pour in just enough water to cover them.
3. Place the pan on the heat but turn it down as soon as the water has almost reached boiling point. Do not allow it to boil.
4. Place the lid on the pan and leave to steep for 3 hours.
5. Turn off the heat and then leave the pan to stand overnight with the lid on.
6. Strain the alder mixture through a sieve and collect the liquid in a bowl. It will be light brown in colour.
7. Rinse the pan and then pour the liquid back into it through a coffee filter.
8. Gently heat the liquid until it reaches the consistency of syrup; it is very important that you do not allow it to boil.
9. Add the potash and stir everything well. The colour will change to a shade of warm brown.
10. Bottle the ink following the instructions on page 29.

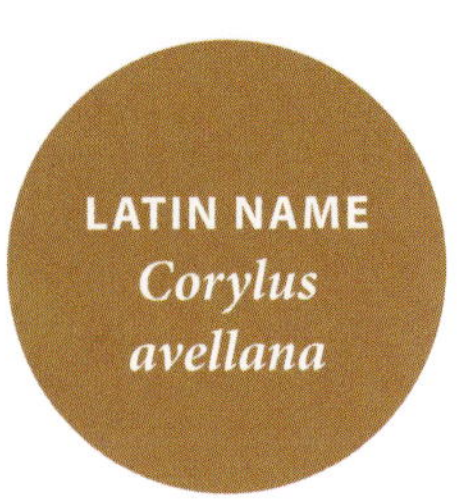

WARM ORANGE

Hazel

Ink from the hazel tree is lightfast +++

Hazels bloom when they still don't have any leaves, which is why they are sometimes known as 'naked bloomers'. The male and female flowers appear on the same tree at different times. The male catkins are a yellow-green colour and about 10cm (4in) long; they contain the pollen. The female (pistillate) flowers grow out of the leaf axils and are bright red. They come out once the male flowers have released their pollen. Hazel is a wind pollinator. It releases its pollen to the wind and a small part of it will end up on the female flowers, which results in hazelnuts. Since the male and female flowers appear on the same tree but are not in bloom at the same time, it means self-fertilization is impossible. By pollinating this way, the tree can ensure strong offspring. Hazel flowers between January and April. When the flowering season is over, the bright red female flowers emerge from the buds on the branches. At this point, the tree is also starting to produce leaves. The leaves are a light green colour and ovoid, with a pointed tip at the bottom and nice, clear striations. Hazels grow in deciduous woods and they are widely planted in parks. They can grow to a height of approximately 6m (19¾ft) and only start bearing fruit after 10 years. Beekeepers love hazels. They like to plant them near their hives because the early bloom provides their bees with their first food.

Ingredients
- 2 handfuls of flowering catkins
- ¼tsp potash

Equipment
- old pan with lid
- sieve and bowl
- coffee filter

METHOD

1. Put the catkins in a pan and pour in just enough water to submerge them.
2. Place the pan on the heat but turn it down as soon as the water has almost reached boiling point. Do not allow it to boil.
3. Place the lid on the pan and leave to steep for 1 hour.
4. Turn off the heat and then leave the pan to stand overnight with the lid on.
5. Strain the mixture through a sieve and collect the liquid in a bowl. It will be light yellow.
6. Rinse the pan and then pour the liquid back into it through a coffee filter.
7. Gently heat the liquid until it reaches the consistency of syrup; do not allow it to boil.
8. Add the potash and stir everything well. The colour first changes to dark yellow and then again to warm orange.
9. Bottle the ink following the instructions on page 29.

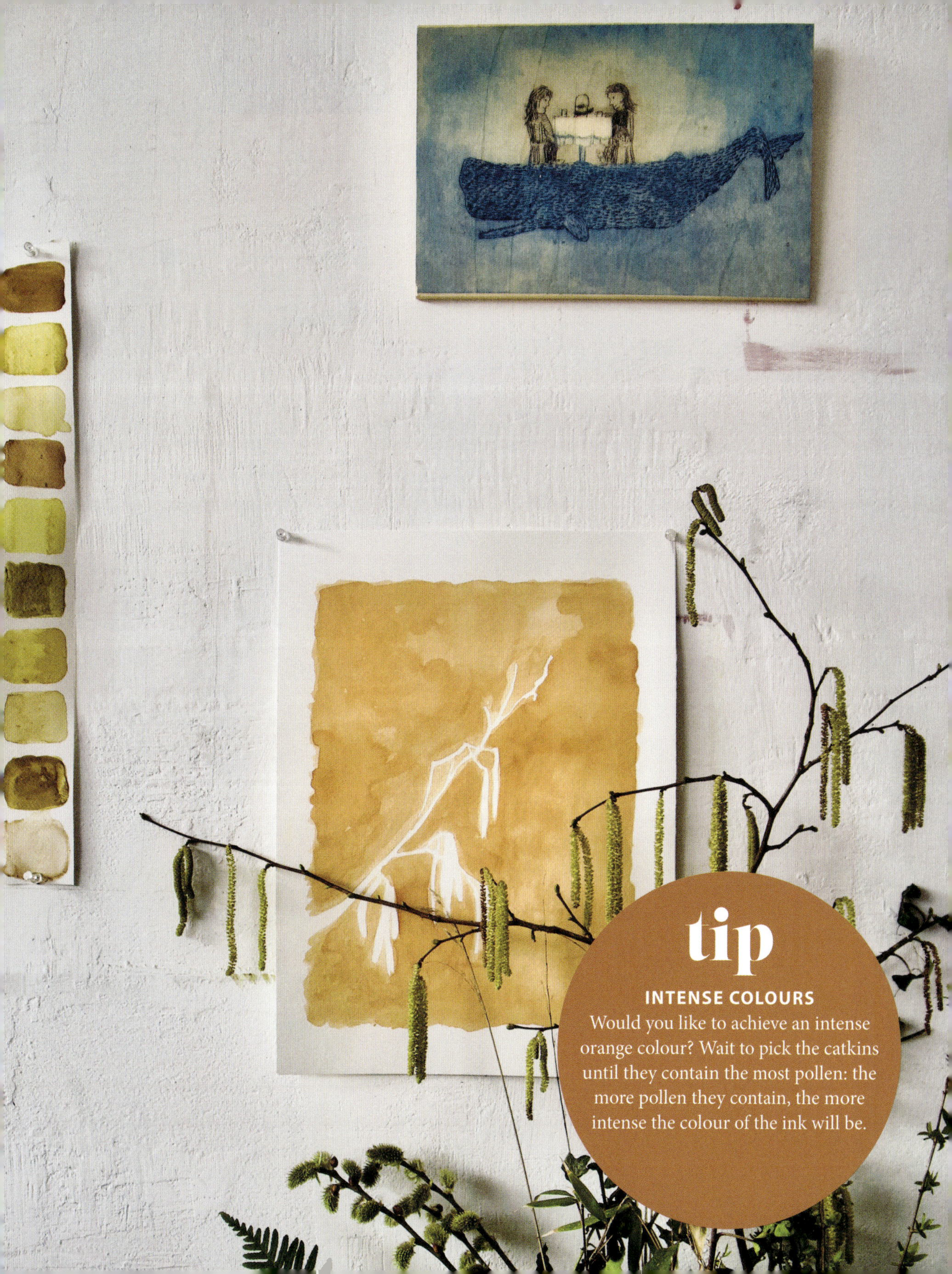

tip

INTENSE COLOURS

Would you like to achieve an intense orange colour? Wait to pick the catkins until they contain the most pollen: the more pollen they contain, the more intense the colour of the ink will be.

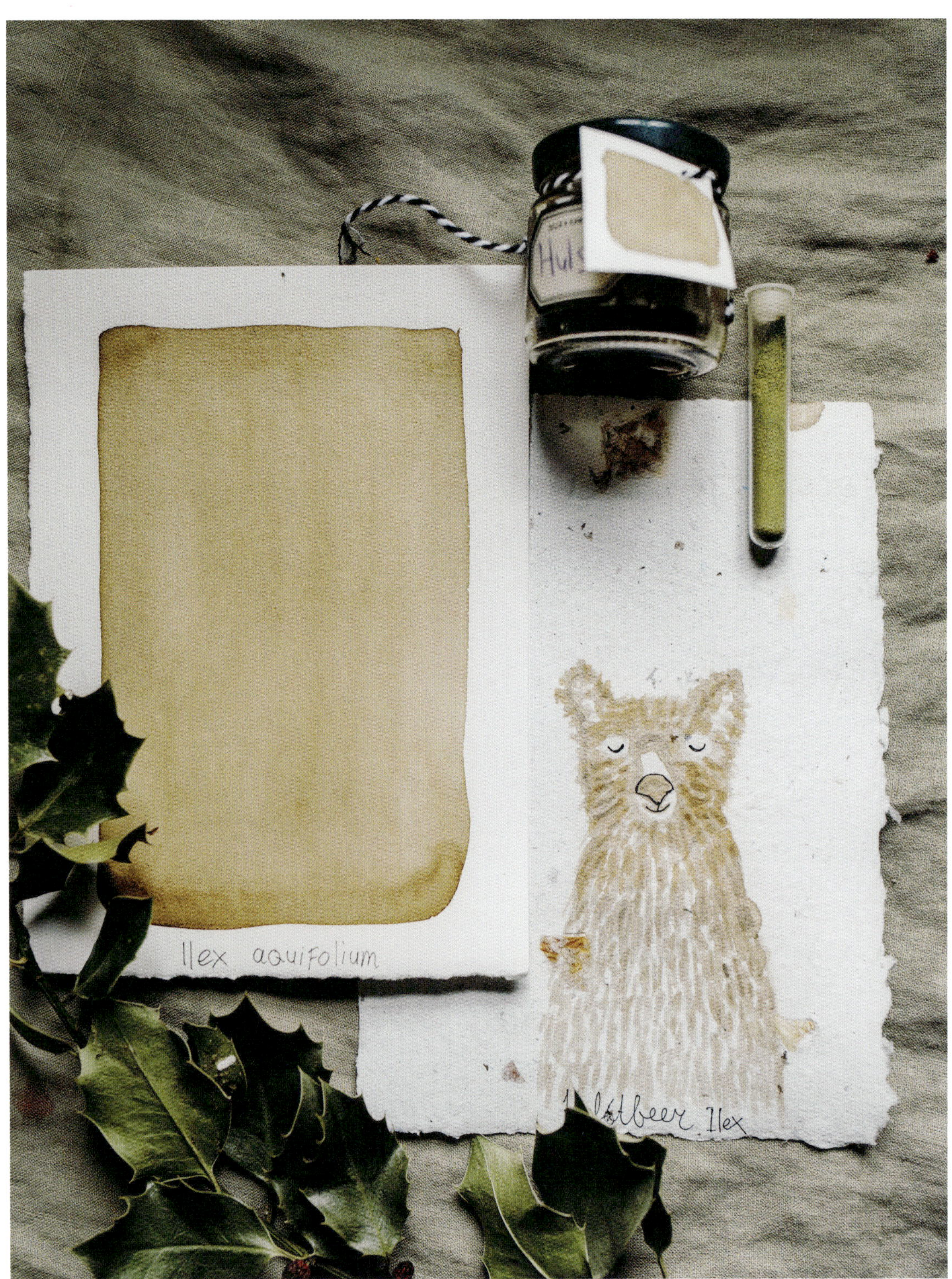
Hul
Ilex aquifolium
Hulstbeer Ilex

Holly

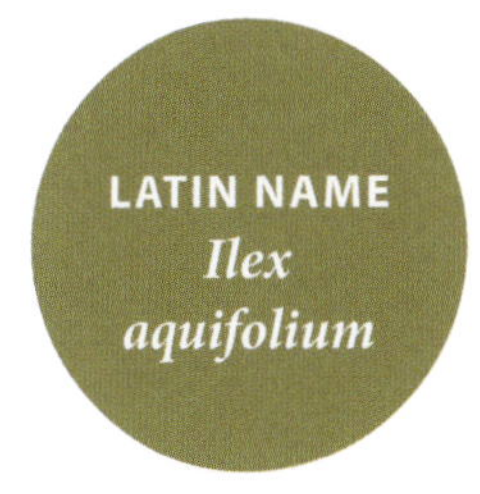

Ink from holly is lightfast +++

Ilex *is the name of the plant genus to which holly belongs. The leaves of lots of* **Ilex** *species resemble the leaves of the evergreen holm oak (***Quercus ilex***). ***Aquifolium*** means 'sharp-toothed leaf'. Holly is a native evergreen shrub. You can find it in deciduous and coniferous woods and on heathland. It has leathery green leaves that are wavy in shape with large spikes. The prickly leaves are mainly found at the base of the shrub. There are still wavy leaves at the top, but the spikes are missing. This is because the holly tree is clever: creatures that live on the ground and don't like spiky leaves would do well to steer clear of this plant. When given enough room to grow, holly can grow up to 10m (33ft) in height. I think large, bushy holly trees are an imposing sight. As Christmas approaches, the holly is popular because of its shiny green leaves and bright red berries. It goes so well in Christmas arrangements. Incidentally, it is only female bushes that grow berries. The male ones flower, but these flowers do not develop into berries.*

Holly stands for hope. When everything seems dead in winter, the evergreen holly tree provides hope that spring will come again: nature's rebirth.

There is a lovely ancient Celtic story about King Oak and King Holly: King Oak represents the summer and King Holly represents the winter. Every year on 21st December, King Oak asks King Holly to bring back the sunshine and light. We know this time as the midwinter solstice. It is when the days start to get longer again, and the light slowly returns. On 21st June, this is reversed when King Holly asks King Oak to make it dark again and introduce a calmness to nature: the midsummer solstice.

Holly

Ingredients
- 4 handfuls of holly leaves

Equipment
- newspaper or baking paper
- old pan with lid
- sieve and bowl
- coffee filter

METHOD

1. Place the holly leaves on the newspaper to air dry them. This will take a few days. It is also possible to dry them in the oven, which is quicker. Preheat the oven to 50°C (120°F). Place the leaves separated from each other on a sheet of baking paper. Dry them in the oven for 30 minutes. You need to monitor this stage and carefully check the leaves to avoid them burning.

2. Cut the holly leaves into very small pieces and put them in a pan.

3. Pour in just enough water to cover the pieces of leaves.

4. Place the pan on the heat but turn it down as soon as the water has almost reached boiling point. Make sure it doesn't boil.

5. Place the lid on the pan and leave it to stand for as long as possible – at least 4 hours. The longer you leave the mixture on the heat, the darker the colour will become.

6. Turn off the heat and then leave the pan to stand overnight with the lid on.

7. Strain the holly mixture through a sieve and collect the liquid in a bowl.

8. Rinse the pan and then pour the liquid back into it through a coffee filter.

9. Gently heat the liquid until it reaches the consistency of syrup; do not allow it to boil.

10. Try the ink on watercolour paper. It will be misty green in colour.

11. Bottle the ink following the instructions on page 29.

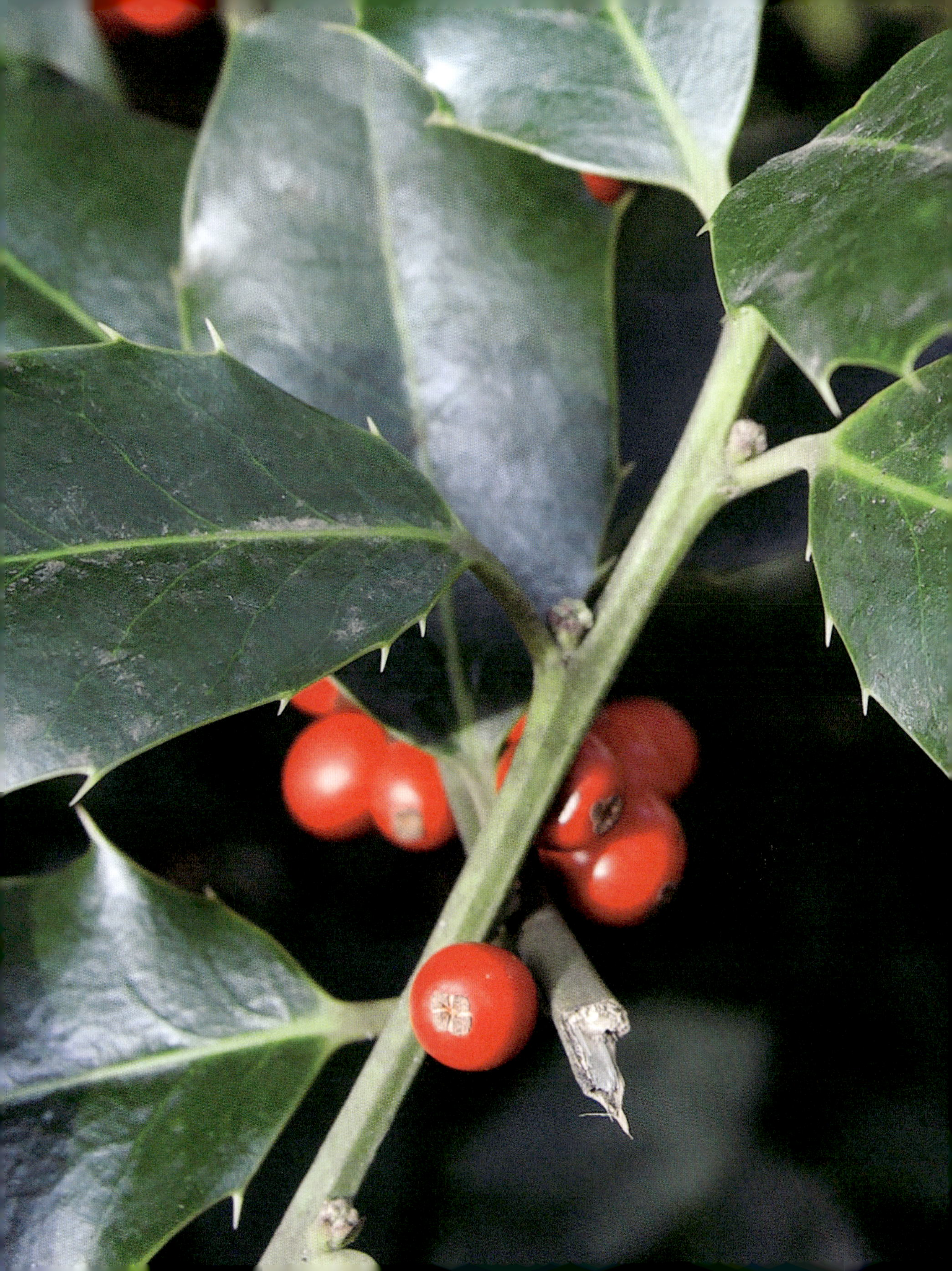

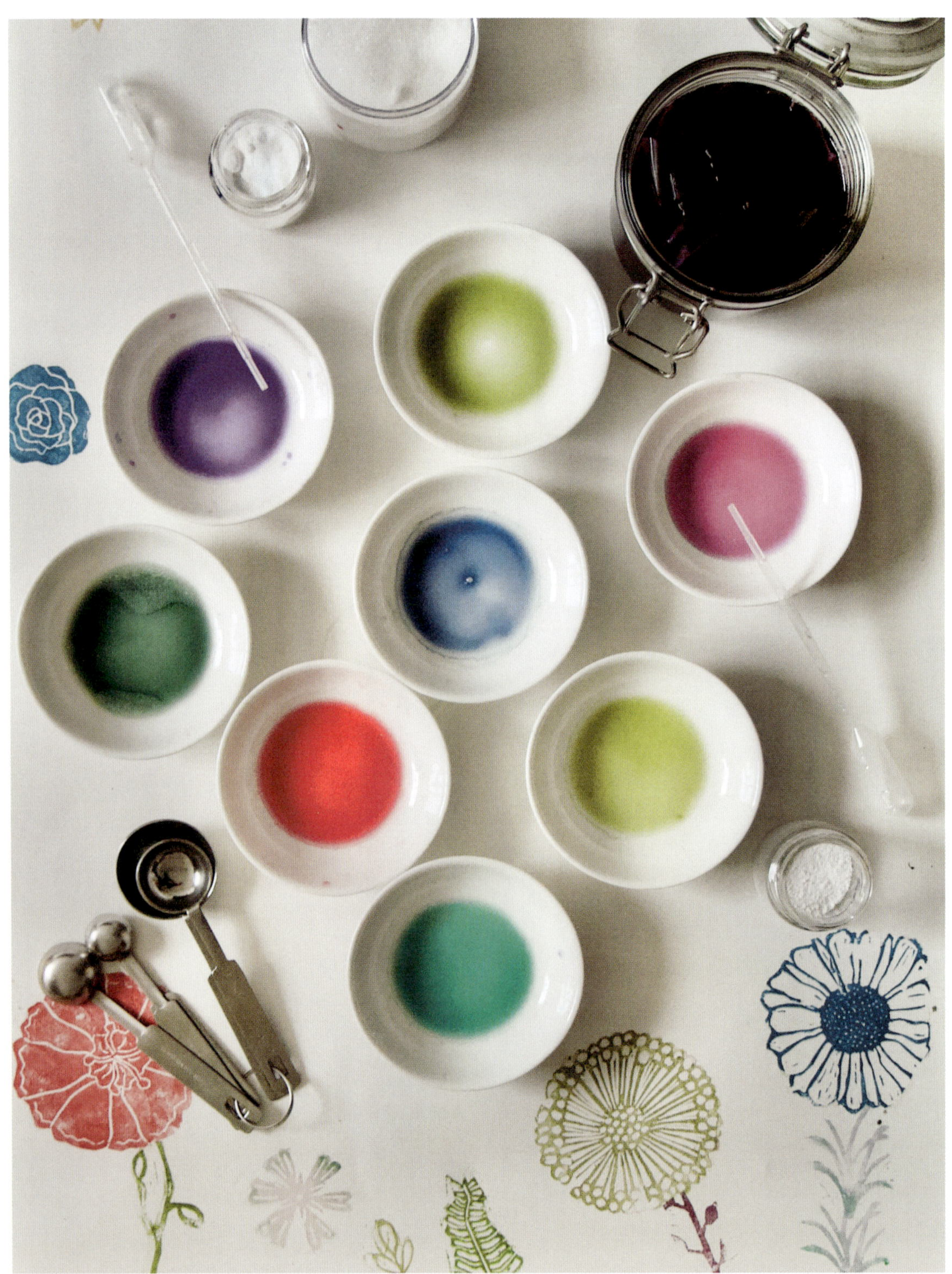

MAGENTA – CYAN – SOFT GREEN – PETROL – PURPLE

Red cabbage

Ink from red cabbage is lightfast +++

Red cabbage would actually be better called 'rainbow cabbage'. It contains a whole range of colours, but bright red is not one of them! The leaves are dark red to purple and can change colour when the pH value, which indicates acidity content, changes. The pH value of the soil also affects the colour because the plant contains the pigment anthocyanin. This is the pigment that gives leaves their red colour in autumn. Anthocyanin is an indicator of whether something is acidic or alkaline. If you add an acid (e.g. vinegar or lemon) to red cabbage, it will turn the magenta colour into pink. If you add an alkaline (e.g. soda or soap), it turns blue into green.

Ingredients
- 1 red cabbage, the 4 outer leaves
- ¼tsp baking soda (optional)
- ¼tsp citric acid (optional)
- ¼tsp alum (optional)
- 1 pinch of iron sulphate (optional)

Equipment
- 500ml (17½oz) sterile preserving jar
- sieve
- pan
- 4 bowls

METHOD

1. Tear up the leaves of the red cabbage into small pieces and place them in the preserving jar.
2. Cover the leaves with boiling water until submerged.
3. Close the jar and leave it to stand overnight. The next day, the liquid will be an indigo colour.
4. Strain the red cabbage liquid through a sieve and collect it in a pan.
5. Place the pan on the heat but turn it down as soon as the liquid has almost reached boiling point. Make sure it doesn't boil. Leave it to heat through gently until it achieves the consistency of syrup. It will be intense purple in colour.
6. Divide the liquid between 4 bowls. Add a different ingredient to each bowl to change the colour.
7. For a green colour, add baking soda.
8. For a magenta colour, add citric acid.
9. For a cyan colour, add some alum.
10. For a petrol colour, add iron sulphate.
11. Bottle the ink following the instructions on page 29.

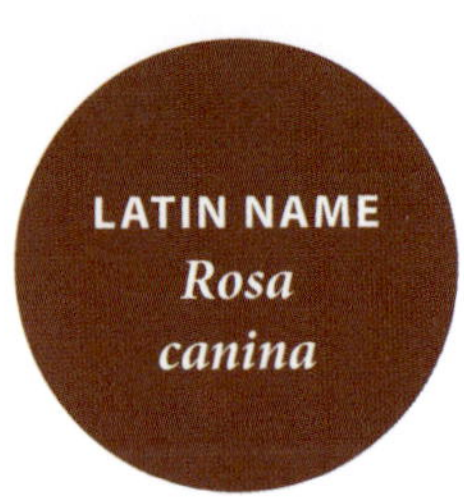

ORANGE-BROWN

Rose

Ink from rose is lightfast ++

A common rose in the UK is the dog rose. It is a very versatile plant. Rose hips can be made into jam, jelly, syrup, tea or a liqueur. You can also use the rose petals to make tea. Dog roses can be found in lots of different places: in gardens, in hedges and bushes along a roadside, on the edges of woods, on the moors and in dunes. They bloom in summertime with large white and pink flowers. Rose hips – which are oval red or orange fruits about 2cm (¾in) in diameter – follow during the autumn. These fruits are full of white seeds. If you are going to make this ink, pay close attention to the hairs that grow at the bottom of the hips as well as the white seeds. The hairs and seeds (which also contain tiny hairs themselves) will cause you to itch terribly if they make contact with your skin.

Since the ink from rose hips is often thick, it is ideally suited for screen printing. The principle behind this technique is called push-through. You literally push ink through the open holes of a stretched piece of gauze (the screen frame) in order to create an image. The artist Andy Warhol made lots of screen prints in this way and his famous multicoloured portraits of Marilyn Monroe were also screen printed.

Ingredients
- 4 handfuls of rose hips

Equipment
- old pan
- potato masher
- spoon
- sieve
- bowl

METHOD

1. Put the rose hips in a pan.
2. Pour in just enough water so that the rose hips are about 2cm (¾in) below the surface.
3. Put the pan on the heat and gently boil the rose hips until they are soft – it will take about 10 minutes.
4. Using a potato masher, mash the rose hips together with the water to form a purée.
5. Squash the rose hip mixture through a sieve using a spoon, leaving the seeds behind. Collect the liquid in a bowl. This will be orange-brown in colour.
6. For screen printing, the ink should have the consistency of thin yoghurt. Dilute the ink with water if it is too thick. Boil the ink slowly if it is too thin.

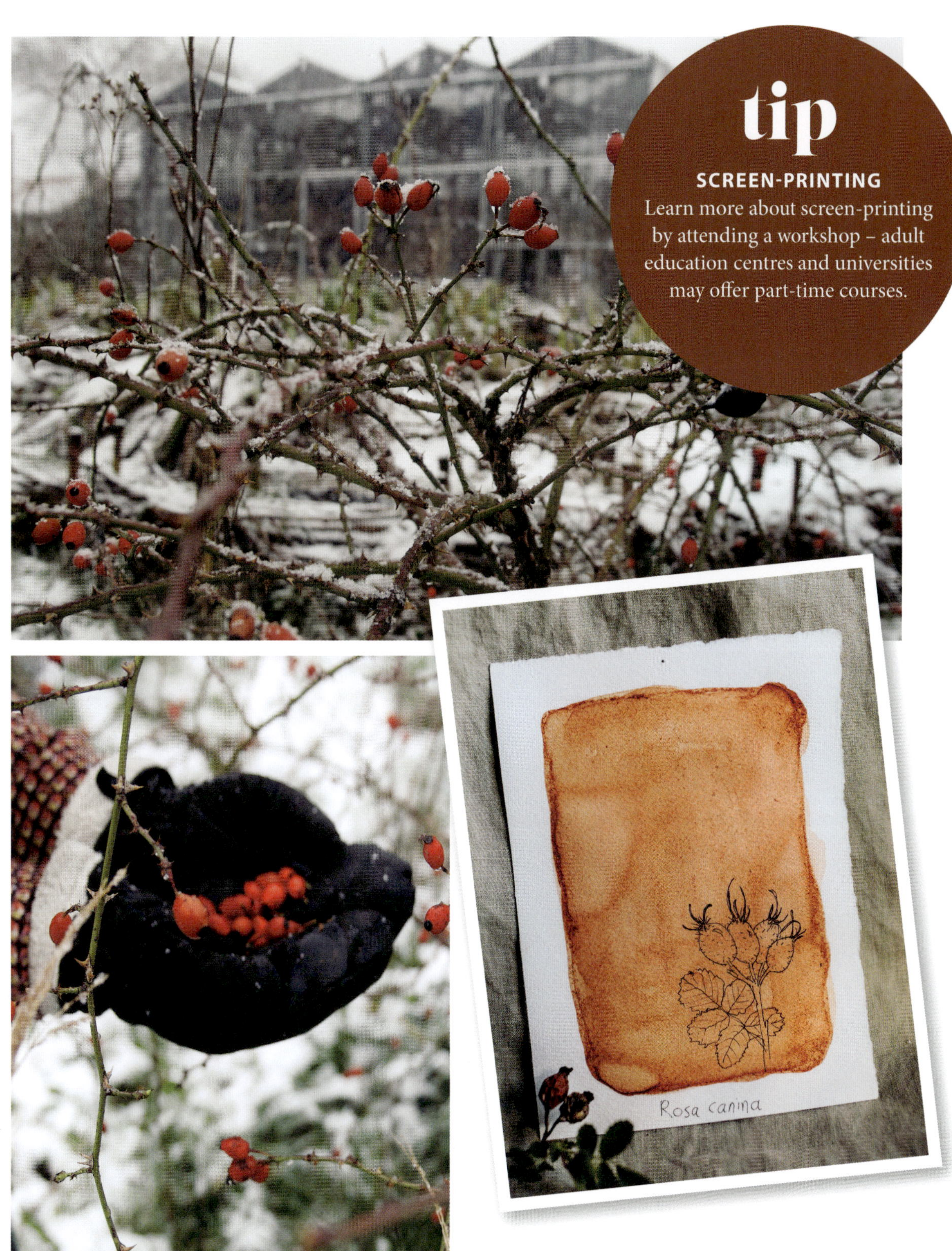

tip

SCREEN-PRINTING
Learn more about screen-printing
by attending a workshop – adult
education centres and universities
may offer part-time courses.

Rosa canina

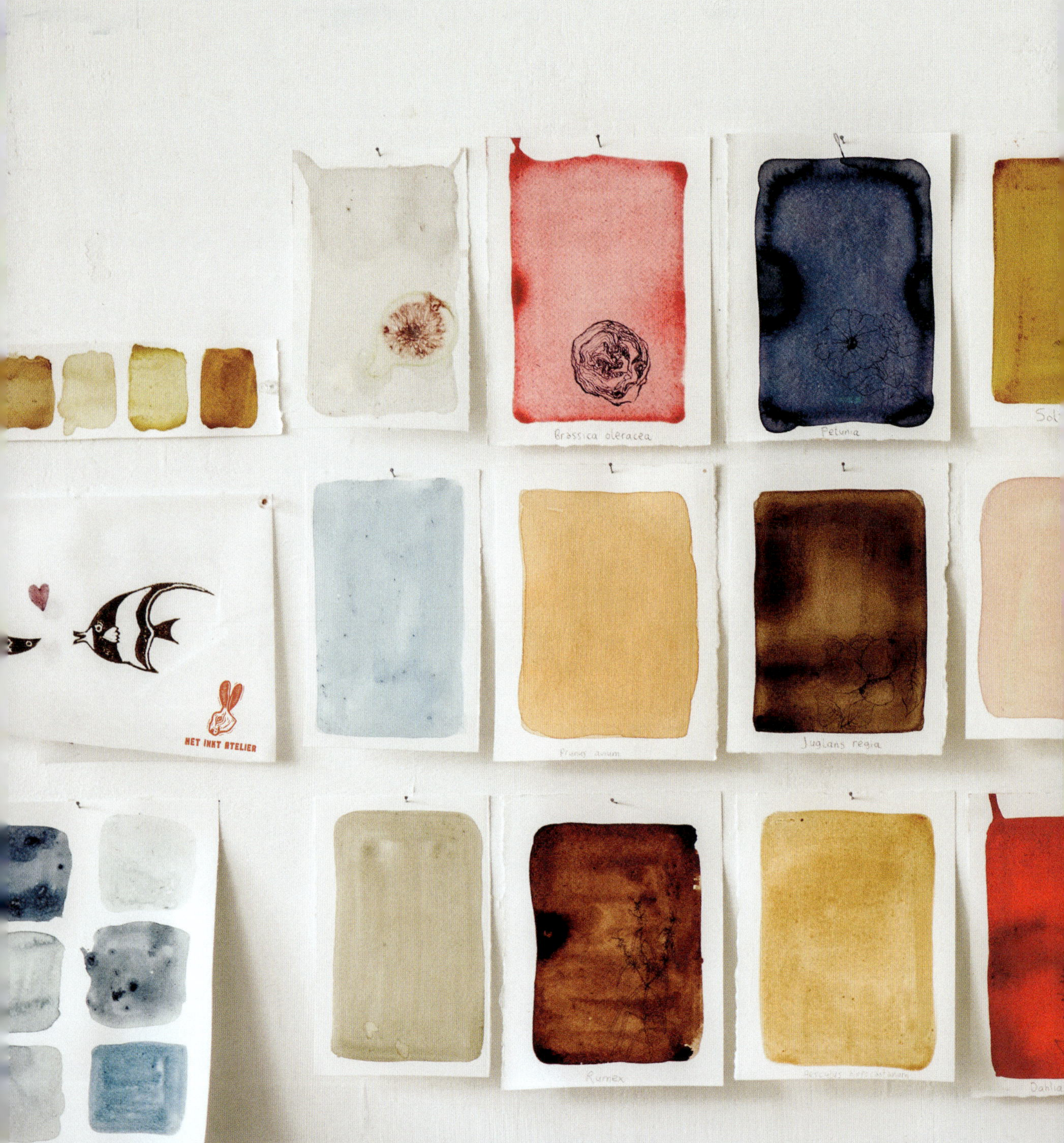

HET INKT ATELIER
Brassica oleracea
Petunia
Sol
Prunus avium
Juglans regia
Rumex
Dahlia

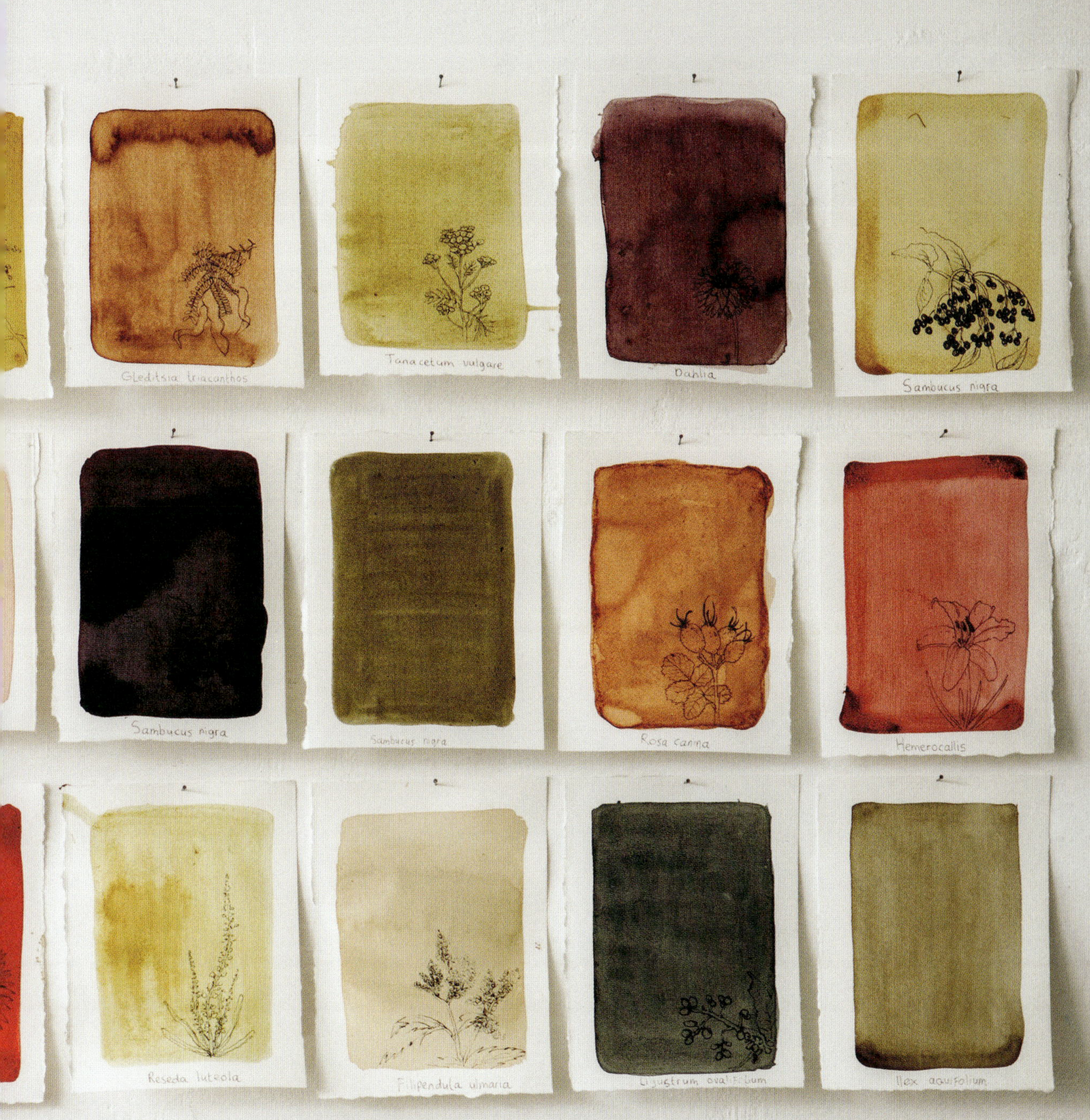

Gleditsia triacanthos
Tanacetum vulgare
Dahlia
Sambucus nigra
Sambucus nigra
Sambucus nigra
Rosa canina
Hemerocallis
Reseda luteola
Filipendula ulmaria
Ligustrum ovalifolium
Ilex aquifolium

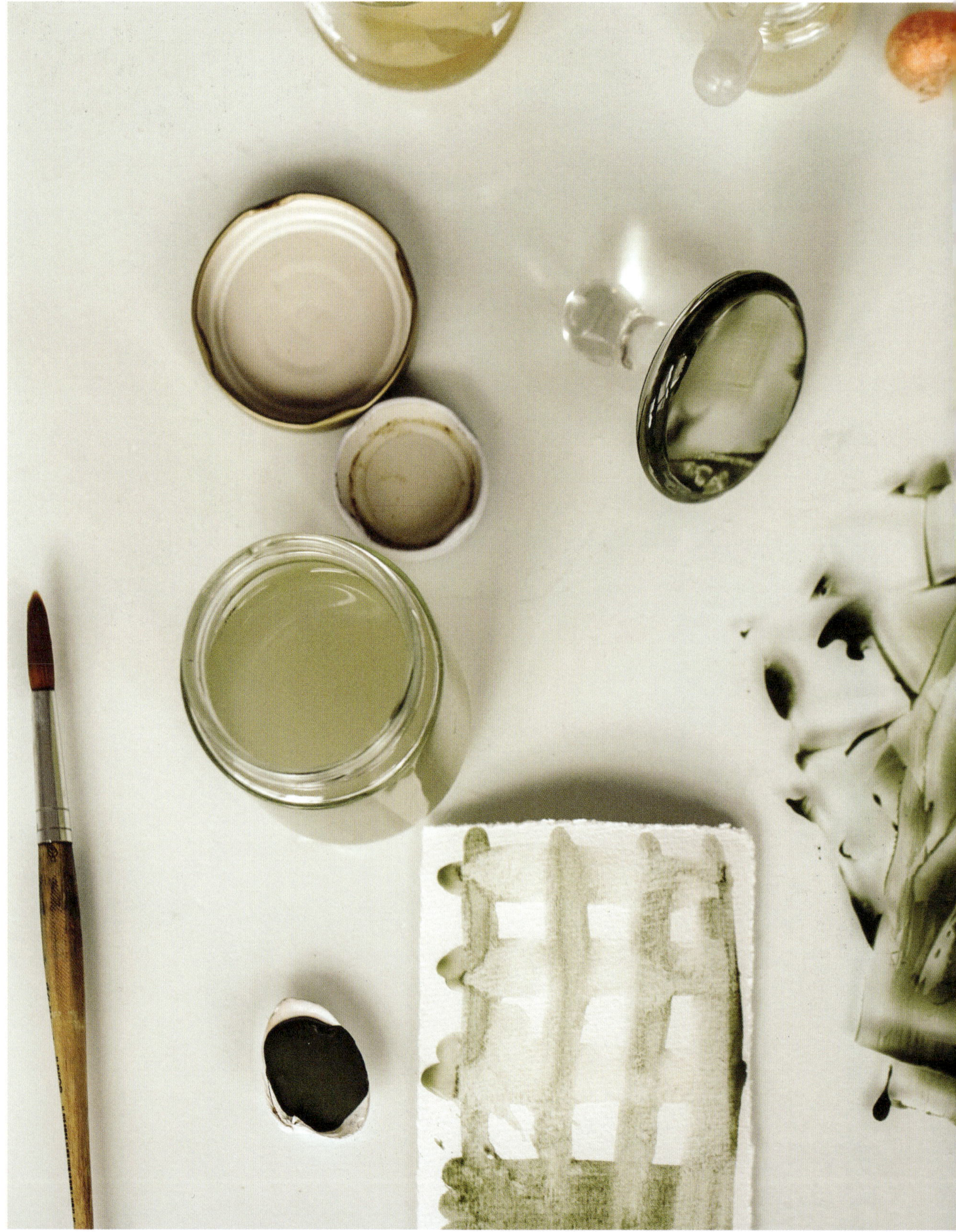

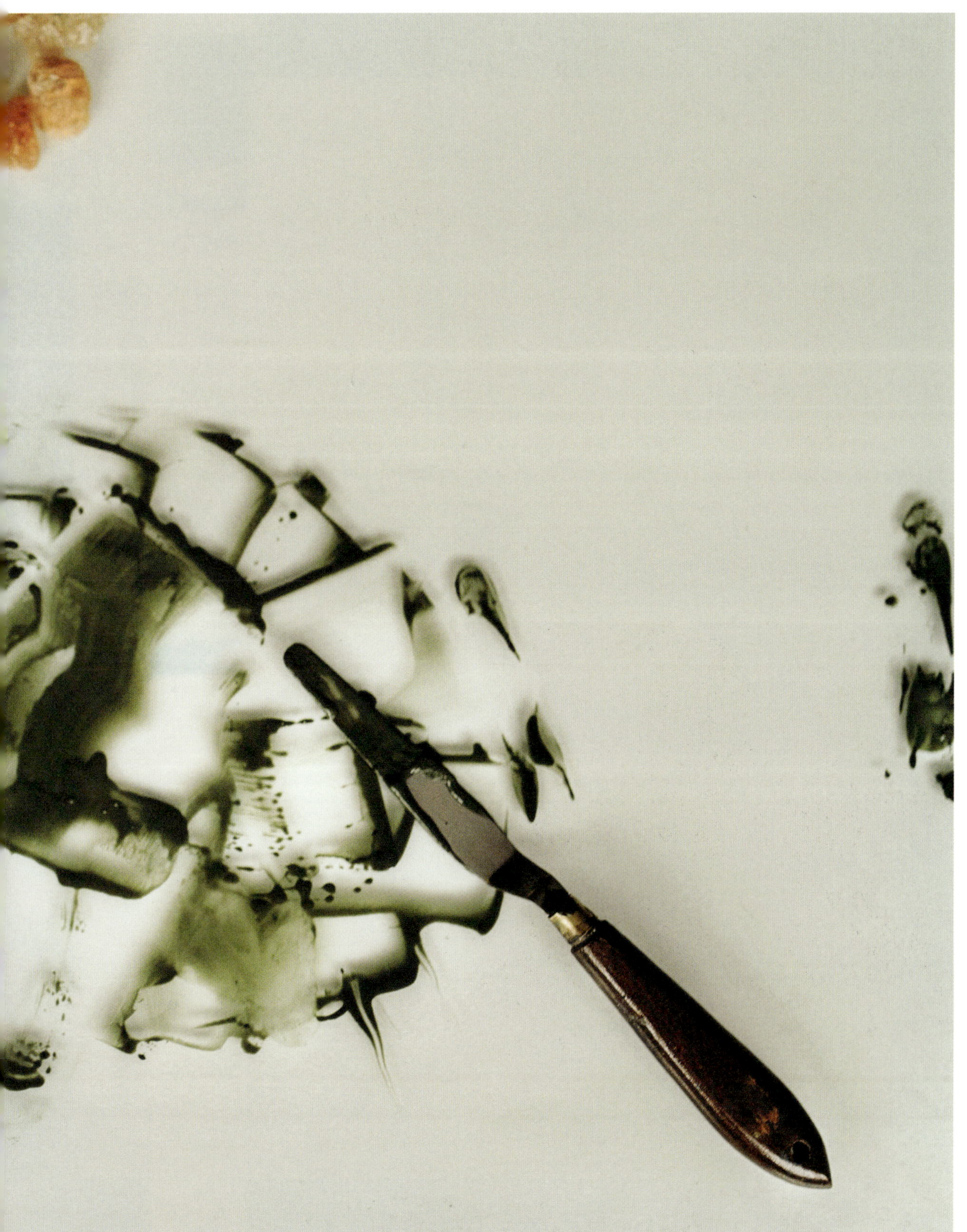

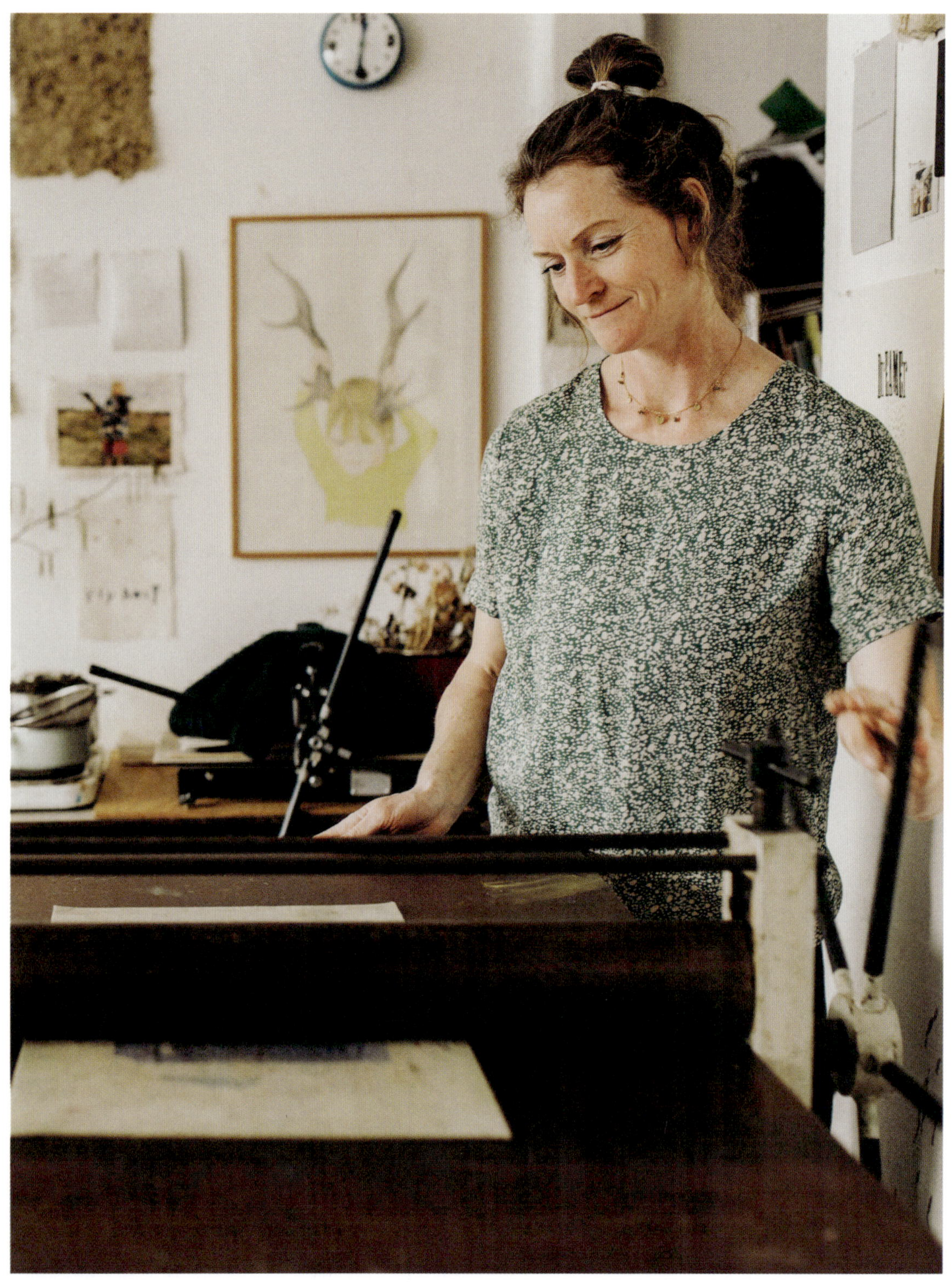

My journey to plant-based printing

Before attending the Academy of Art and Design in Den Bosch, I had already been introduced to linocut and etching techniques, letterpress and an intaglio technique. With linocutting, the image you print is the raised portion; what you don't want to print, you cut away. This is basically the same as a stamp technique. With etching, the image you end up with is the lower portion: you scratch the image into the etching plate. When I was introduced to the graphic workshop at the academy, I was simply amazed. It smelt of printing ink and I love the smell of printing ink, although I know not everyone agrees with me! The wall was full of prints and everywhere you looked you saw large pots of ink, bottles filled with interesting liquids, pipettes, palette knives, rollers and reams of paper. There were also countless printing presses. In fact, my heart skipped a beat looking at all those beautiful things.

The craftsmanship involved in the process, the deferred result (you invest time and energy into making a printing plate but you have to wait a while before you can print with that plate and see the result), working with print runs, the ability to change colours quickly – I simply loved everything about it.

What bothered me at the time was the amount of chemicals used as part of the process. Many printing inks were oil-based or – worse still – solvent-based, meaning that tools had to be cleaned with turpentine. It was a common occurrence for me to end up retiring to my dorm room each evening with a really bad headache. After the academy, I started working at the Grafisch Atelier Den Bosch. There, we swapped turpentine for an organic cleaning product, which was a big improvement. Thank goodness that solvent-based inks are now banned in many countries! I worked at the Grafisch Atelier Den Bosch for 10 years and the people there still hold a very special place in my heart.

When working in my own studio, I don't work with oil-based printing inks. All of my inks are water-based, which is why they are sustainable and friendly to every living thing. My love of plant-based inks has taken me on a quest for appropriate printing inks. I started trying out different binders and experimenting with making my own vegetable-based paints. It was this very quest that gave me the idea for this book.

In the following chapters, I'll explain about different pigments and how to make paint and printing ink from them.

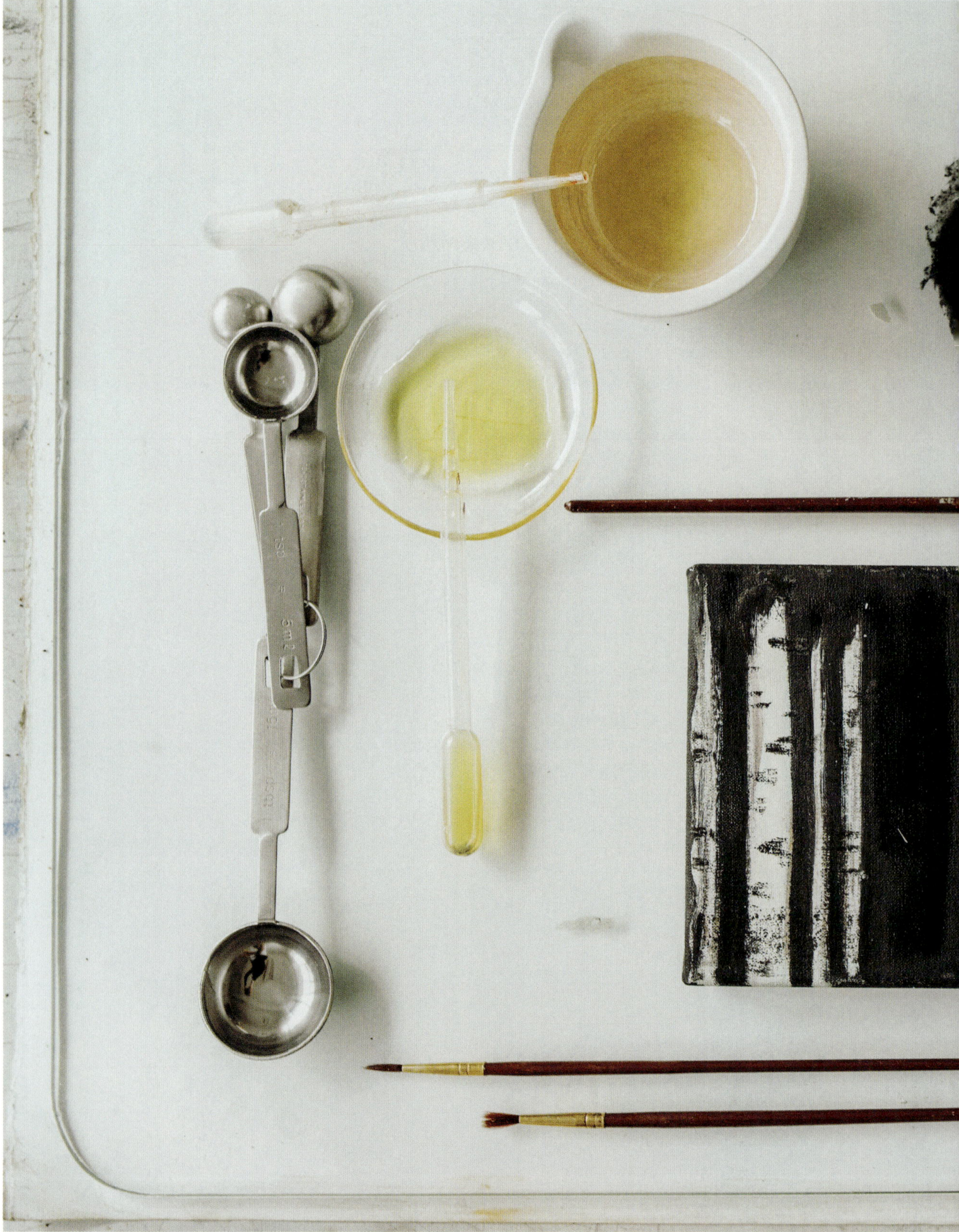

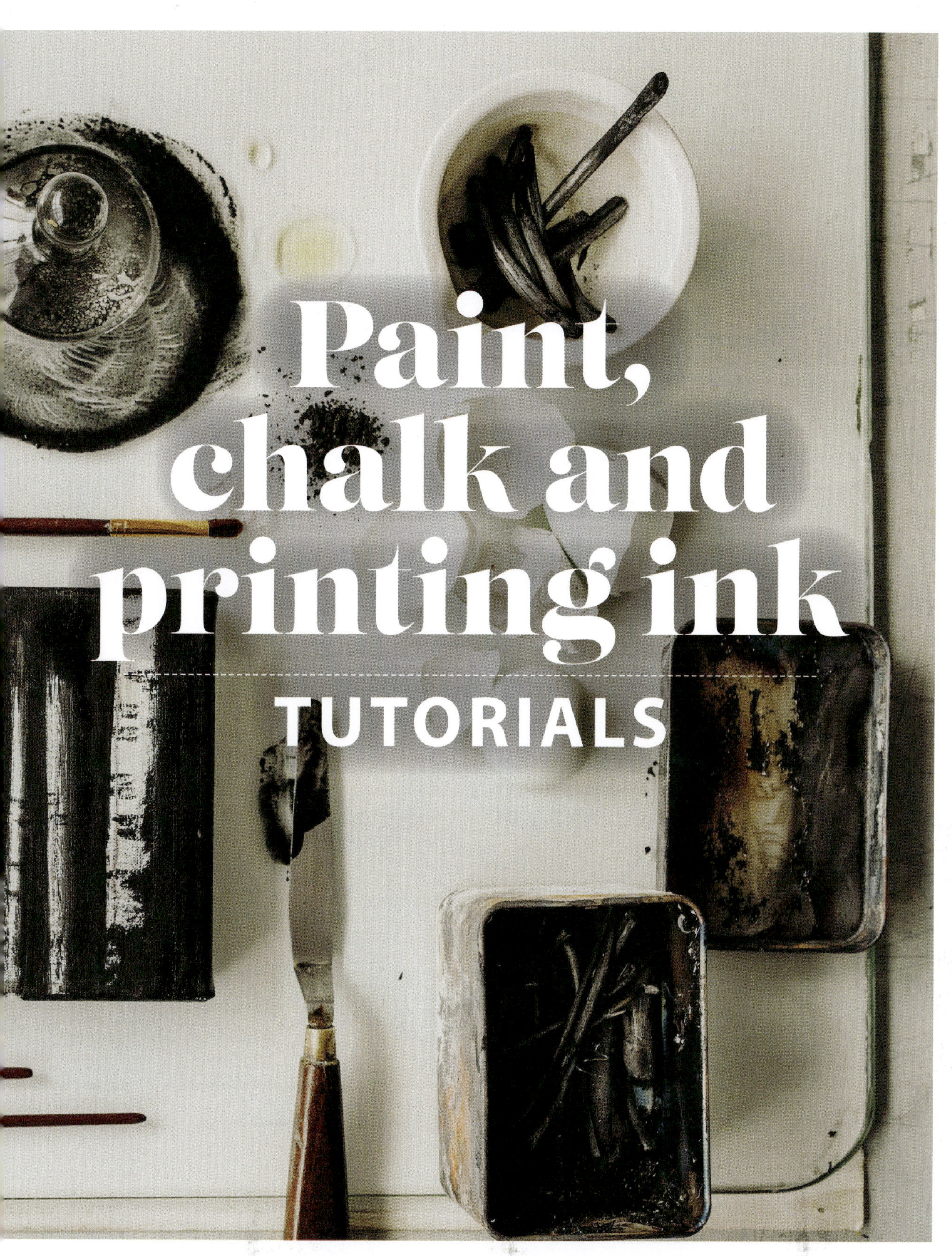

Paint,
chalk and
printing ink
TUTORIALS

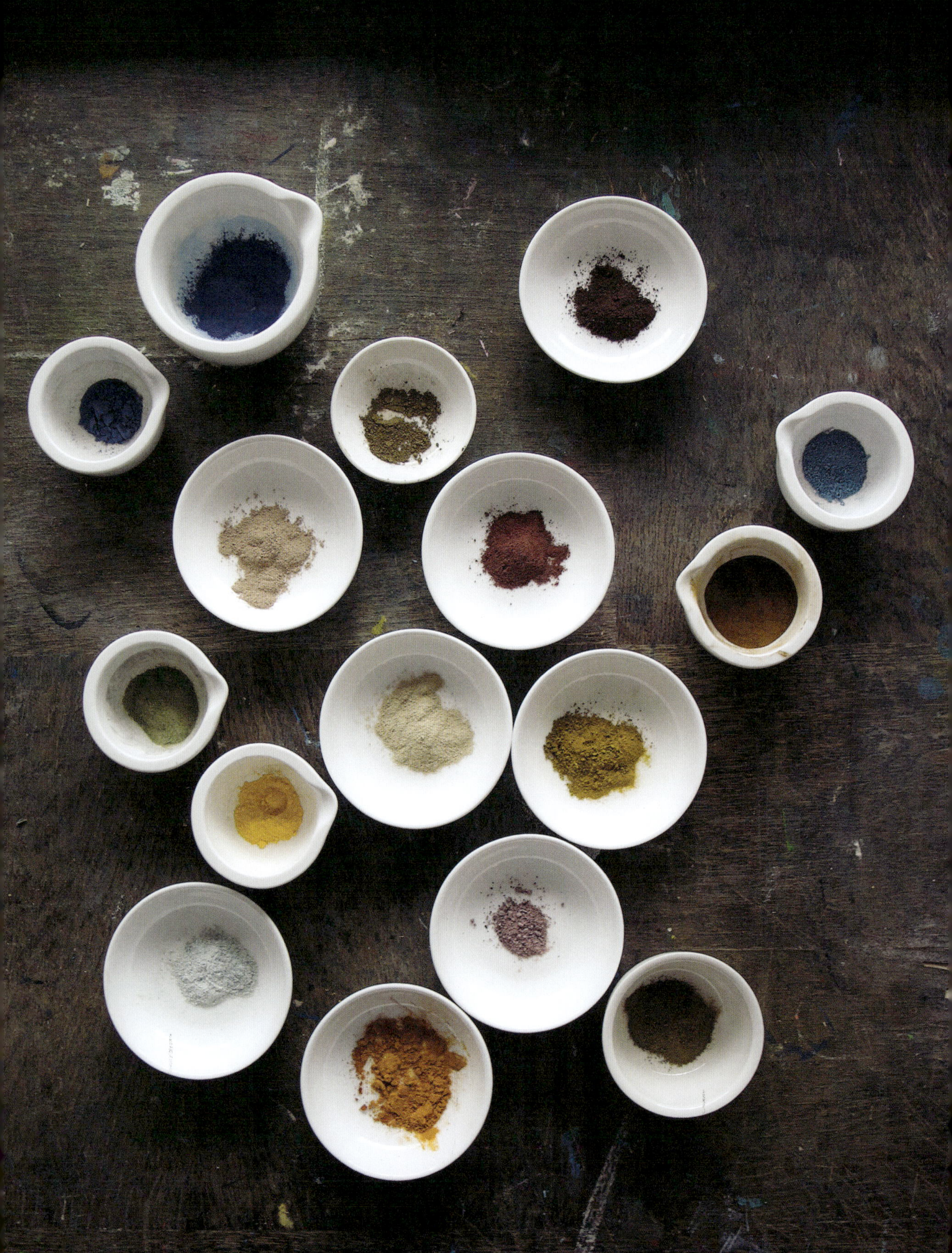

Pigment

A pigment is a dry substance that is used to add colour to paint and printing ink, among other things. Pigments are also insoluble in water. In order to be able to use a pigment, you will need a binder, such as oil for oil paint. Pigments do not dissolve in binders but stay in granular form. The finer you grind the granules of pigment, the more evenly the pigment granules are distributed throughout the binder, which in turn makes the paint smoother and better.

There are three types of pigments:

- *Organic pigments* are extracted from animals and plants. This includes colours like magenta, which is extracted from cochineal insects. This pigment is used to add pink colouring to cakes and other items.
- *Inorganic pigments* are extracted in the form of minerals. This includes earthy colours such as sienna, umber and ochre.
- *Lake pigments* are pigments that have been produced using chemicals. The method for making a lake pigment can be found on page 140.

Today, lots of pigments are made synthetically.

Organic pigments are made by boiling plant tea until it is completely dry, or by allowing the water to evaporate in the sun. The dry pigment can then be scraped off the bottom of the container.

Inorganic pigments can be made by drying out beautifully coloured earth or clay before grinding it to form a powder.

Lake pigments give a greater yield than the methods used for organic pigments. This is because soda and alum are added to the pigment. These substances remain partially present in the pigment, meaning lake pigments are less pure than organic or inorganic pigments.

Lake pigment

A lake pigment is extracted from a coloured liquid using metal salts. By pouring boiling water over different parts of plants, you can extract the dye from the plants. The amount of leaves you will need for this will depend on the quantity of dye within a plant. It all comes down to trial and error. Basically, you make a tea from the plants. You then add two metal salts to this plant tea – firstly, alum, which makes the colour particles stick together. You then add soda, which causes the colour particles to precipitate in the water and fall to the bottom. By using a filter, it is possible to remove the colour particles from the water and leave them to dry. Once they have dried, grind up the colour particles in a mortar or a coffee grinder until they resemble a fine powder. This is lake pigment.

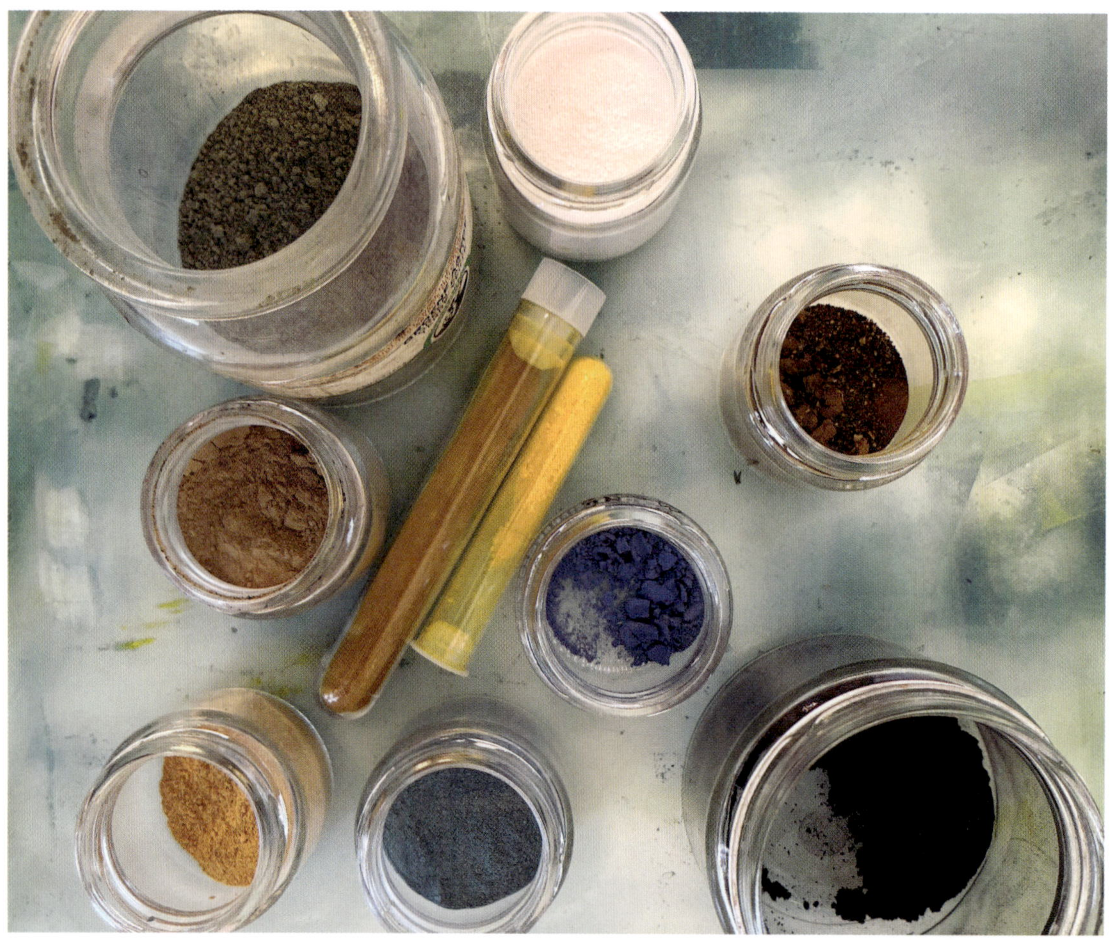

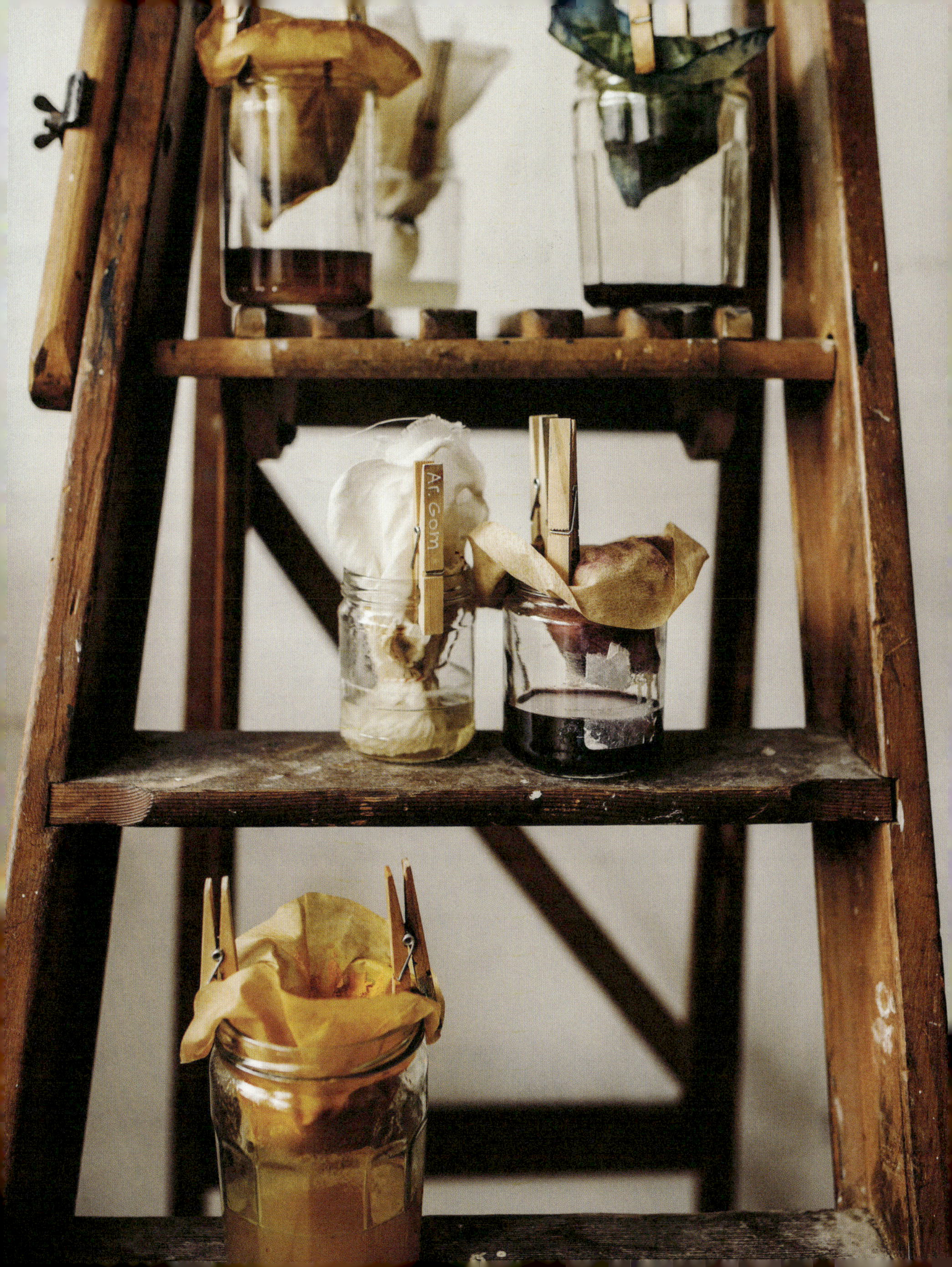

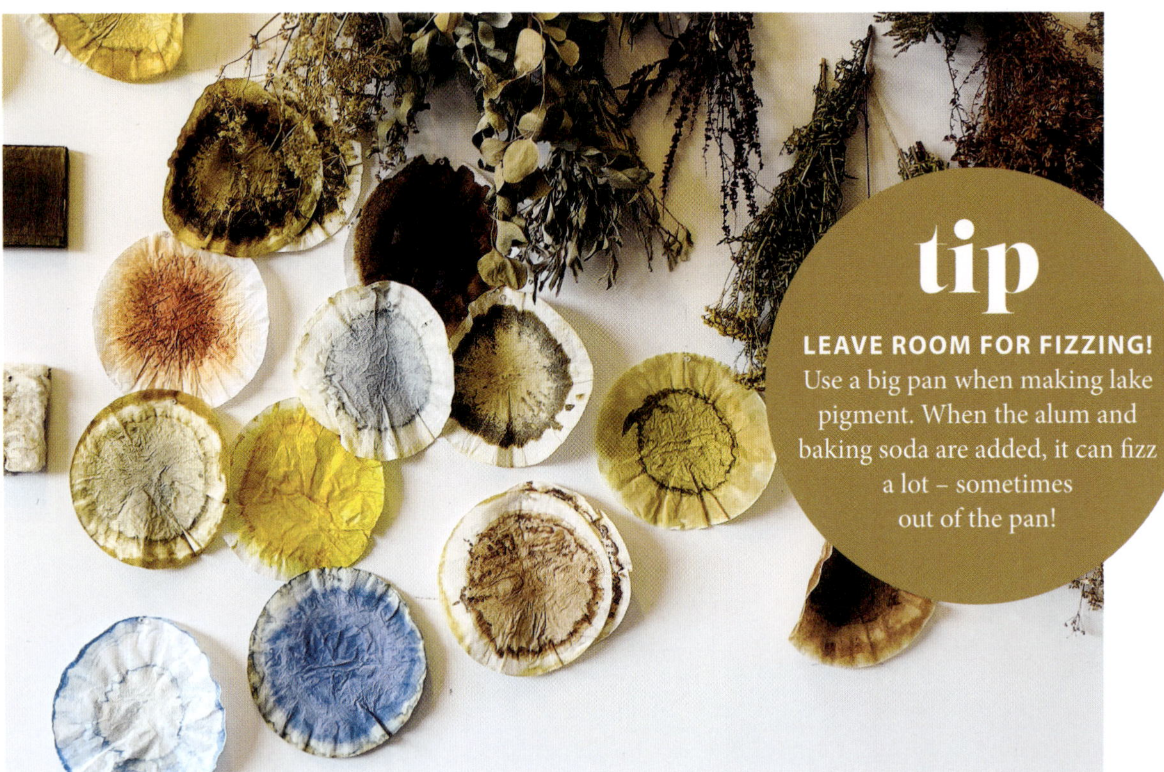

<table>
<tr><td>

Ingredients
- 4 handfuls of elder leaves
- 1.5l (50fl oz) of water
- 10g (⅓oz) alum
- 10g (⅓oz) fine washing soda (sodium carbonate)

</td><td>

Equipment
- large old pan with lid
- hand-held blender
- sieve
- plastic container
- measuring cup
- 7 coffee filters
- thermometer
- 2 cups
- litmus paper
- sterile glass jar
- filter holder or 2 pegs
- pestle and mortar or coffee grinder
- glass jar to store the pigment

</td></tr>
</table>

METHOD FOR LAKE PIGMENT FROM ELDER LEAVES

1. Cut the elder leaves until they are finely shredded and put them in a large pan.
2. Pour 1.5l (50fl oz) of water into the pan over the shreds.
3. Puree them with the hand-held blender until they resemble pulp.
4. Bring the leaf pulp to the boil and simmer on very low heat for 3 hours.
5. Turn off the heat and then leave the pan to stand overnight with the lid on.
6. Pour the pulp through a sieve and squeeze out all of the liquid; collect this liquid in a plastic container.
7. Pour the leaf liquid through a coffee filter to clarify it.
8. Pour the leaf liquid into a measuring cup and check that you have 1l (35³⁄₁₆fl oz) of liquid; top it up with water if you need to. Then put it back in the pan and heat to 70°C (160°F).
9. Put the alum in one cup and the washing soda in a second cup.
10. Pour warm water over the alum and washing soda and stir until the crystals dissolve. The alum will take longer to dissolve than the washing soda.
11. Add the alum solution to the leaf liquid and stir the mixture well.
12. Add the washing soda solution to the leaf liquid and stir the mixture well. The liquid should fizz; this is a chemical reaction that occurs between the two metal salts.
13. Use litmus paper to check whether the pH level is around 7 (neutral). If it is lower than 7, the liquid is too acidic so add some extra washing soda. If it is higher than 7, the liquid is too alkaline so add some extra alum.
14. After a while, you will start to see a sifting process: the colour particles sink to the bottom and a layer of clear water is visible on top. This may take several hours.
15. Carefully pour off the clear water.
16. Put together two coffee filters and place them in the filter holder or attach the filters to the rim of a glass jar using two pegs.
17. Slowly pour the remaining coloured sludge from the pan through the filters. Do it a little bit at a time to avoid them tearing. It may take several hours for everything to filter through.
18. Pour away the liquid that has filtered through into the glass jar and rinse the jar.
19. Pour the wet sludge back into the jar and fill it with clean water.
20. Vigorously shake the jar.
21. Pour the liquid through the coffee filters again. This stage is to rinse the pigments so that the soda is flushed out.
22. Repeat steps 19 to 21 twice.
23. Allow the remaining sludge to dry completely in the filters. This might take several days.
24. Scrape the dry colour particles off the filters and place them in a mortar.
25. Grind the colour particles together until they resemble a fine powder. Alternatively, you could use a coffee grinder.
26. Store the pigment in a glass jar and put a label on it showing the plant's name.

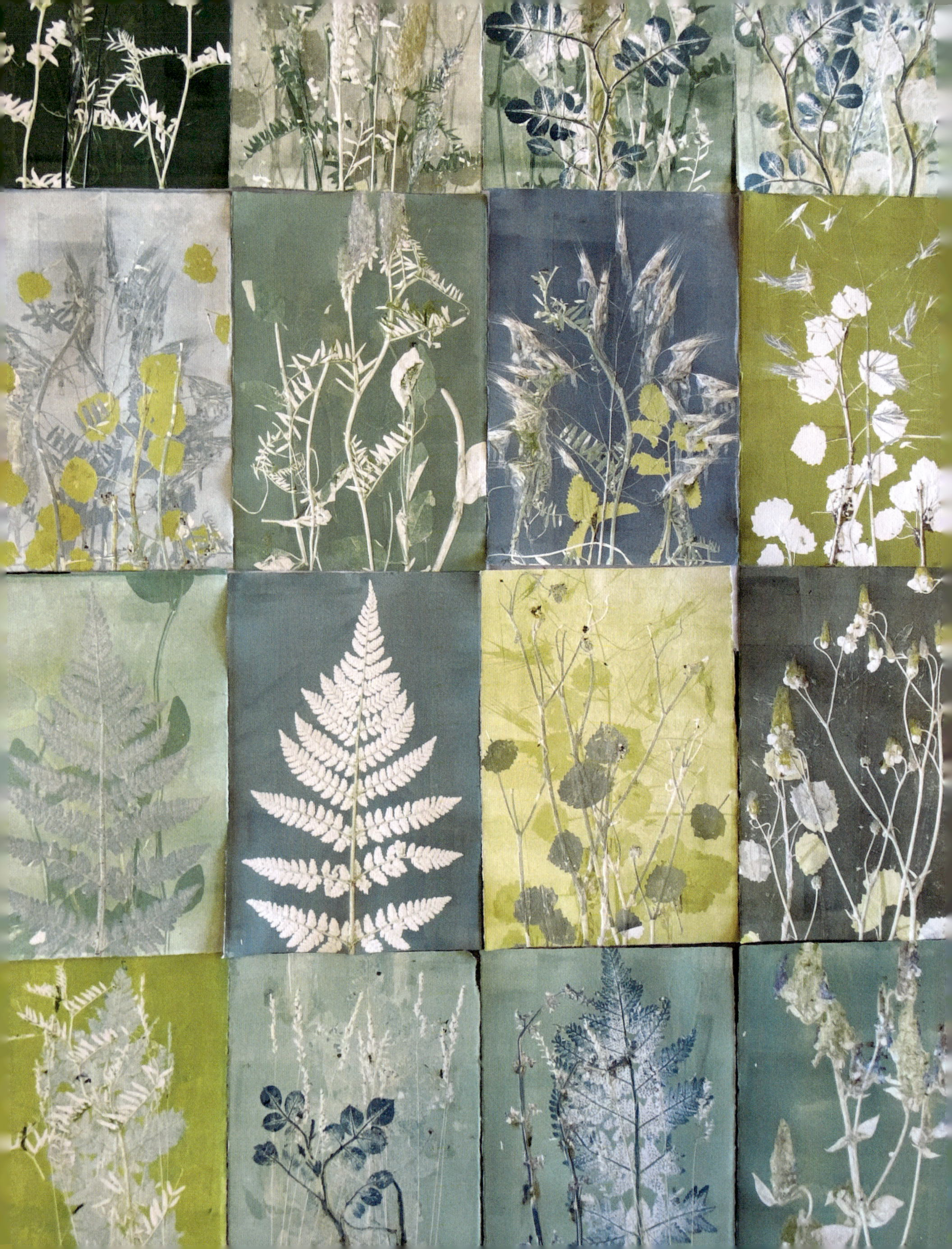

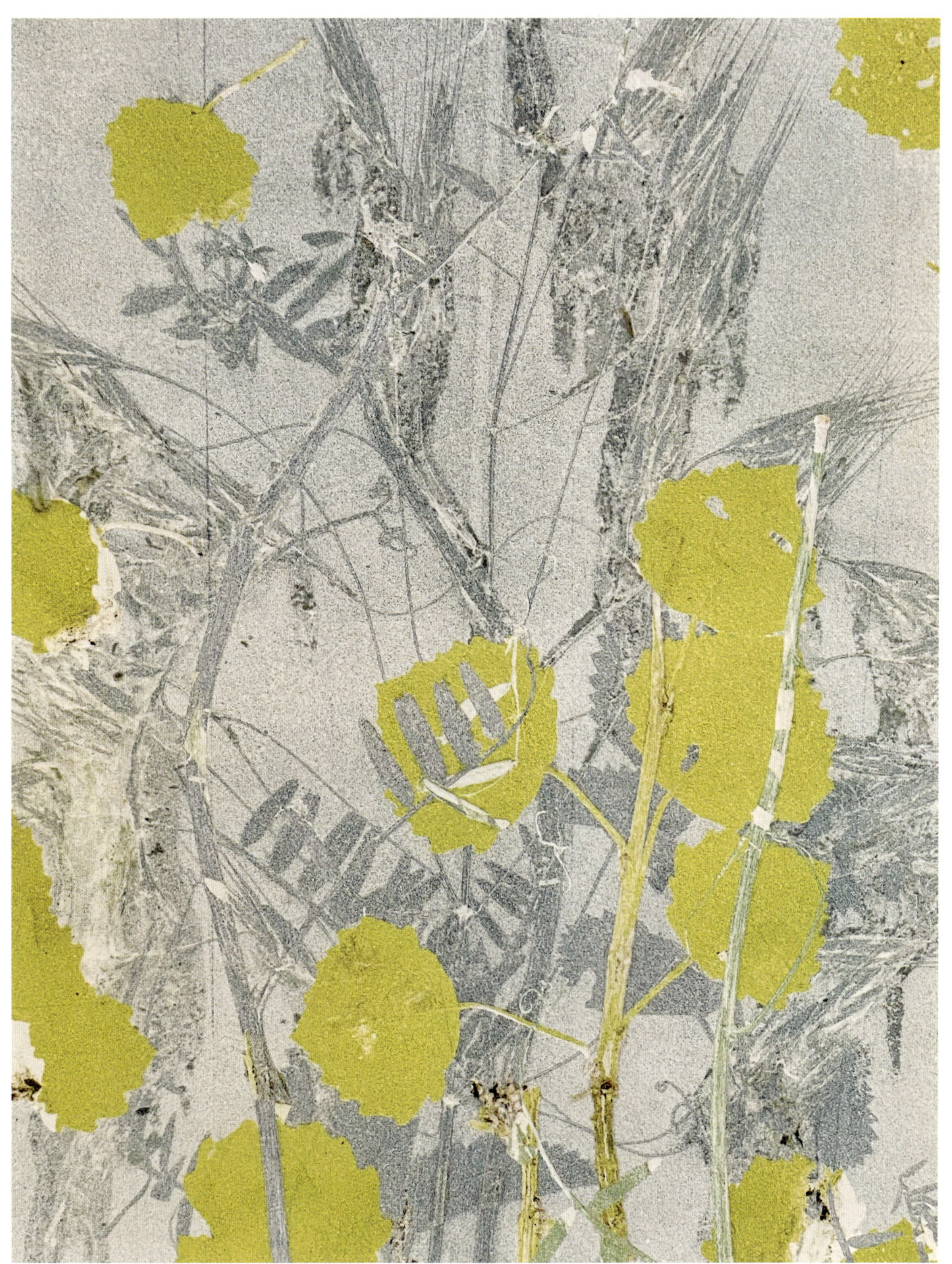

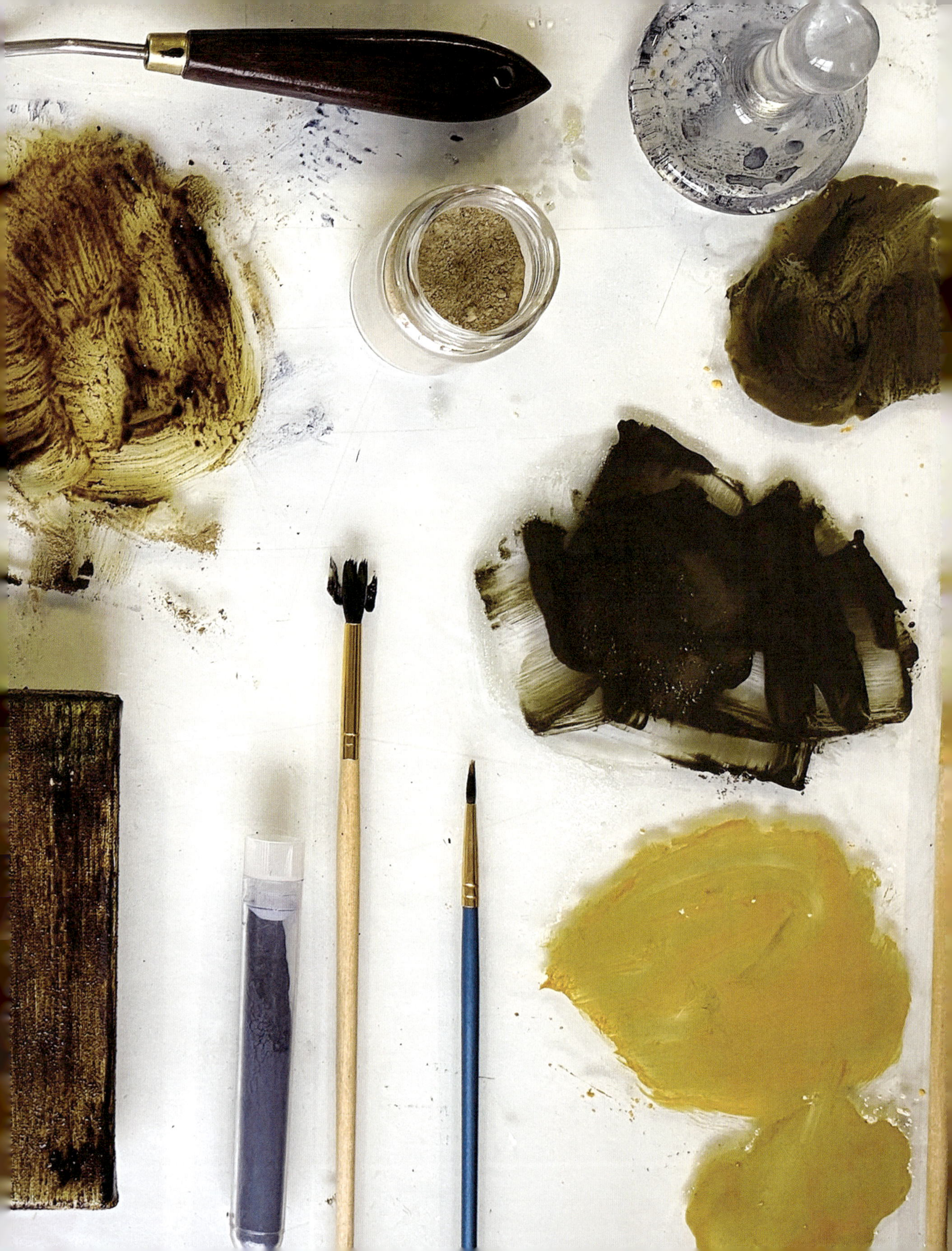

Oil paint

Oil paint is a type of paint that is made from a pigment and a plant-based oil, often linseed oil. This paint applies beautifully to canvas. You can work with thick, paste-like paint as well as in transparent layers. Oil painting first became very popular in the Middle Ages. Lots of painters also made their own paint and it has been the most commonly used paint since 1700.

In order to make oil paint you will need a medium, as well as pigment and oil. If you only mix the pigment together with the oil, the paint will crack. Using a medium makes sure this does not happen; it also helps the paint to dry faster. I use damar varnish as the medium in this recipe. For this, you first need to make damar varnish and then you can make damar varnish medium. You can also apply damar varnish as a final coat over your oil painting. Just make sure your painting is completely dry before varnishing. Oil colours work best on linen, but linen canvas can be quite expensive. A cotton cloth will also work perfectly well and is cheaper. It's even possible to purchase oil paint paper if you wish.

Damar varnish

<table>
<tr><td>

Ingredients
- 1 part damar resin chunks
- 3 parts gum turpentine

</td><td>

Equipment
- stocking(s)
- sterile glass jar with lid
- elastic band

</td></tr>
</table>

METHOD

1. Put the damar resin chunks into one stocking.
2. Roll the stocking over a sterile glass jar and secure the band to the rim using an elastic band. Make sure the toe of the stocking is suspended just above the base of the jar.
3. Pour in the gum turpentine.
4. The damar resin chunks will dissolve in the gum turpentine. This takes about 2 days.
5. Seal the jar of damar varnish and store in the fridge.

Damar varnish medium

<table>
<tr><td>

Ingredients
- damar varnish (3 parts, as prepared above)
- stand oil (1 part) – see page 174

</td><td>

Equipment
- sterile glass jar with lid

</td></tr>
</table>

METHOD

1. Pour the damar varnish into a sterile glass jar.
2. Pour in the stand oil and stir the mixture well.
3. The damar varnish medium is now ready for use.
4. Seal the medium in the jar and store it in the refrigerator.

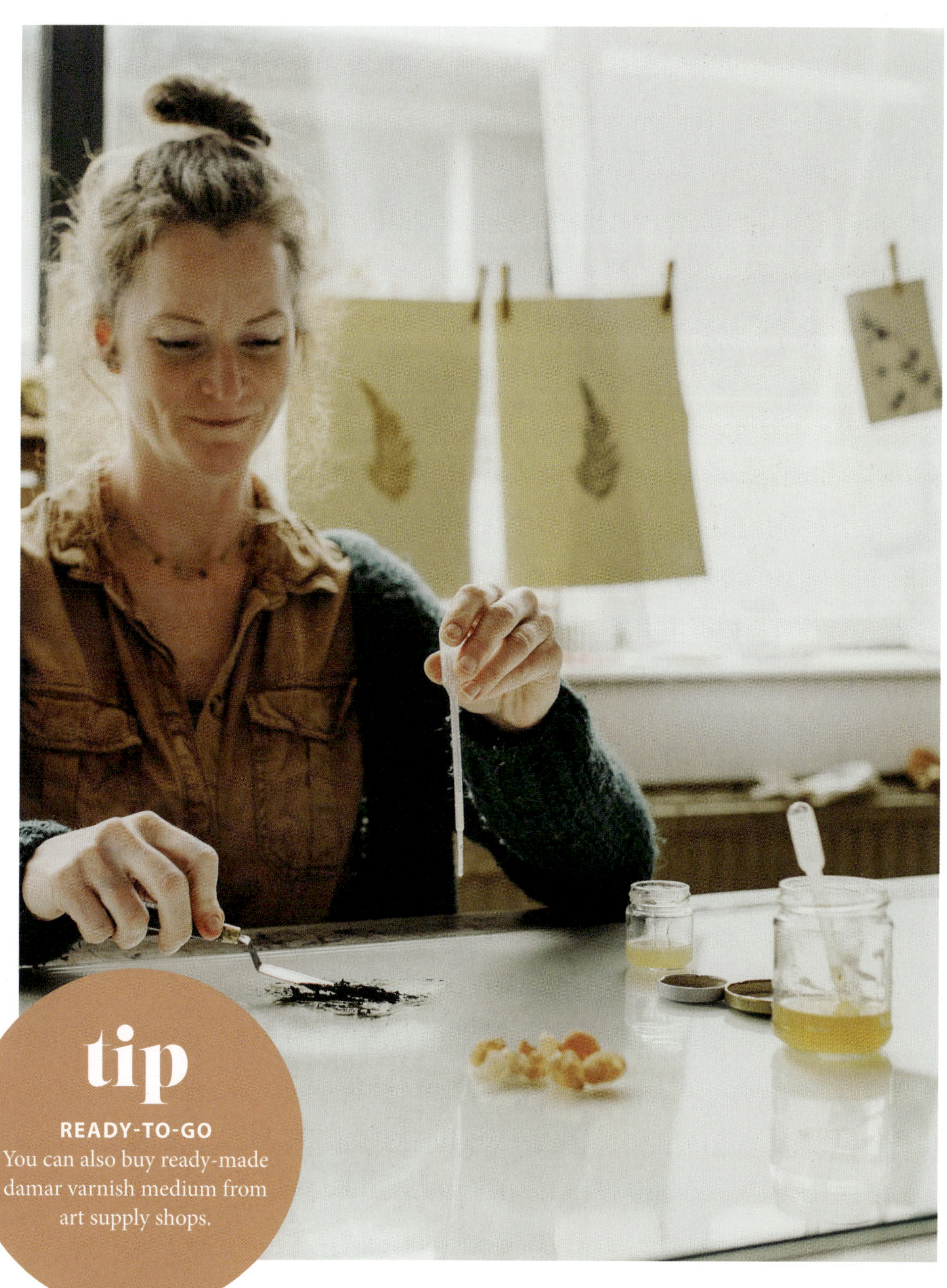

tip
READY-TO-GO
You can also buy ready-made damar varnish medium from art supply shops.

Oil colours

Ingredients
- 2tsp lake pigment (see page 138)
- 4 drops linseed oil
- damar varnish medium
  (see page 146)
- gum turpentine

Equipment
- glass plate
- pipette
- palette knife
- glass muller
- sterile jar or empty tube

METHOD

1. Scoop the pigment onto a glass plate in a pile.
2. Make a small well in the top of the pile, and use the pipette to drip the linseed oil into it.
3. Using the palette knife, mix the pigment and the linseed oil together so that a thick paste forms (you may need more drops of oil, depending on the pigment).
4. Drizzle the damar varnish medium on top of that. The more drops you use, the thinner your paint will be.
5. Thoroughly mix the pigment paste and damar varnish medium together.
6. Place the glass muller on top of the paint and rub over the glass plate in circular motions. All of the pigment particles must be coated with the oil and varnish.
7. The paint is now ready to use. You can always thin out the paint using some more damar varnish medium.
8. Scoop the paint into a sterile jar or an empty tube to store it.
9. Clean your tools with the gum turpentine..

Egg tempera

'Tempera' comes from the Latin word *temperare*, which means 'to mix'. Egg tempera is a mixture of egg yolk and pigment. Before oil paint was invented, this was the type of paint that was most commonly used. It is actually an easy paint to make. The only downside is that it's not possible to store the paint because you are working with raw egg and it spoils very easily. Make sure you make only the amount you need to use each day. Once the paint has dried, it won't spoil at all and is actually very durable. Tempera paintings dating back to the Middle Ages are still in great condition today. The technique involves painting thin layers on top of each other. The paint dries very quickly, allowing another layer to be painted on after each coat has dried. The previous layers will remain visible. I find egg tempera to be a wonderfully smooth paint, and the good thing about making your own paint is that you have the choice to make it as thick or as thin as you want. Tempera can be used to paint on canvas or on sturdy paper.

Ingredients
- 1 egg
- 1tsp white wine
- 1tsp lake pigment (see page 138)

Equipment
- 2 bowls
- tea towel
- palette knife
- teaspoon
- glass plate
- pipette
- glass muller

METHOD

1. Separate the egg yolk from the egg white into two bowls. Don't break the yolk.
2. Roll the yolk from one hand to the other; each time you do so, wipe your hand dry with the tea towel. Do this about six times, until the yolk feels dry.
3. Taking the yolk between your thumb and forefinger, hold it over a bowl and then poke a hole in it using the palette knife.
4. Drain the yolk into the bowl and discard the membrane.
5. Stir the yolk smoothly with a teaspoon.
6. Add the white wine and stir until you see a nice, even emulsion forming.
7. Scoop the lake pigment powder on to a glass plate and make a small well in it.
8. Use the pipette to add the smooth emulsion into the well, one drop at a time and then mix it together with the palette knife.
9. Place the glass muller on top of the mixture and, using circular motions, work the lake pigment powder and smooth emulsion together into paint. Decide how thick or thin you want the paint to be.

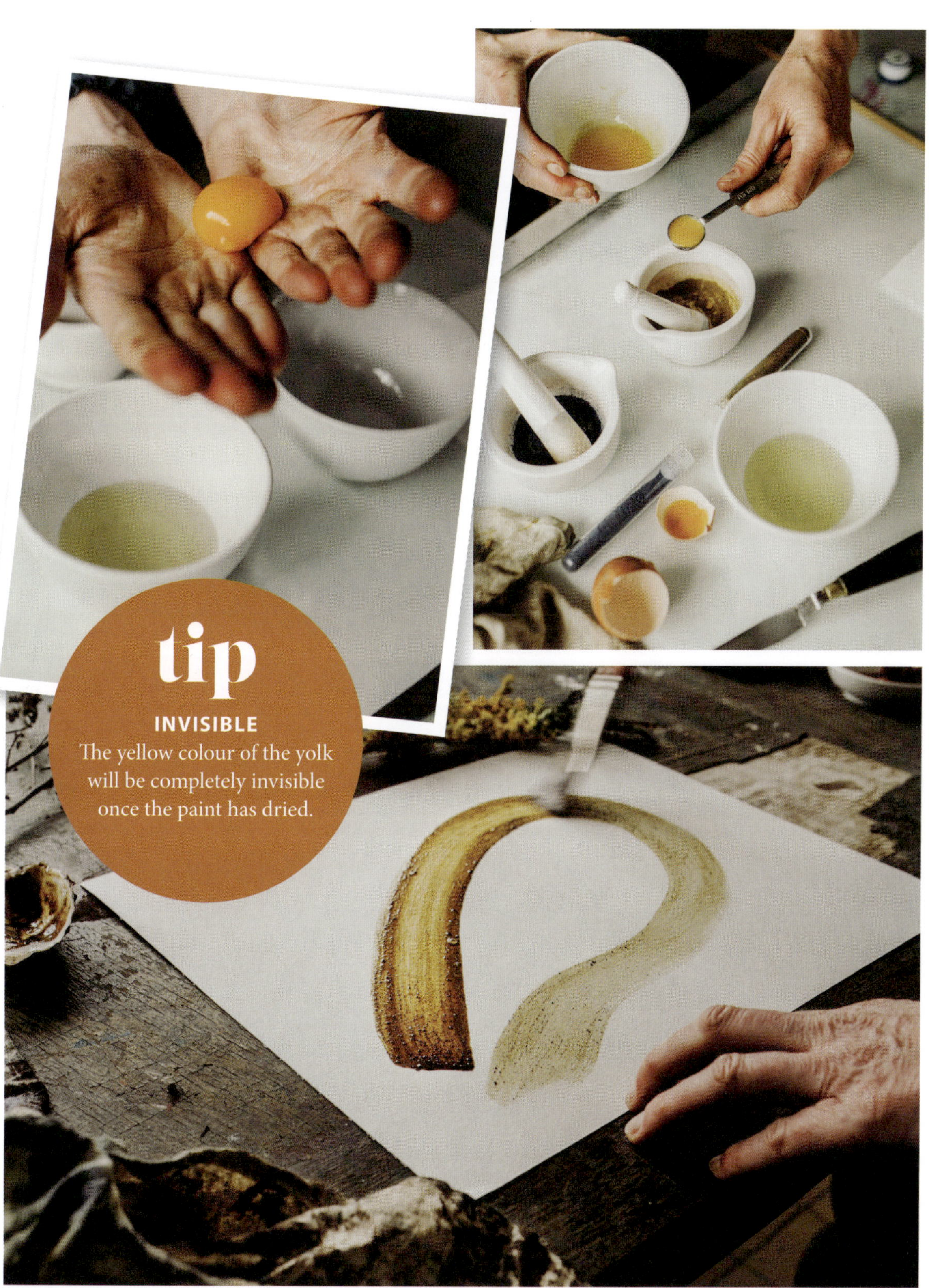

tip

INVISIBLE
The yellow colour of the yolk
will be completely invisible
once the paint has dried.

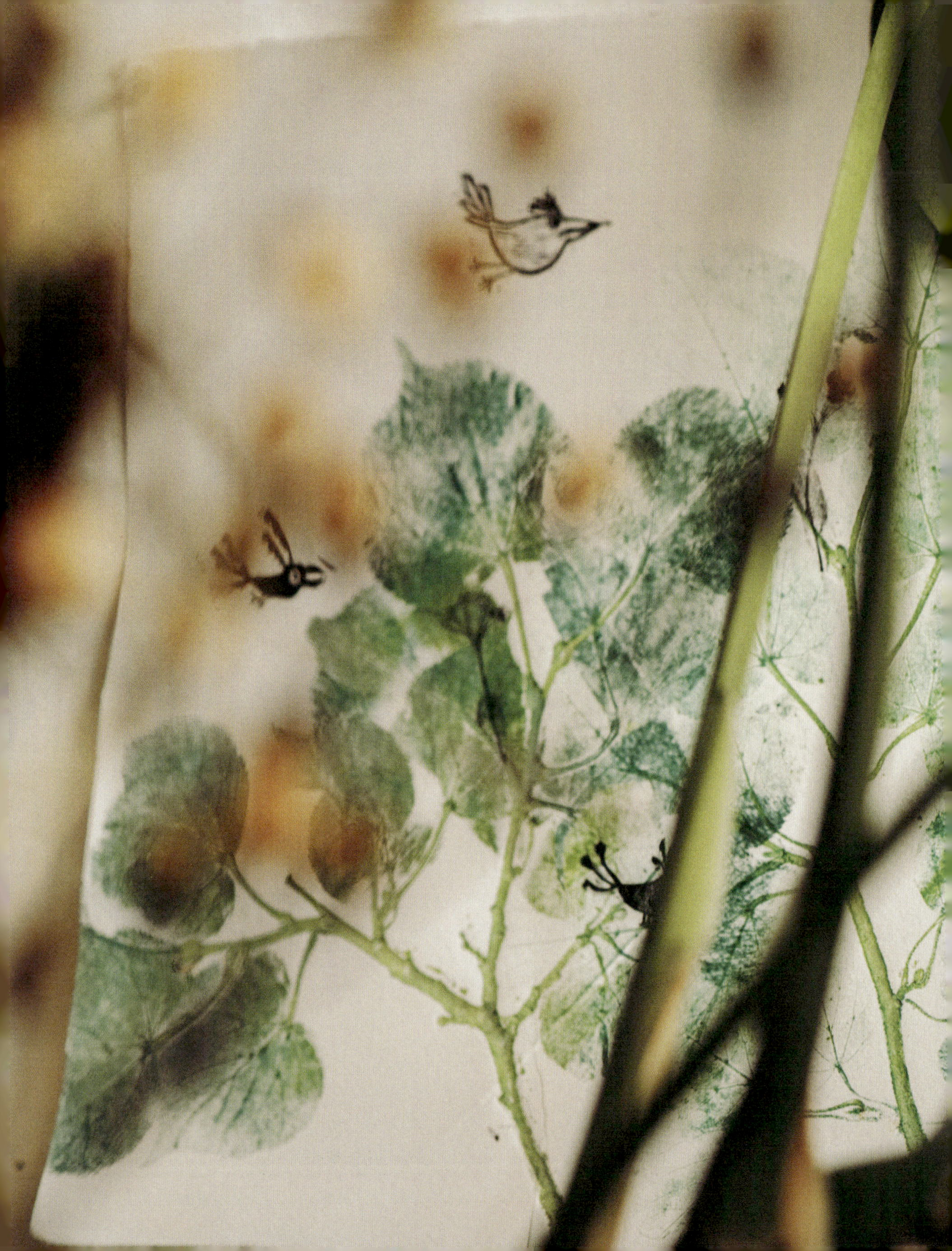

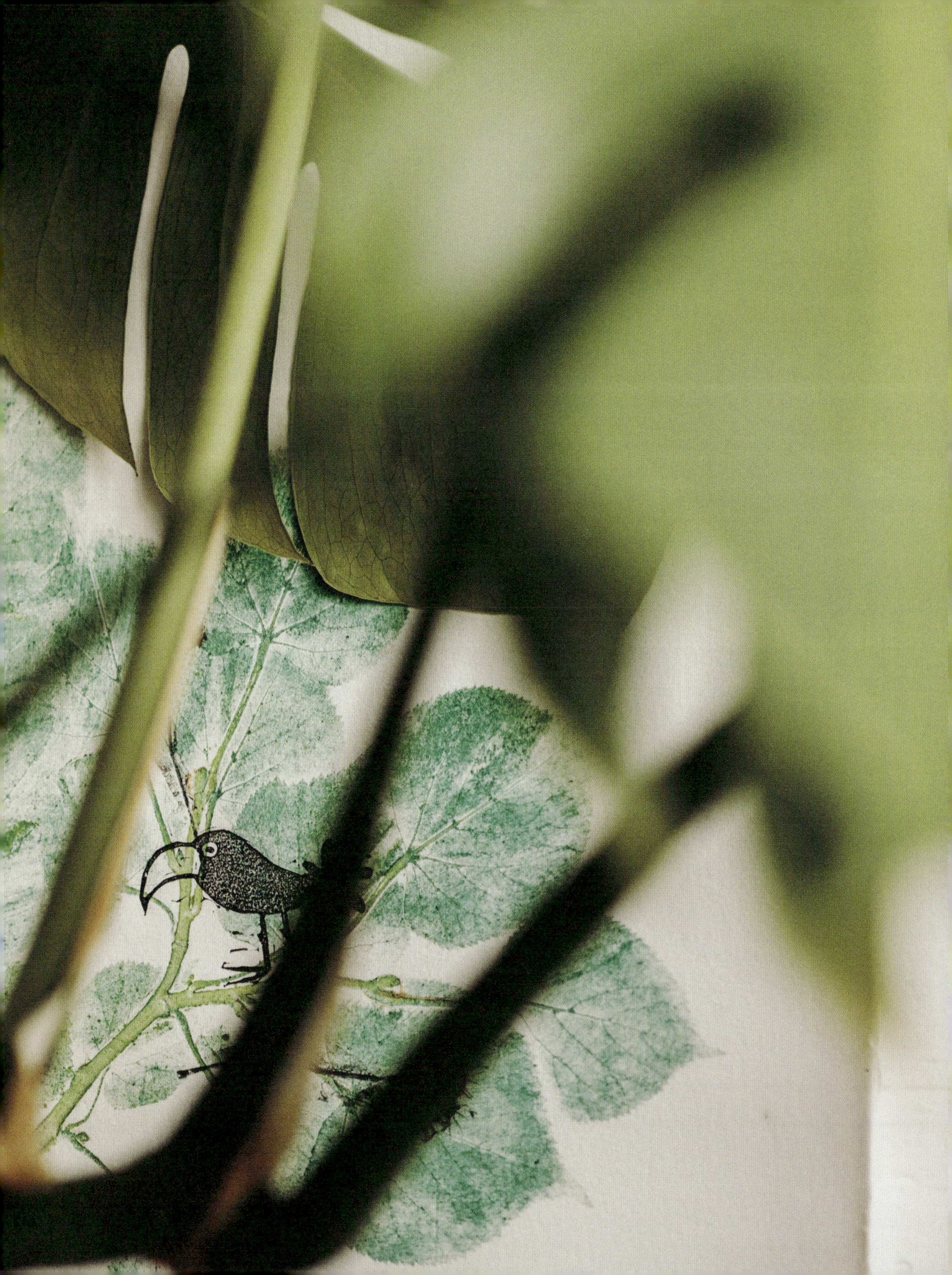

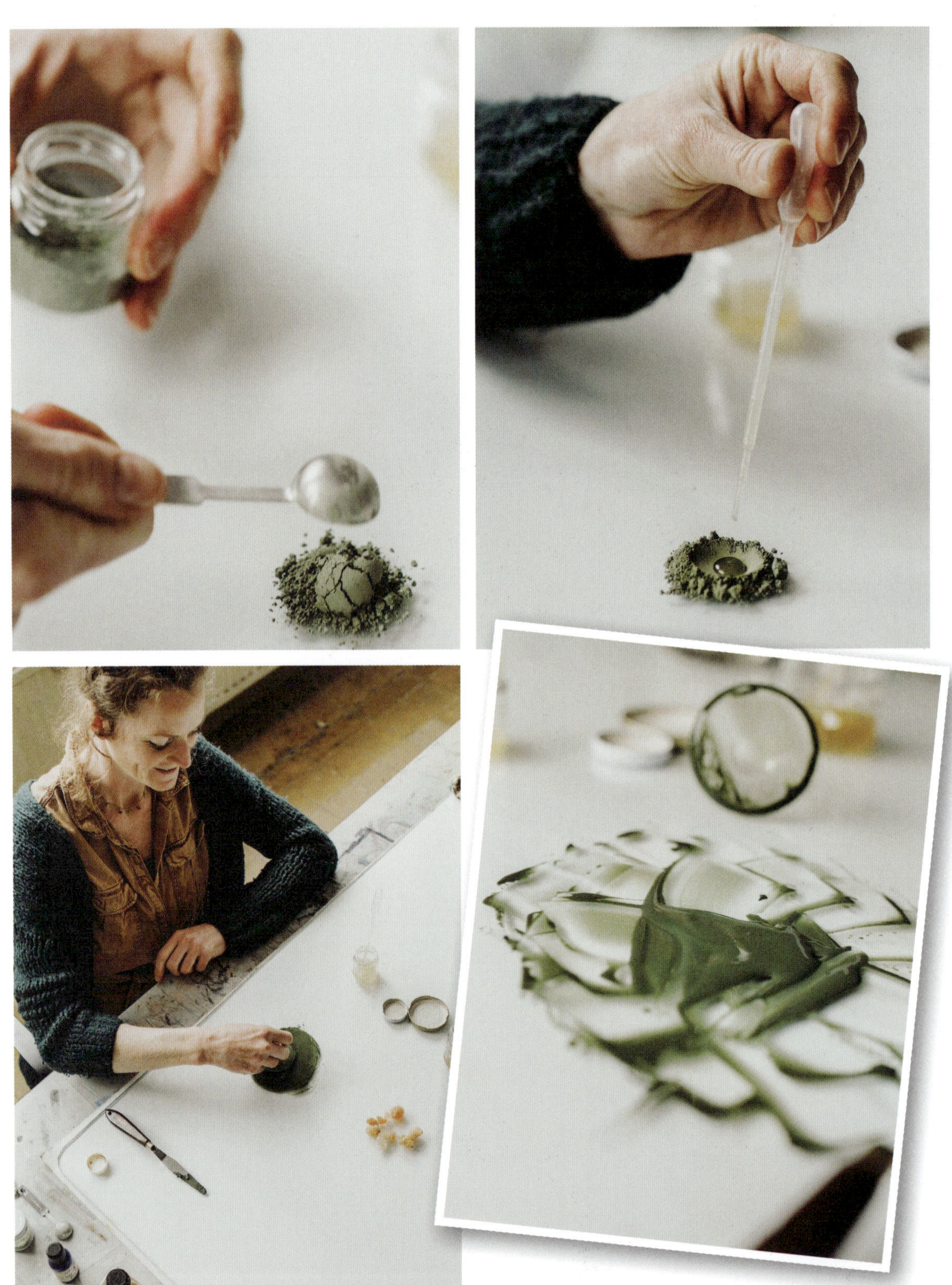

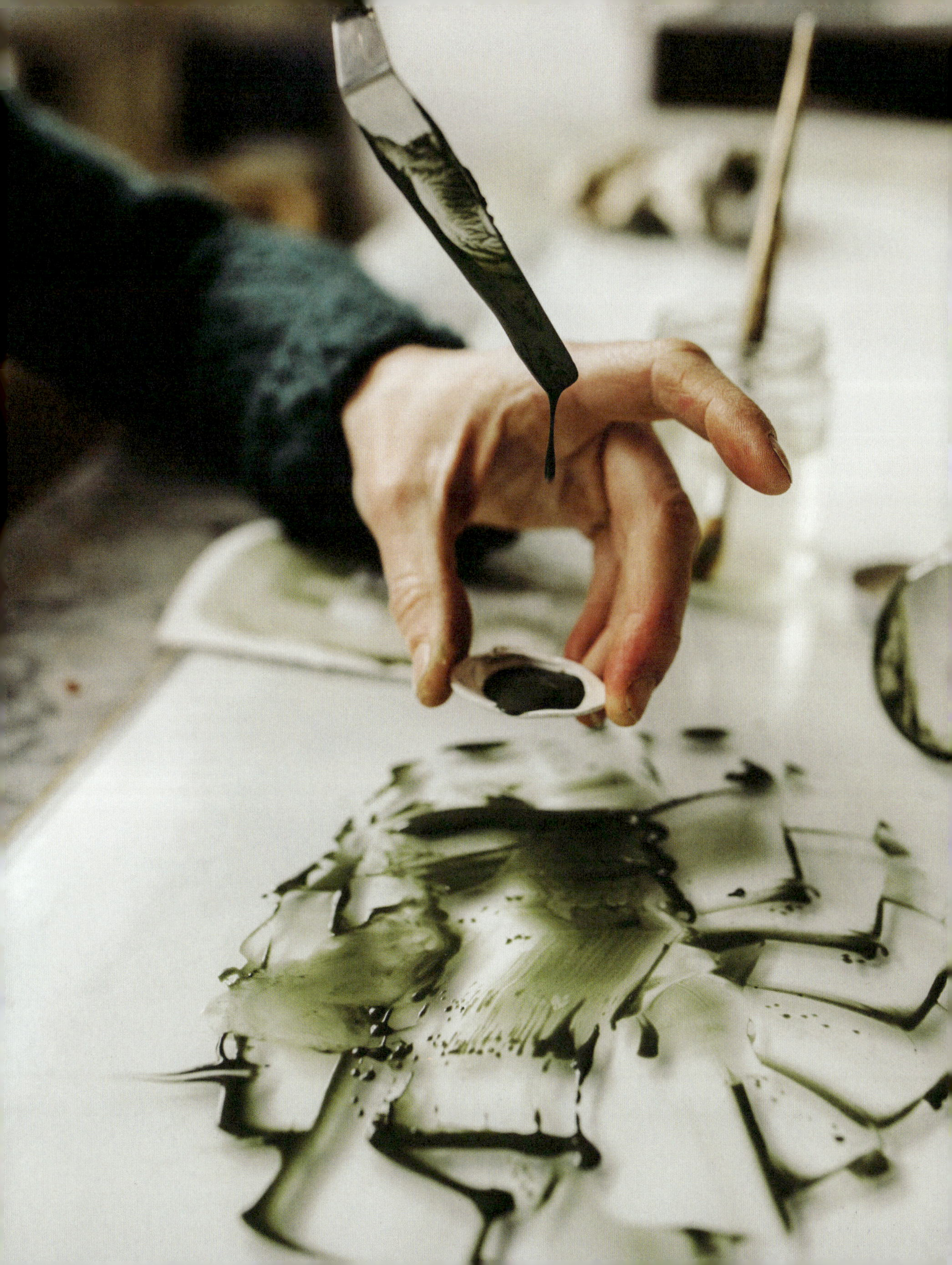

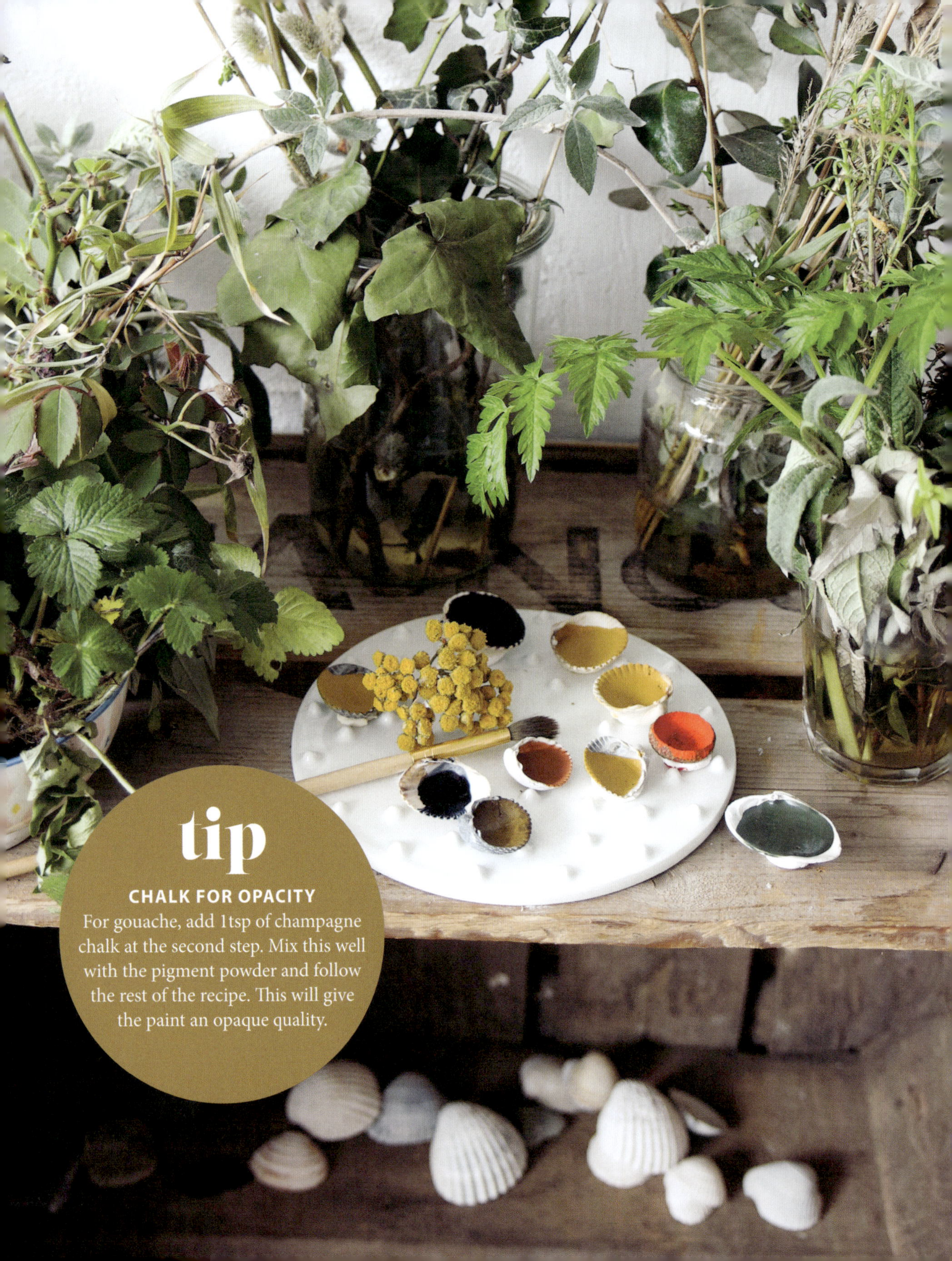

tip

CHALK FOR OPACITY

For gouache, add 1tsp of champagne
chalk at the second step. Mix this well
with the pigment powder and follow
the rest of the recipe. This will give
the paint an opaque quality.

Watercolour paint and gouache

Watercolour paint is a water-soluble paint that can be used on thick watercolour paper. It consists of pigment powder mixed with a combination of gum arabic, glycerine and ox gall. Gum arabic functions as a binder. Glycerine will make the paint flow nicely when applied to wet surfaces. It also allows any dry paint to be reactivated with a wet brush. Ox gall helps to stop any drips forming (beading). With this recipe, I also add clove oil as a preservative. Allow the watercolour paint to dry completely in an acorn shell, sea shell or milk cap. As with any paint, it is important that the pigment powder you use is as fine as possible. This is because the pigment particles do not dissolve in the paint, but instead float around in it. The finer the particles, the smoother the paint will be. Gouache is also a watercolour. The difference is that gouache is made opaque by adding chalk. Watercolours and gouache paints are best applied to thick watercolour paper containing a high quantity of cotton fibres, thereby allowing the paper to hold a lot of water without warping.

Ingredients
- 6tbsp gum arabic
- 1tbsp glycerine
- ¼tbsp ox gall
- 1 drop of clove oil
- 1tsp lake pigment (see page 138)

Equipment
- sterile glass jar
- glass plate
- pipette
- palette knife
- glass muller
- sea shell or milk cap

METHOD

1. First of all, make the watercolour medium. In a glass jar, thoroughly mix together the gum arabic, glycerine and ox gall. Add the clove oil.
2. Scoop the lake pigment powder onto a glass plate and make a small well in it.
3. Using a pipette, add the watercolour medium one drop at a time and mix it together with a palette knife until all of the pigment particles have been coated with the medium.
4. Add more drops of the medium until the paint becomes liquid.
5. Place the glass muller on top of the paint and, using circular motions, work the pigment and the medium into a smooth paint. The paint might be quite wet.
6. Scoop up the paint and put it in a sea shell or milk cap using a palette knife; leave until completely dry. This may take a few days. Dry watercolour paint can be stored indefinitely.

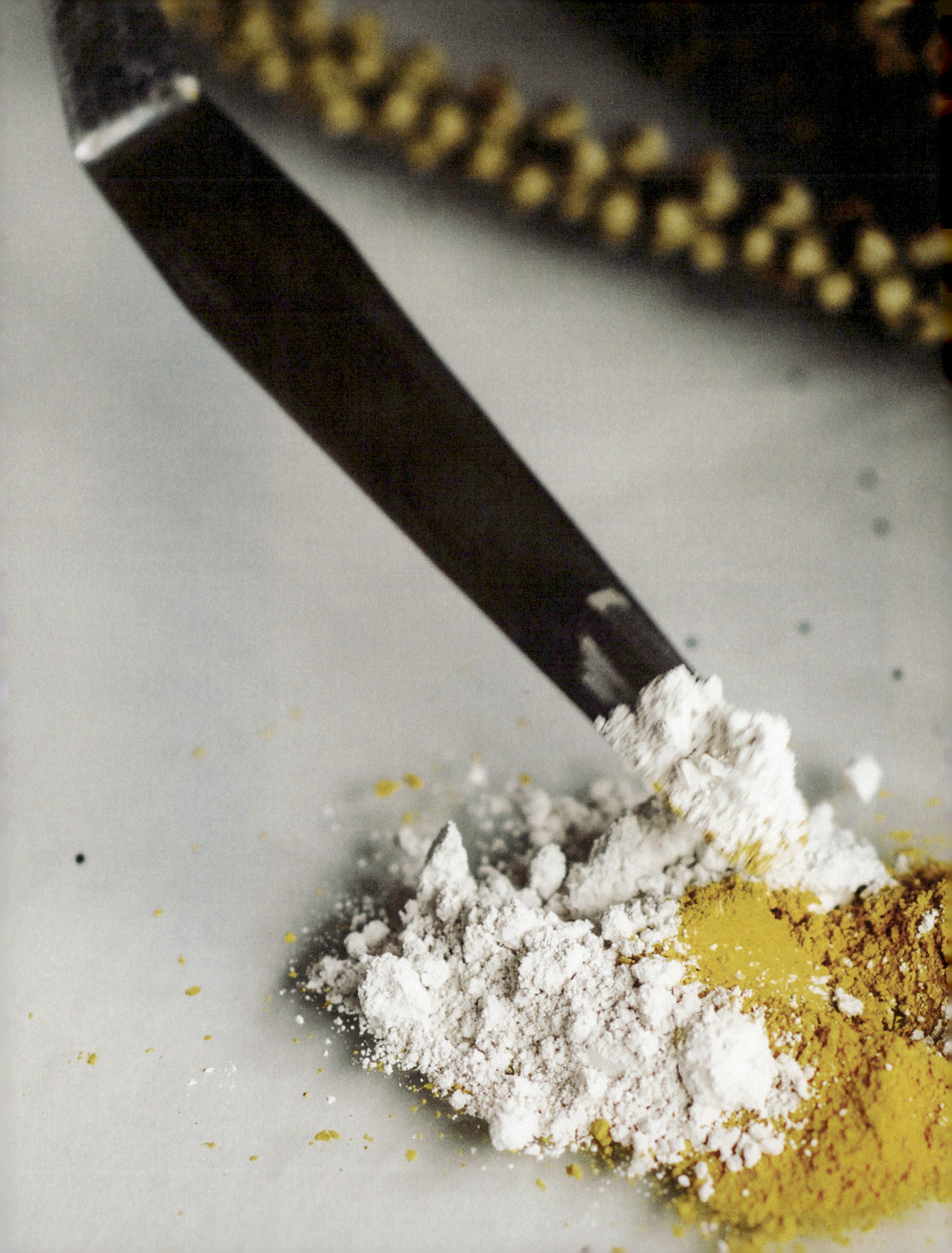

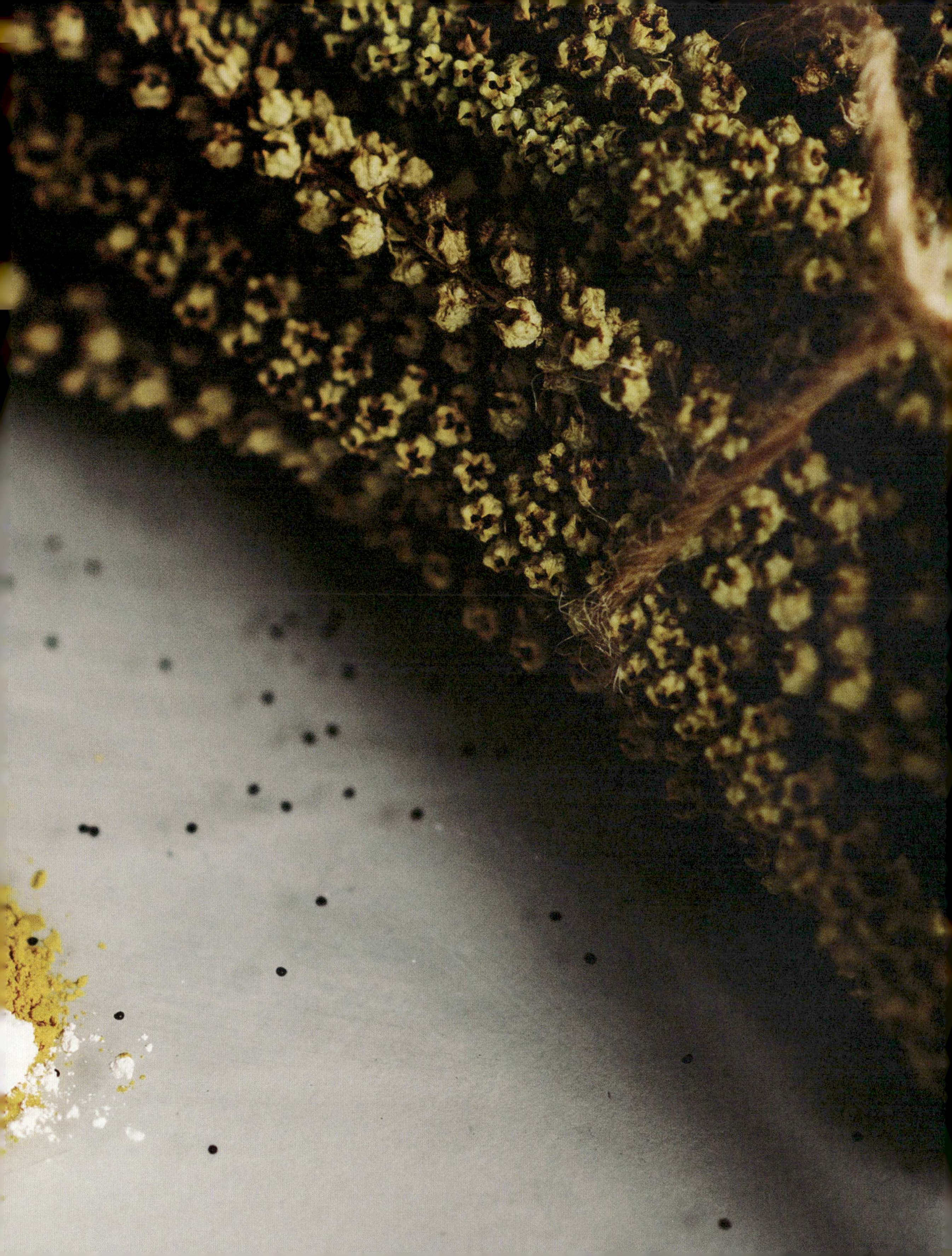

Chalk pastels

I used to love drawing on the pavement with chalk. I covered entire pavements with my drawings and my stories could be found all over the neighbourhood. When it rained, my drawings would disappear and I would once more be free to tell new stories. I can clearly remember how dry and rough my hands were, completely dried out by the chalk. I didn't have very many colours at the time.

At the academy, I experimented with a chalk pastel that my teacher gave me. It created such a rich colour: very different from the faded pavement chalk colours that I remembered from childhood. When I visited an art supply shop, I discovered that a whole range of chalk pastel colours were available. I also learned that the name 'pastel' has nothing to do with the soft muted colours that I knew and disliked. I saw pastel colours that were intense and bright. They were beautiful, full and rich in colour. Each colour has a number and is made up of a series of ten shades. Any chalk with full colour intensity is given the number .5; this is for pastel chalks containing pure pigment. The numbers increasing to .10 are mixed with increasing quantities of white chalk, taking on an ever-softer hue. The numbers decreasing to .1 are mixed with increasing quantities of black chalk. These colours become deep and heavy.

You can use chalk pastels in a manner similar to painting: chalk pastels can be blended together on the paper, enabling soft colour transitions. Since chalk pastels are opaque, you can even work with them on black paper. Light-coloured chalks can be used to add highlights. Chalk pastels will also wash away if you brush over them using a wet brush. It's easy to make chalk pastels. You will need to use gum tragacanth (see page 172) as a binder for the pigment. Depending on the shades you want, you can mix in champagne chalk (see page 171) to lighten the colour or add powdered charcoal to darken it. Hard and soft chalk pastels and oil pastels are available in shops. This recipe is for soft chalk pastels. This chalk works best on a thick paper that has a light grain. Special pastel paper can be bought at art supply shops.

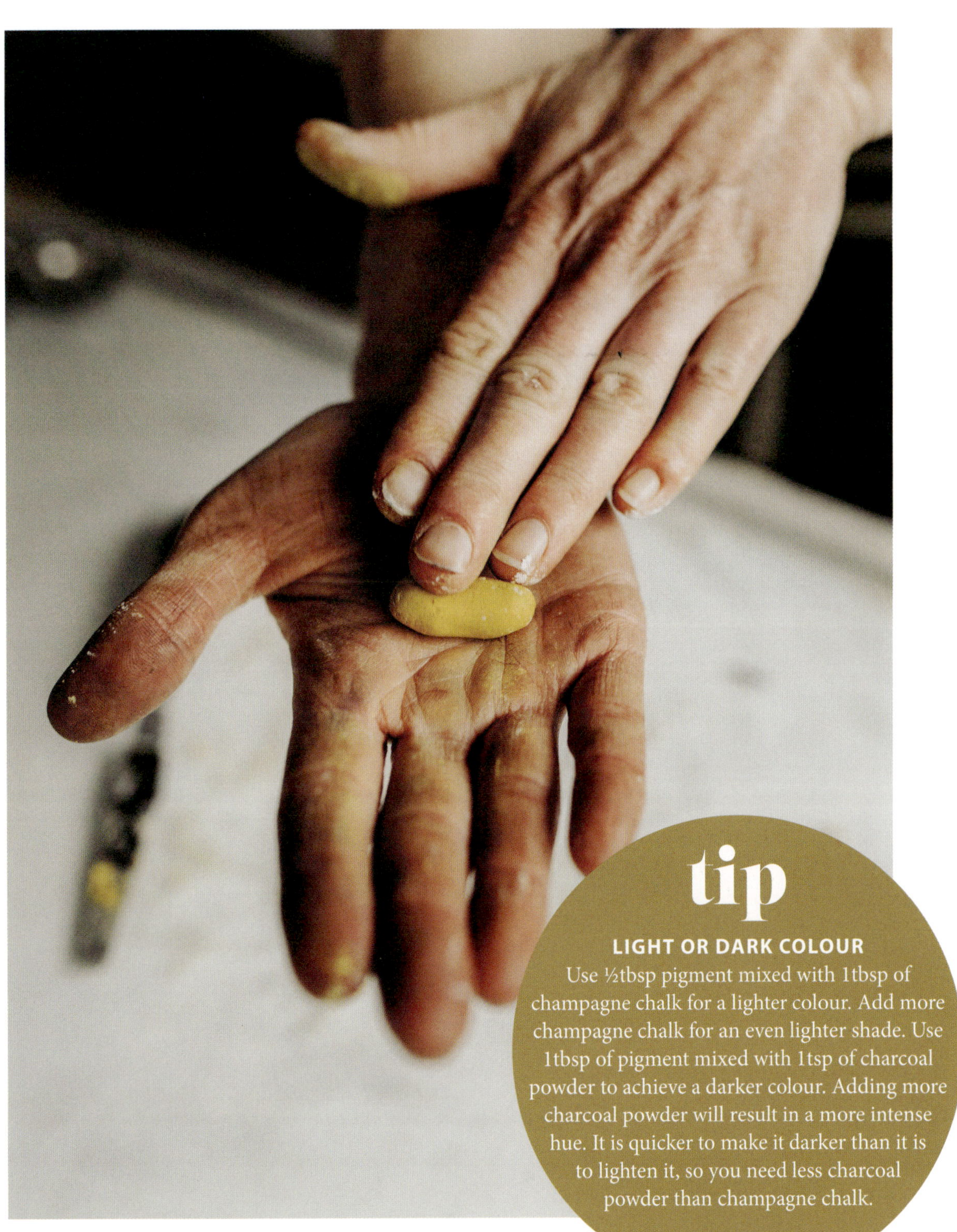

tip

LIGHT OR DARK COLOUR

Use ½tbsp pigment mixed with 1tbsp of champagne chalk for a lighter colour. Add more champagne chalk for an even lighter shade. Use 1tbsp of pigment mixed with 1tsp of charcoal powder to achieve a darker colour. Adding more charcoal powder will result in a more intense hue. It is quicker to make it darker than it is to lighten it, so you need less charcoal powder than champagne chalk.

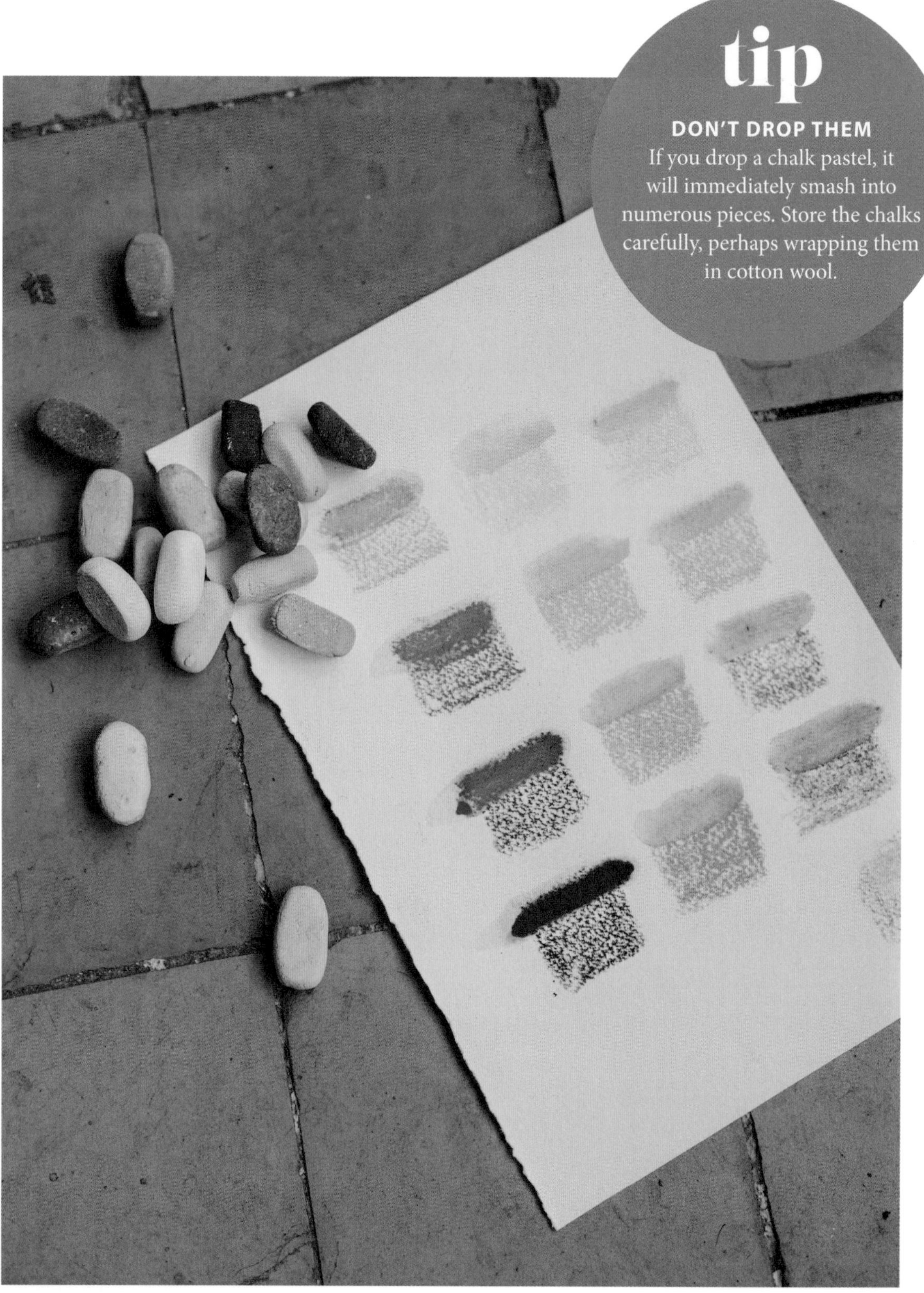

tip

DON'T DROP THEM
If you drop a chalk pastel, it
will immediately smash into
numerous pieces. Store the chalks
carefully, perhaps wrapping them
in cotton wool.

Chalk pastels

Ingredients
- 5g (³⁄₁₆oz) gum tragacanth powder
- ½l (17½fl oz) water
- 1tbsp lake pigment
  (see page 138)
- 1tbsp champagne chalk
  (optional)
- 1tsp charcoal powder
  (optional)

Equipment
- sterile glass jar
- wooden stirring stick
- glass plate
- pipette
- palette knife

METHOD

1. First of all, make the chalk pastel medium. In a glass jar, mix the gum tragacanth powder with ½l (17½fl oz) of cold water. Stir it all together well using a wooden stirring stick. The gum tragacanth will slowly dissolve in the water. It will take a day to do so. Eventually, a thick jelly-like mix will form, similar to wallpaper paste.

2. Scoop the pigment powder onto a glass plate and make a small well in it.

3. Using a pipette, drizzle the gum tragacanth into the well. The chosen pigment will determine how many drops you need. Work it in, drop by drop.

4. Mix the pigment powder and gum tragacanth together using a palette knife.

5. Keep mixing it well until you have a thick clay-like mass. Continue to add the gum tragacanth in very small quantities because you do not want it to get too wet.

6. The mixture is ready when it no longer sticks to the glass plate.

7. Take the mass into your hands and shape it into a ball.

8. Roll out the ball on the table to form a thick stick.

9. Allow the stick to air dry overnight.

10. Store your chalks carefully. See tip, opposite.

Screen-printing ink

Ingredients
- ¼tsp cornflour (corn starch)
- 250ml (8¾fl oz) plant tea
  (see page 29)

Equipment
- 2 bowls
- pan

METHOD

1. Put the cornflour (corn starch) in a bowl and add 2tbsp of plant tea. Fully mix together the cornflour (corn starch) and plant tea, ensuring that there are no lumps.
2. Pour the rest of the plant tea into a pan and heat it until it almost reaches boiling point.
3. Add the cornflour (corn starch) mixture while stirring continuously.
4. Pour the ink into another bowl and allow it to cool completely.
5. The screen-printing ink is ready to use. It should be the same consistency as thin yoghurt.
6. If the screen-printing ink is too thick, dilute it with the plant tea.

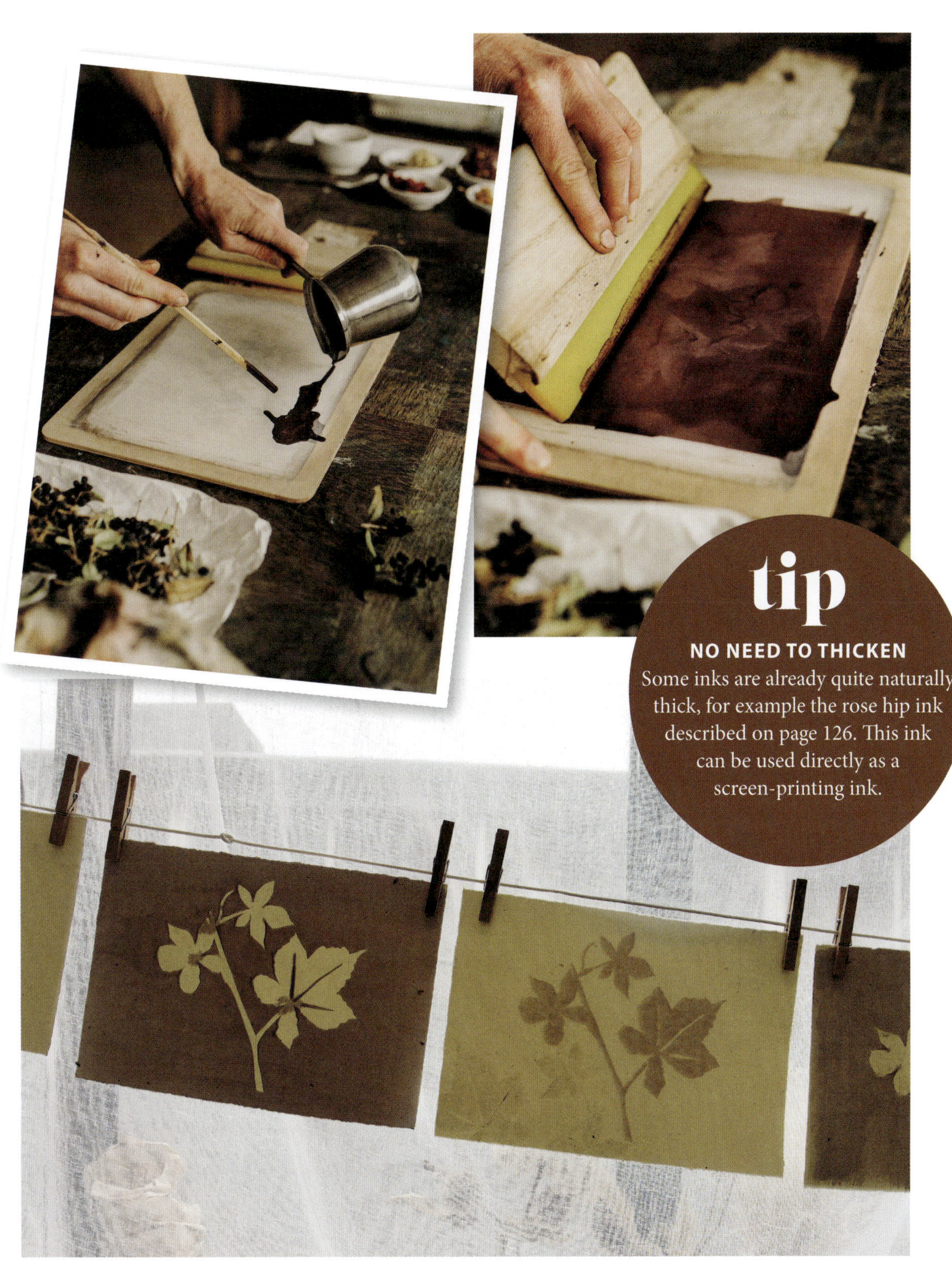

tip

NO NEED TO THICKEN
Some inks are already quite naturally
thick, for example the rose hip ink
described on page 126. This ink
can be used directly as a
screen-printing ink.

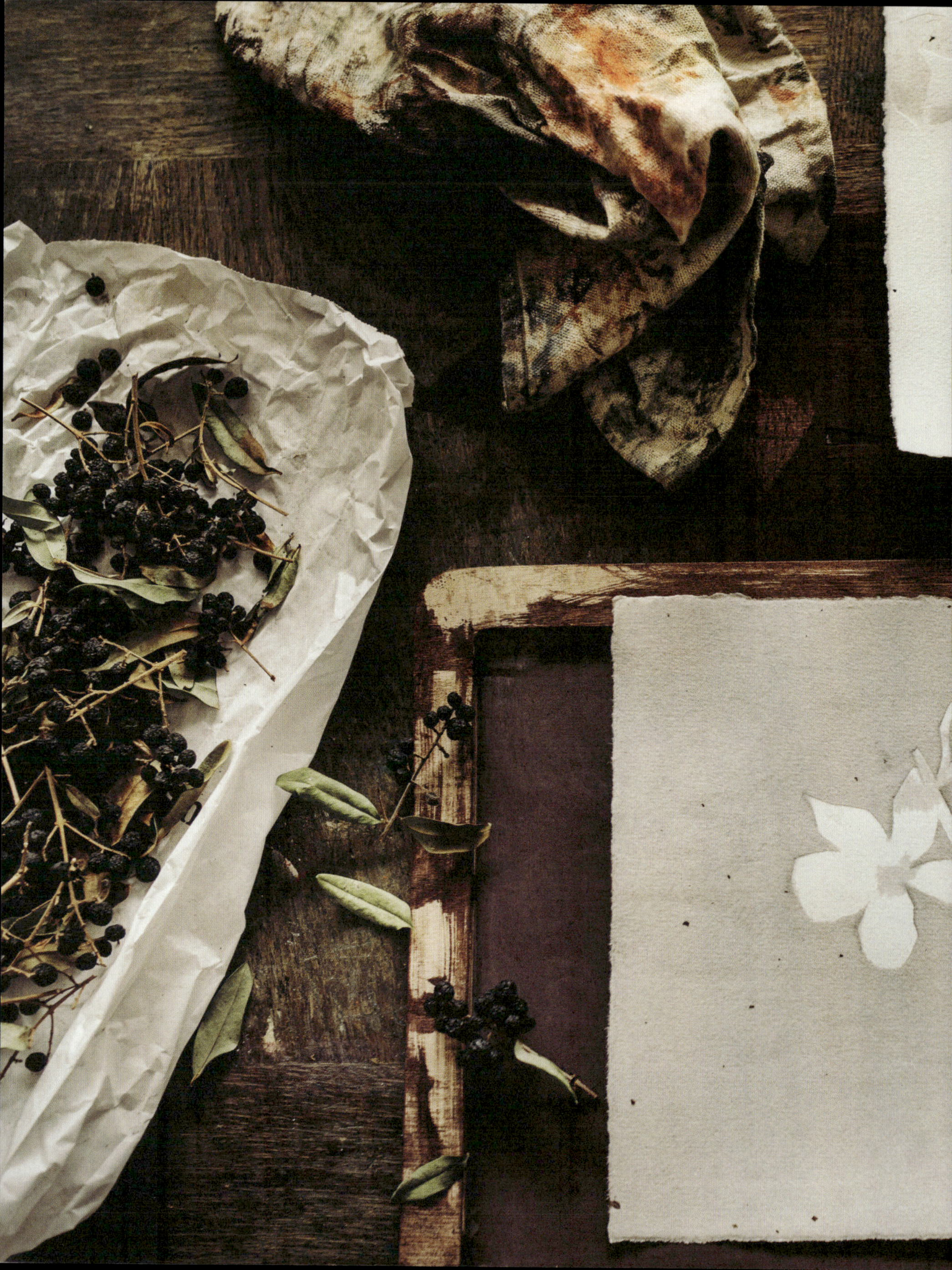

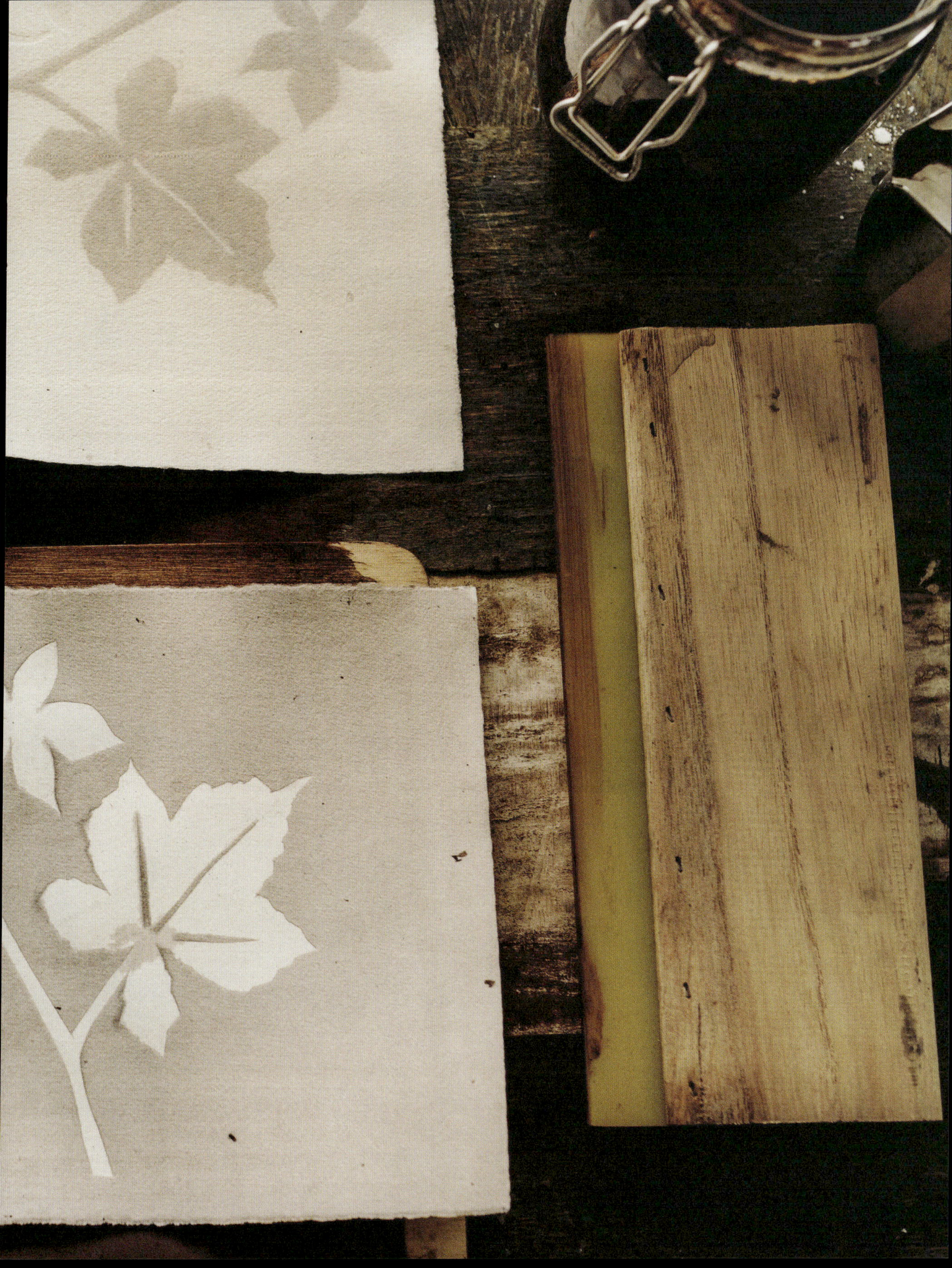

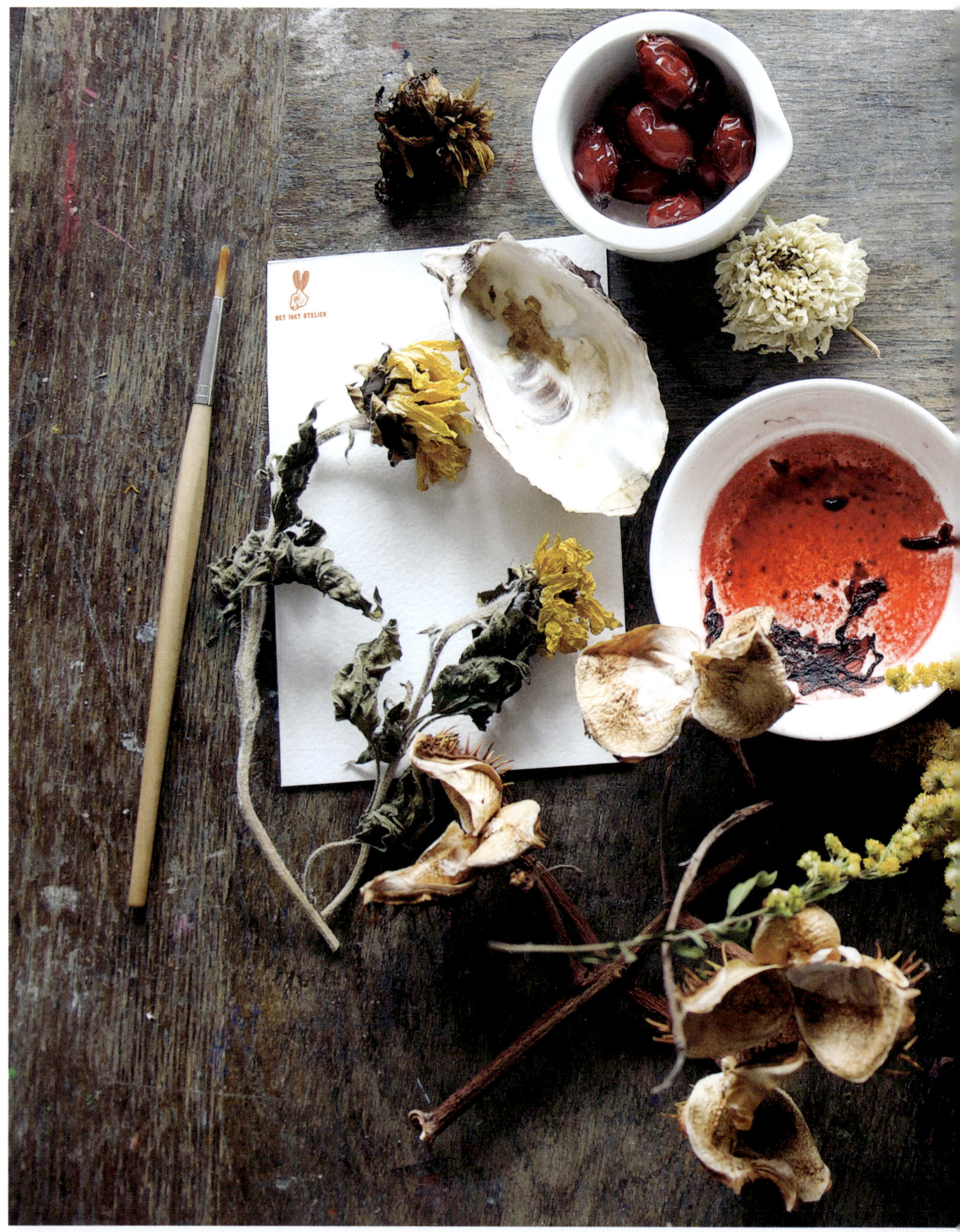
HET INKT ATELIER

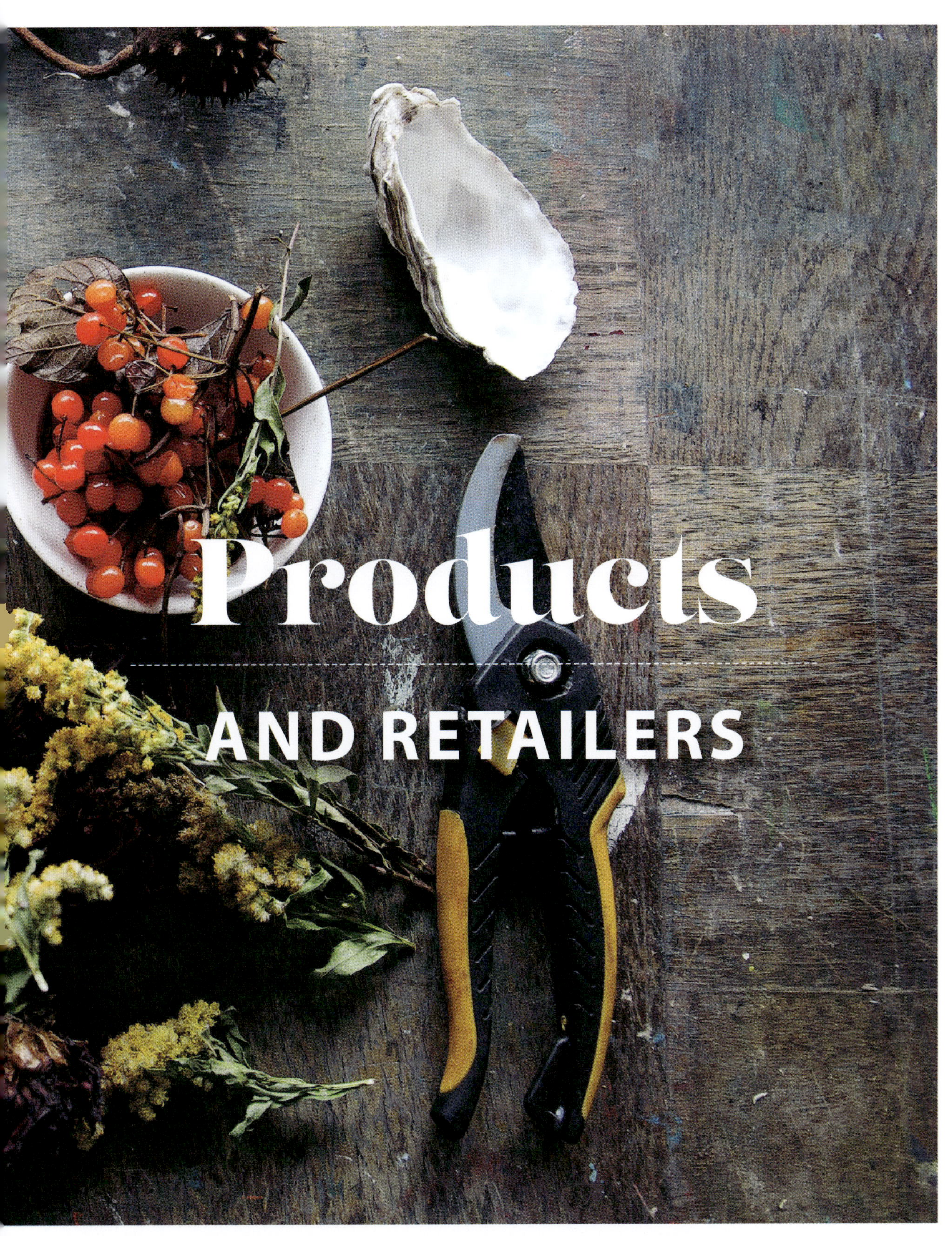
Products
AND RETAILERS

Product information

ALUM is a white metallic salt. You use it to make lake pigments. It adheres to the colour particles, allowing them to be separated from any surrounding moisture. Alum can also be used to change the colour of ink or create a more intense colour. Alum has been used for dying textiles since ancient times. Today, alum is used in the food industry for pickling vegetables. It is also used in deodorants. Alum can also be used to help stop the flow of blood, so it can be used if you happen to cut yourself while shaving.

 **Available at art supply shops, among others.**

BAKING SODA, also called sodium bicarbonate or bicarbonate of soda, is a white powder. It can be used to change the colour of ink or create a more intense colour. In bakeries, baking soda is added to make dough rise.

 **Available at supermarkets and international food shops, among others.**

BONE GLUE is purchased as yellow grains, the size of bulgur wheat. It is a glue that is made from animal bones: it dissolves in warm water and can be used in liquid form. In this book, the glue is used in old ink recipes. The best thing about it is that it is reversible. Once the glue is dry, all you need to do to turn it liquid again is to heat it in a bain-marie.

 **Available at art supply shops, among others.**

CELLULOSE is a substance found in plants. It is the basic ingredient in paper. In this book, I often talk about paper that is made from 100 per cent cellulose. This paper is naturally pure and does not change the colour of the ink. It is also made exclusively from cotton (rags). It is, however, more expensive. The most common paper is made from wood pulp fibres. If a label says the paper is 'wood-free', it does not mean that no wood at all has been used, but instead means that lignin – the substance that turns things yellow – has been removed from the fibres.

 **Available at top-end art supply shops that stock an extensive range of paper, among others.**

CHAMPAGNE CHALK is a fine sedimentary rock that is used as a filler in various different paints. It provides coverage. Champagne chalk is also used in chalk pastels. By adding different amounts of the chalk, you can vary the different shades.

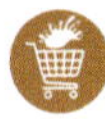 **Available at art supply shops and specialist paint shops.**

CITRIC ACID was extracted from citrus fruits in the past, but nowadays it is made on an industrial scale. It comes in white crystals. Citric acid is used by graphic artists for etching. In this book, I use it to change the colour of ink or create a more intense colour.

 **Available at health food shops, among others.**

CLOVE OIL is an essential oil that has been extracted from cloves using a distillation process. Clove oil is used as a natural preservative as it prevents the growth of bacteria and fungus. The oil has a very strong smell and can irritate skin upon contact. One drop of oil in a 30ml (1oz) bottle of ink is enough to preserve the ink.

 **Available at health food shops and shops that sell essential oils, among others.**

DAMAR RESIN is a natural resin extracted from hardwoods of the *Dipterocarpaceae* family (tropical trees). In this book it is used in the preparation of oil paint, but it can also be used as a varnish. Damar resin dissolves in turpentine.

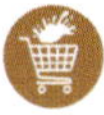 **Available at art supply shops and specialist paint shops, among others.**

GLYCERINE is a substance that has been extracted from vegetable or animal oils; but it is also a naturally occurring compound in the body. It is a white transparent liquid. Glycerine is used in watercolour paint: it makes the dry paint water down properly when you pass over it with a wet brush.

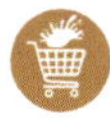 **Available at pharmacies and art supply shops.**

GUM ARABIC is a resinous gum that is extracted from the acacia tree. The gum dissolves slowly in water. It is used as a binder in ink, helping to create a smooth flow, preventing the ink from bleeding and adding a nice shine. Gum arabic is also needed when preparing watercolours and gouache. Gum arabic is a natural glue, which becomes sticky as soon as it gets damp. This is why envelopes sometimes use gum arabic for the gummed strip; stamps used it in the past, too. In the food industry, the gum is widely used in liquorice and soft sweets.

 **Available at art supply shops and organic food shops, among others.**

GUM TRAGACANTH is gum that has been extracted from milkvetch (*Astragalus*), a plant in the legume family. The gum is dried and then ground into a powder. This powder dissolves in water and forms a thick transparent gel. In this book, you will use it to make chalk pastels (see page 163).

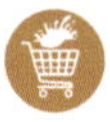 **Available at art supply shops and baking supply shops, among others.**

GUM TURPENTINE is a thin and transparent liquid that is obtained by distilling conifer resin. It is a natural product and smells rather nice, unlike turpentine, which is made from petroleum.

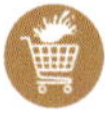 **Available at art supply shops and specialist paint shops, among others.**

IRON SULPHATE is an iron salt with sulphuric acid and looks like small green crystals. It can be used to darken ink. It is one of the main ingredients in the historical ink *atramentum librarium*. In farming and agriculture, iron sulphate is used to kill mosses, while the water purification industry uses it to remove excess phosphate from drinking water.

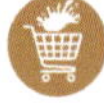 **Available at art supply shops, shops that stock grass seed (such as garden centres) and DIY stores, among others.**

LINSEED OIL is made by pressing flax seeds (also known as linseeds). The flax cake that remains after it has been pressed is used as cattle feed. For centuries, flax has been grown to make linen. It is a versatile product. The long flax fibres are used in construction boards, insulation boards and in the making of rope, while shorter flax fibres are used by the paper industry. Flax, alongside wool, was the most important raw material in the production of textiles until the 18th century, before cotton became more important in the 19th century. Linseed oil is used as a binder in oil paint. It is also found in lots of different products, such as linoleum, soap, synthetic resin and bread.

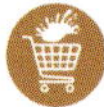 **Available at art supply shops and specialist paint shops, among others.**

LITMUS PAPER is a strip of paper that is used to measure the pH, or acidity, of a liquid. Litmus is taken from lichen through an extraction process. It is ground into a purple powder, which changes colour when it comes into contact with an acid or alkali. Red indicates an acidic substance, whereas blue indicates alkaline. In this book, I use litmus paper to measure the pH level when making pigments. Litmus is also used to measure the pH level of garden soil, urine, fishponds and swimming pools, among other things.

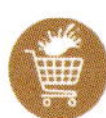 **Available at pond and swimming pool supply shops and pharmacies, among others.**

OX GALL is found in the liver of cattle, and it can be extracted from offal. It binds together fats and proteins, making it a good stain remover. In this book, however, we use it to make watercolour paint. By adding a few drops of ox gall to the watercolour mixture, you can prevent the paint from beading.

 **Available at art supply shops, among others.**

POTASH was originally made by burning beech and oak. The subsequent wood ash was then dissolved in water, filtered and then evaporated. Because it was historically traded in pots, it was called potash. It takes a lot of trees to produce potash, so people looked for other ways to make it. Today, potash is a mixture of salts; mainly made from potassium carbonate, it has a base that is similar to that of soda. Potash is used to change the colour of ink or create a more intense colour.

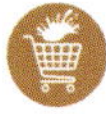 **Available at art supply shops, among others**

SHELLAC is the product secreted by lac insects. It takes the form of yellow translucent flakes that are water soluble. Shellac makes ink waterproof.

 **Available at art supply shops, among others.**

STAND OIL is linseed oil that has been thickened and boiled.

 **Available at art supply shops, among others.**

WASHING SODA is a salt derived from sodium and carbonic acid. Soda is the best and cheapest product you can use to degrease things – a real household favourite. Do you have a pan that is caked in grease? Fill it with a layer of water and a tablespoon of soda and then bring the water to the boil. After half an hour, your pan will be like new again. Got a blocked drain? Pour in a tablespoon of soda and then pour boiling water over the soda. Your drain will fizzle and run clean. If you have sore feet, you can soak them in a foot bath with soda. Are ants bothering you? Sprinkle some soda around the place and they're sure to disappear. In this book, we will be using washing soda to change or intensify the colour of ink and to make lake pigments.

 **Available at supermarkets, among others.**

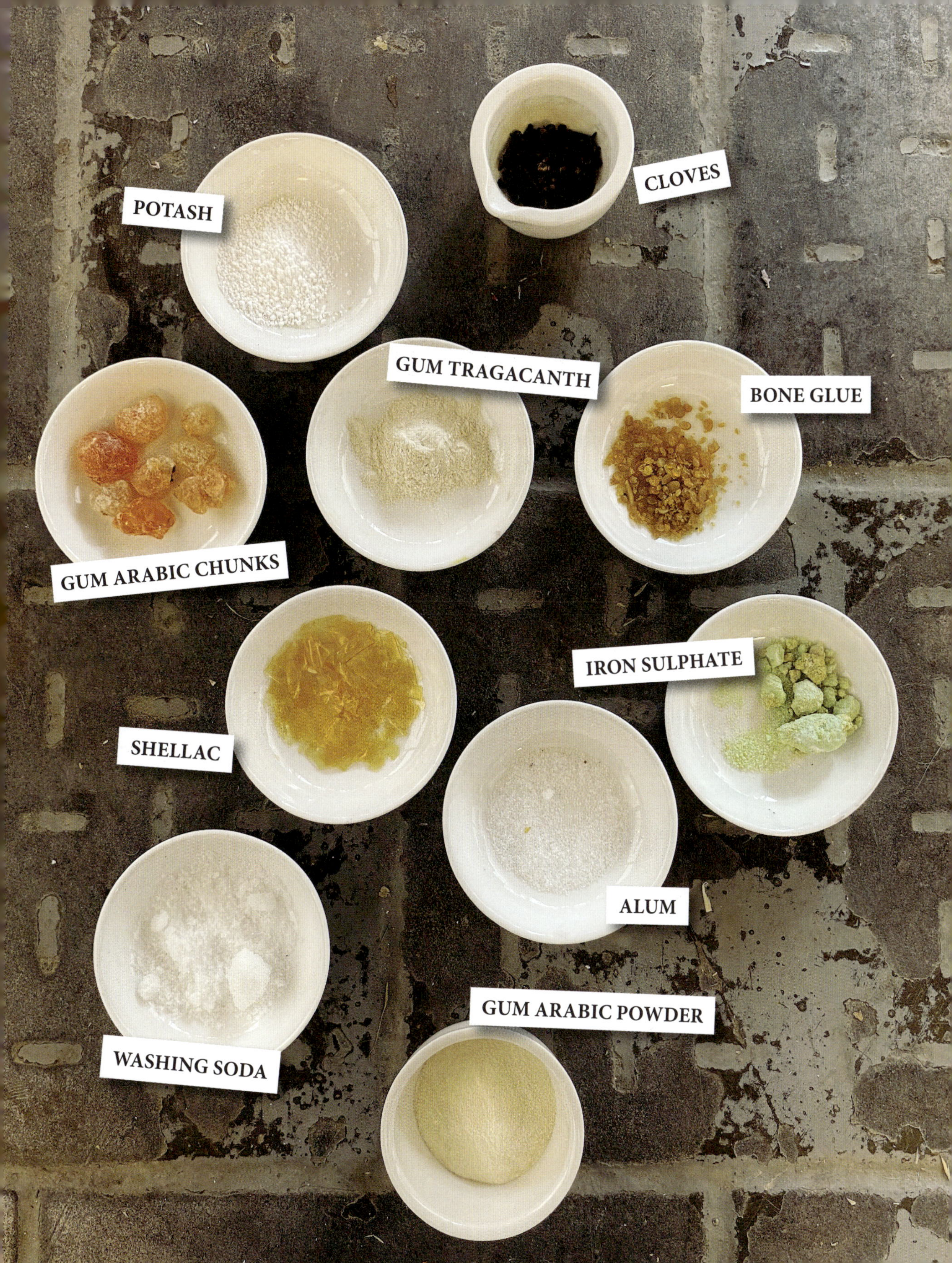

POTASH
CLOVES
GUM TRAGACANTH
BONE GLUE
GUM ARABIC CHUNKS
SHELLAC
IRON SULPHATE
ALUM
WASHING SODA
GUM ARABIC POWDER

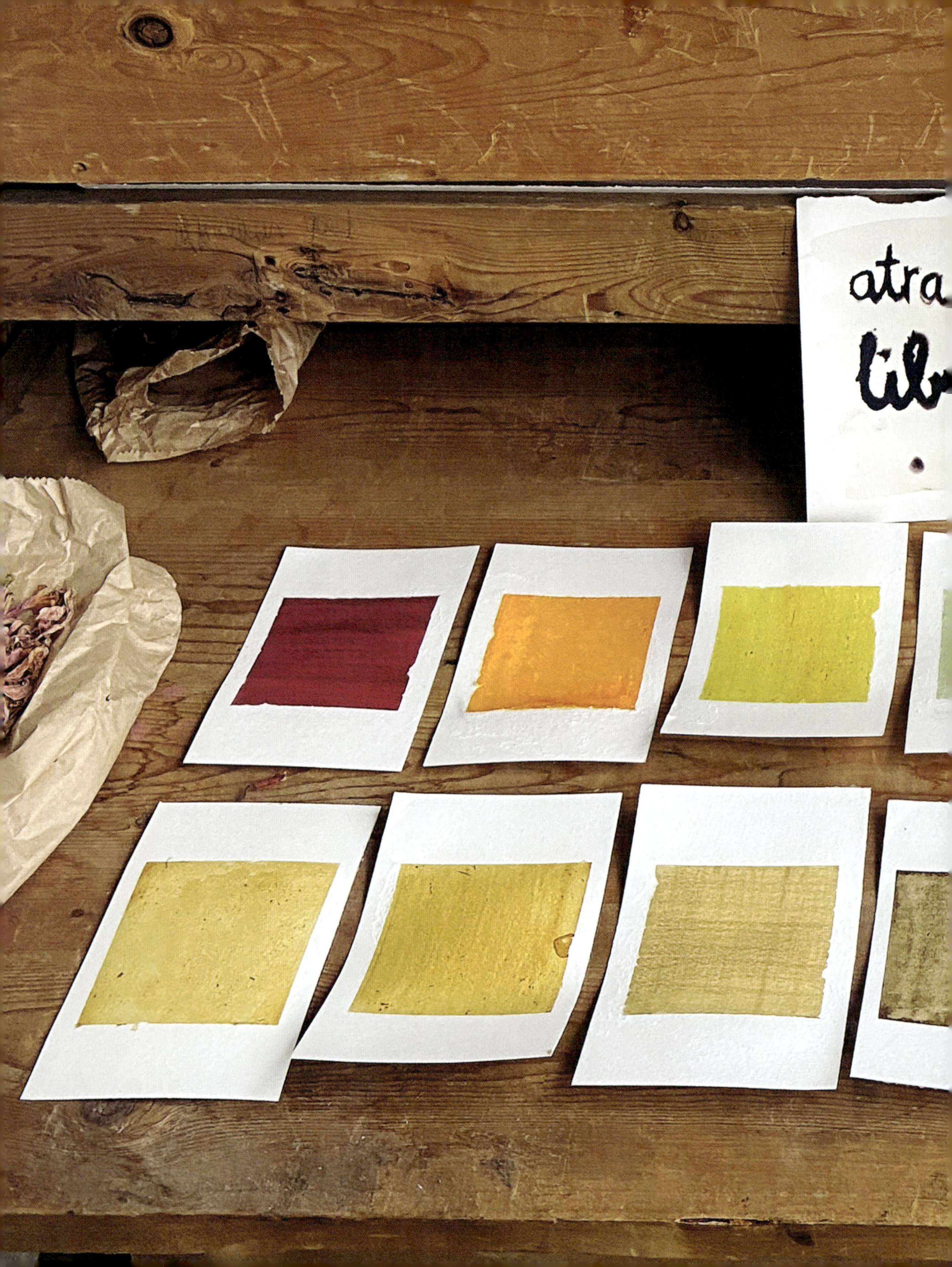

atra
libr

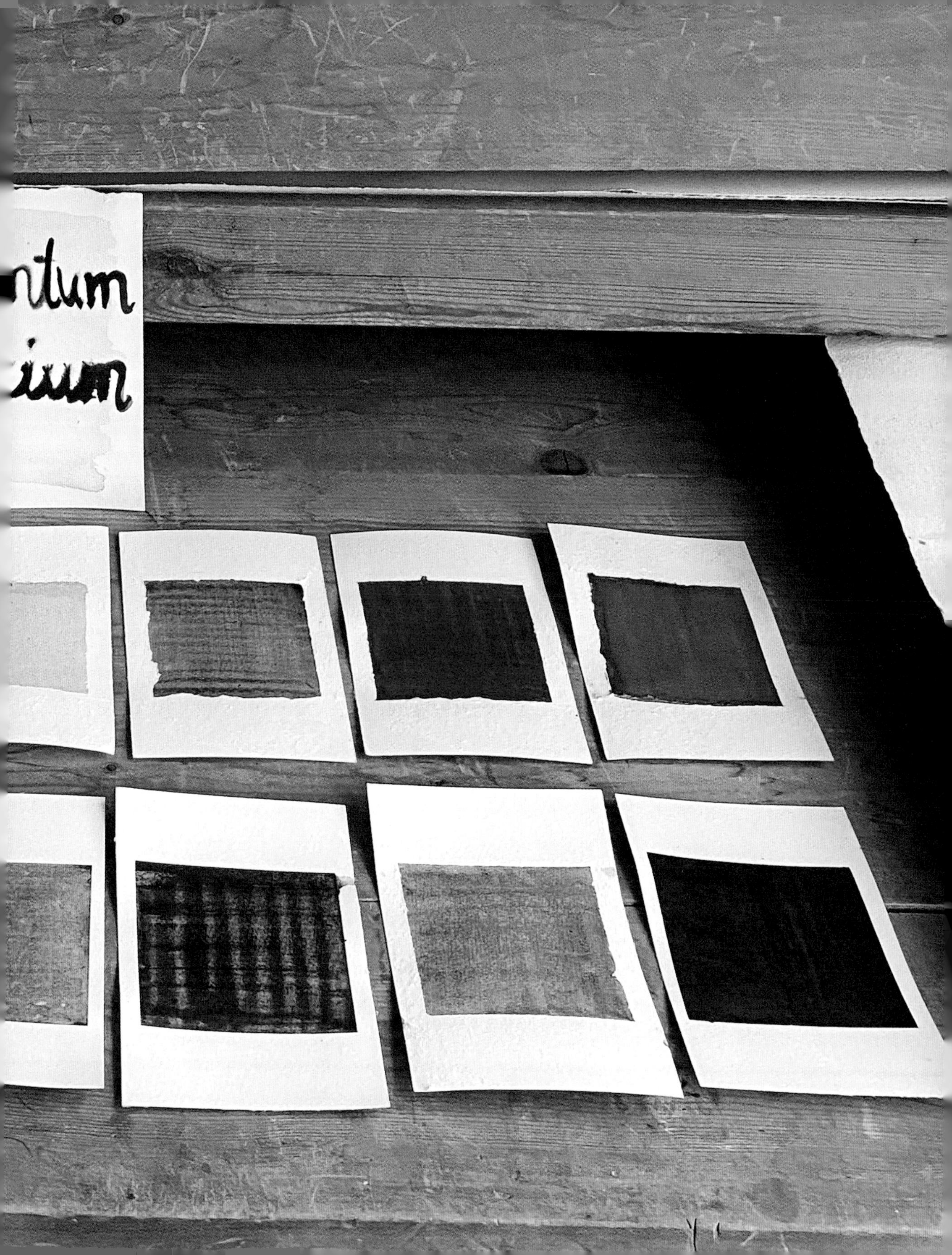
ntum
ium

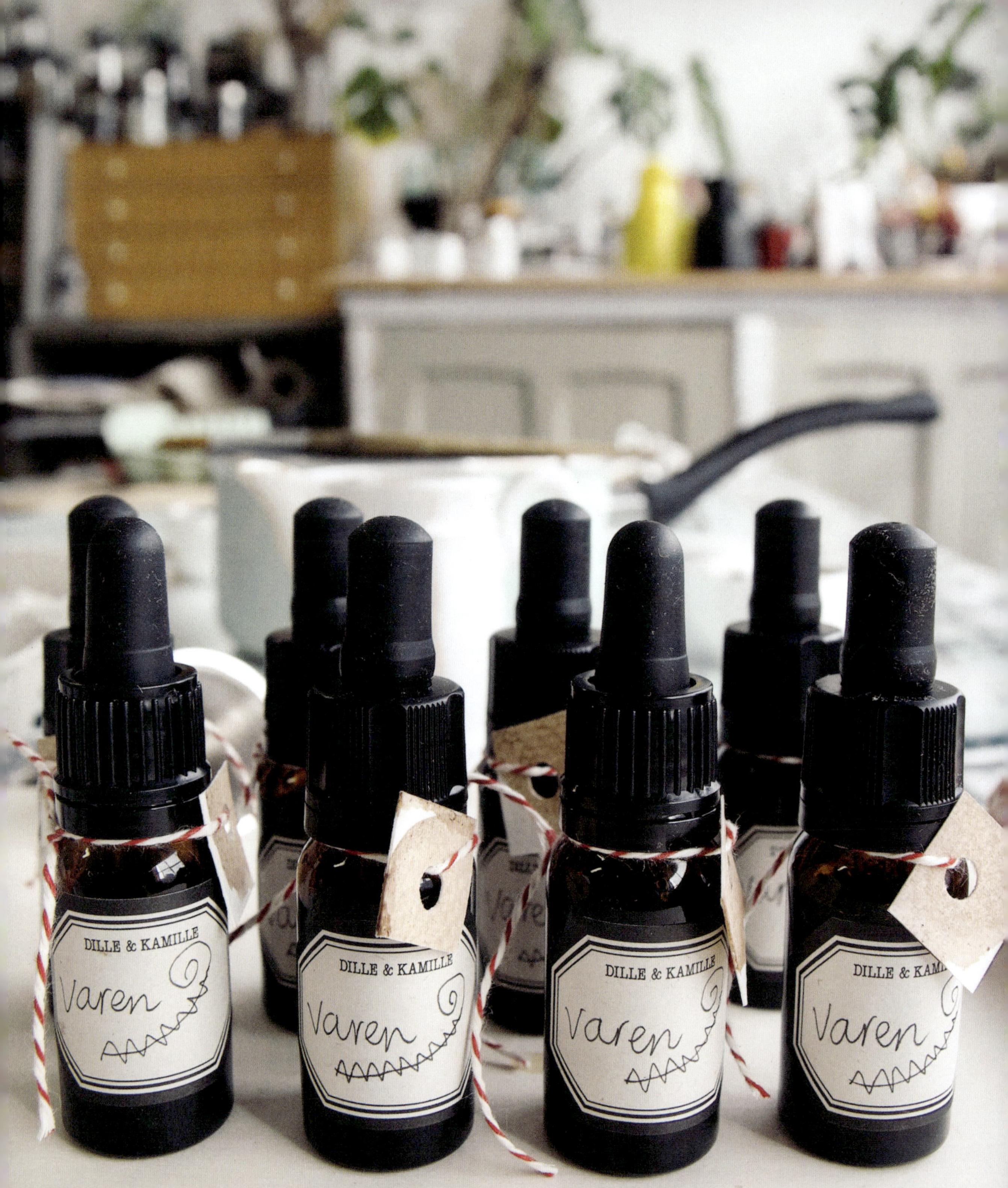

Bracken

Useful addresses

In the UK
DT CRAFT AND DESIGN
www.dtcrafts.co.uk

JACKSONS ART SUPPLIES
www.jacksonsart.com

HOBBYCRAFT
www.hobbycraft.co.uk

GREATART
www.greatart.co.uk

In the US
BLICK ART MATERIALS
www.dickblick.com

NATURAL PIGMENTS
www.naturalpigments.com

In Australia
ART SHED ONLINE
www.artshedonline.com.au

ECKERSLEY'S ART AND CRAFT
www.eckersleys.com.au

LINCRAFT
lincraft.com.au

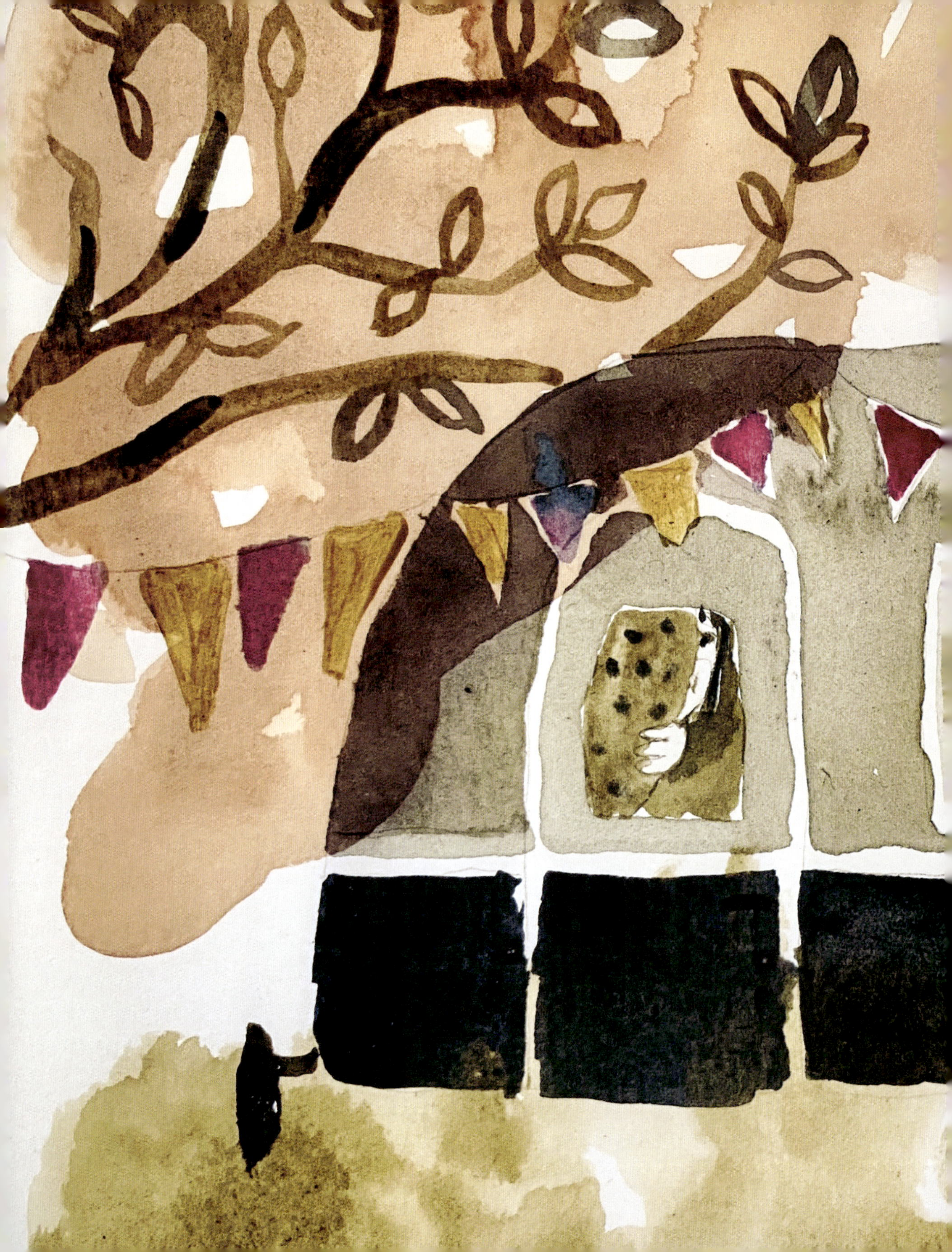

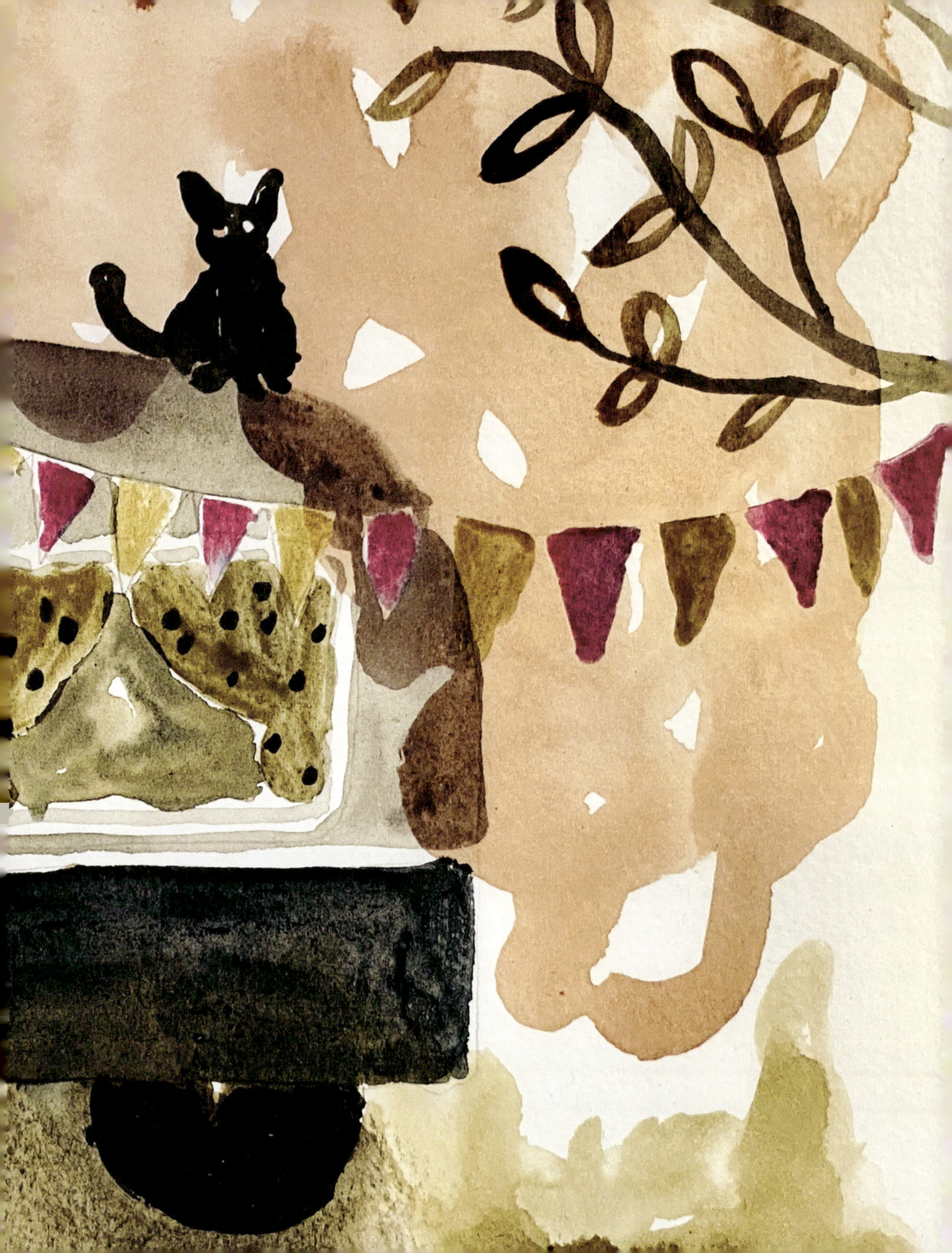

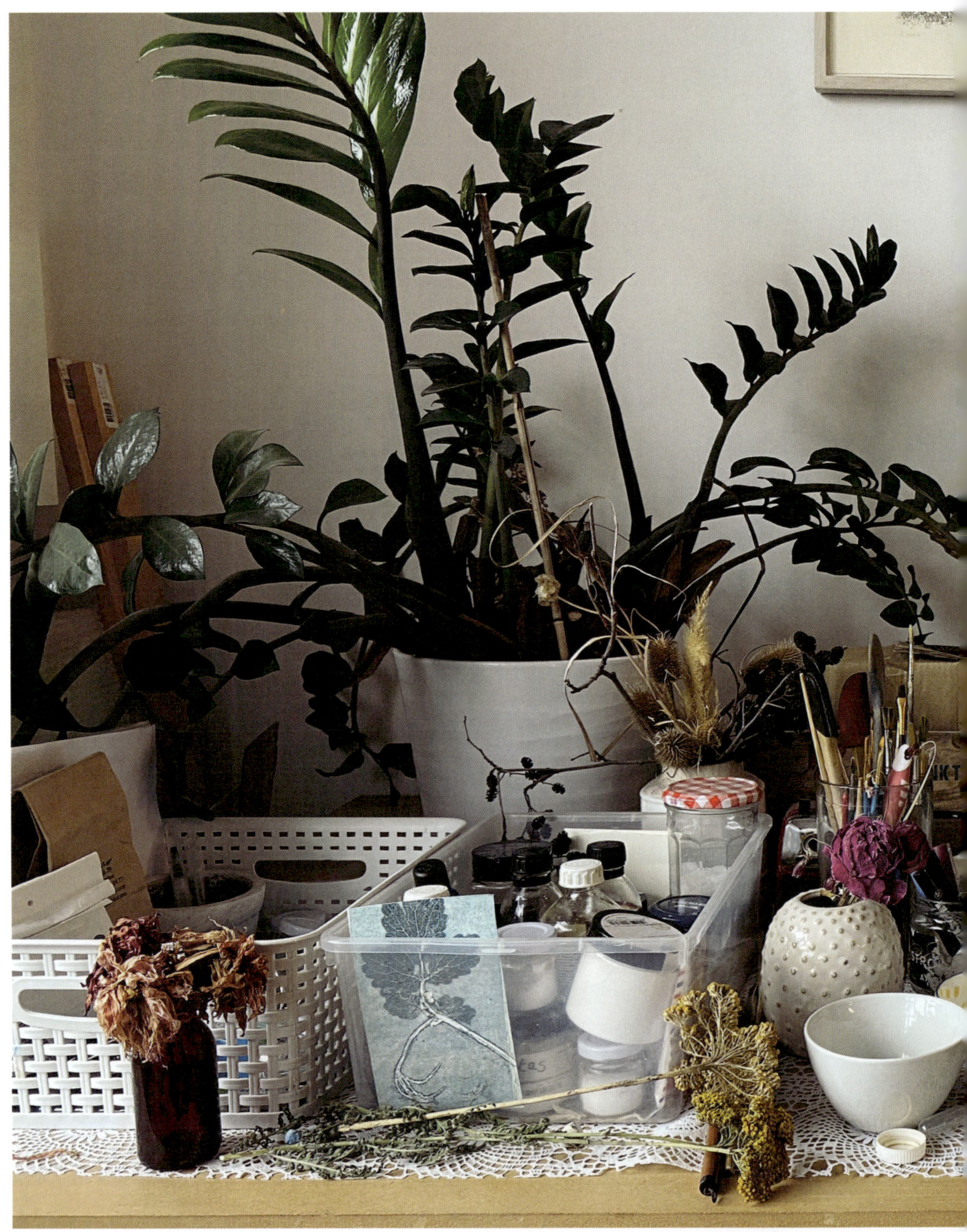

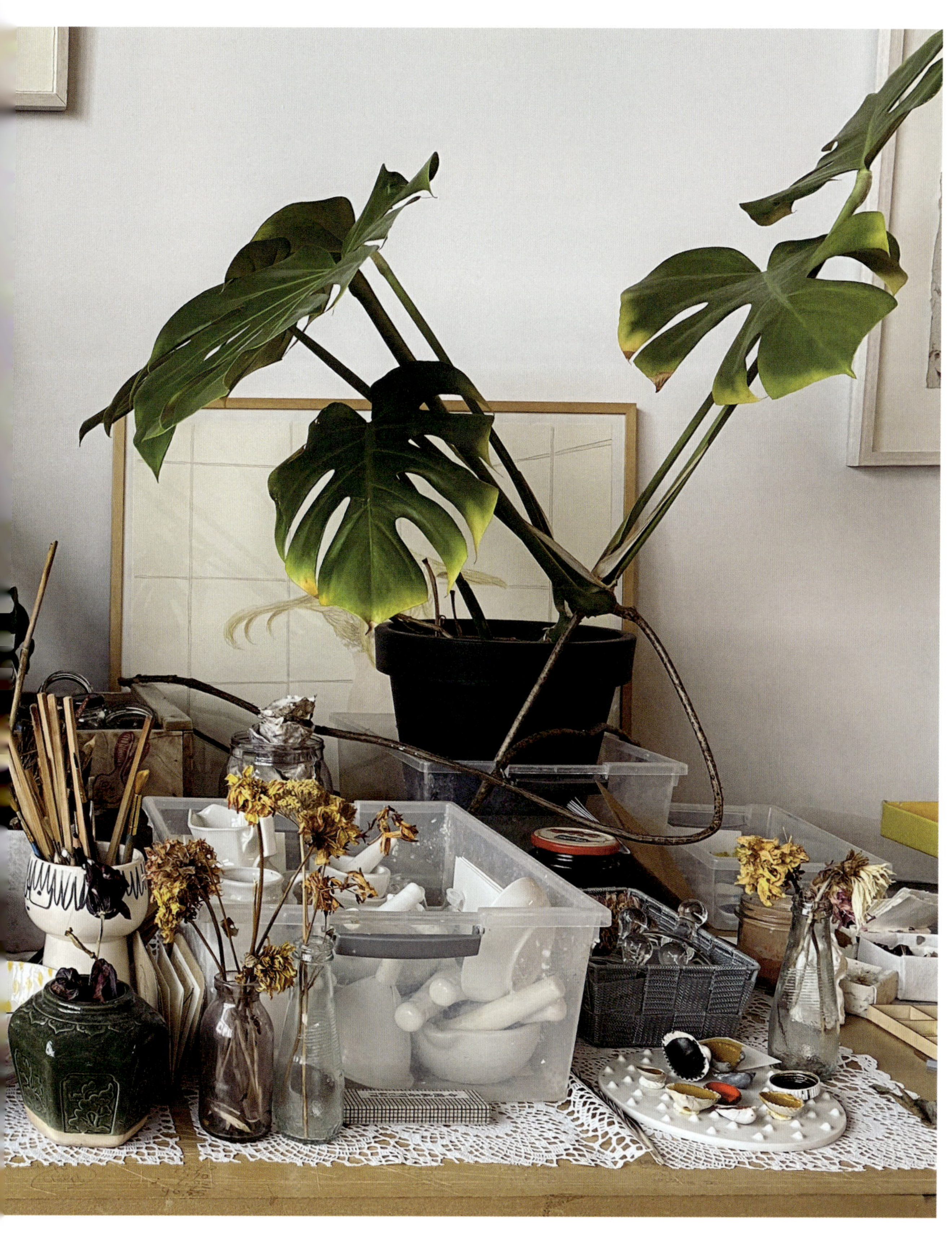

Index

Pink

Black hollyhock (pink) 62–65
Bracken (pale pink) 52–53
Poppy (pink) 82–85
Red cabbage (magenta) 124–125

Purple

Dahlia (purple) 74–75
Elder (deep purple) 86–87
Hibiscus (purple, violet) 80–81
Poppy (indigo) 82–85
Red cabbage (purple) 124–125

Red

Dahlia (deep red) 74–75
Hibiscus (red) 80–81
Madder (red) 36–39
Poppy (red) 82–85
Privet (burgundy) 98–99

Yellow

Birch (warm yellow) 96–97
Cow parsley (yellow-green) 54–55
Daffodil (warm yellow) 58–59
Elder (gold-green) 88–89
Goldenrod (warm yellow, golden
    yellow, chartreuse) 76–79
Horse chestnut (warm ochre)
    100–101
Tansy (soft yellow, lime yellow,
    dark chartreuse) 70–73
Weld (sunny yellow) 44–45

INDEX OF ENGLISH PLANT NAMES

INDEX OF LATIN PLANT NAMES

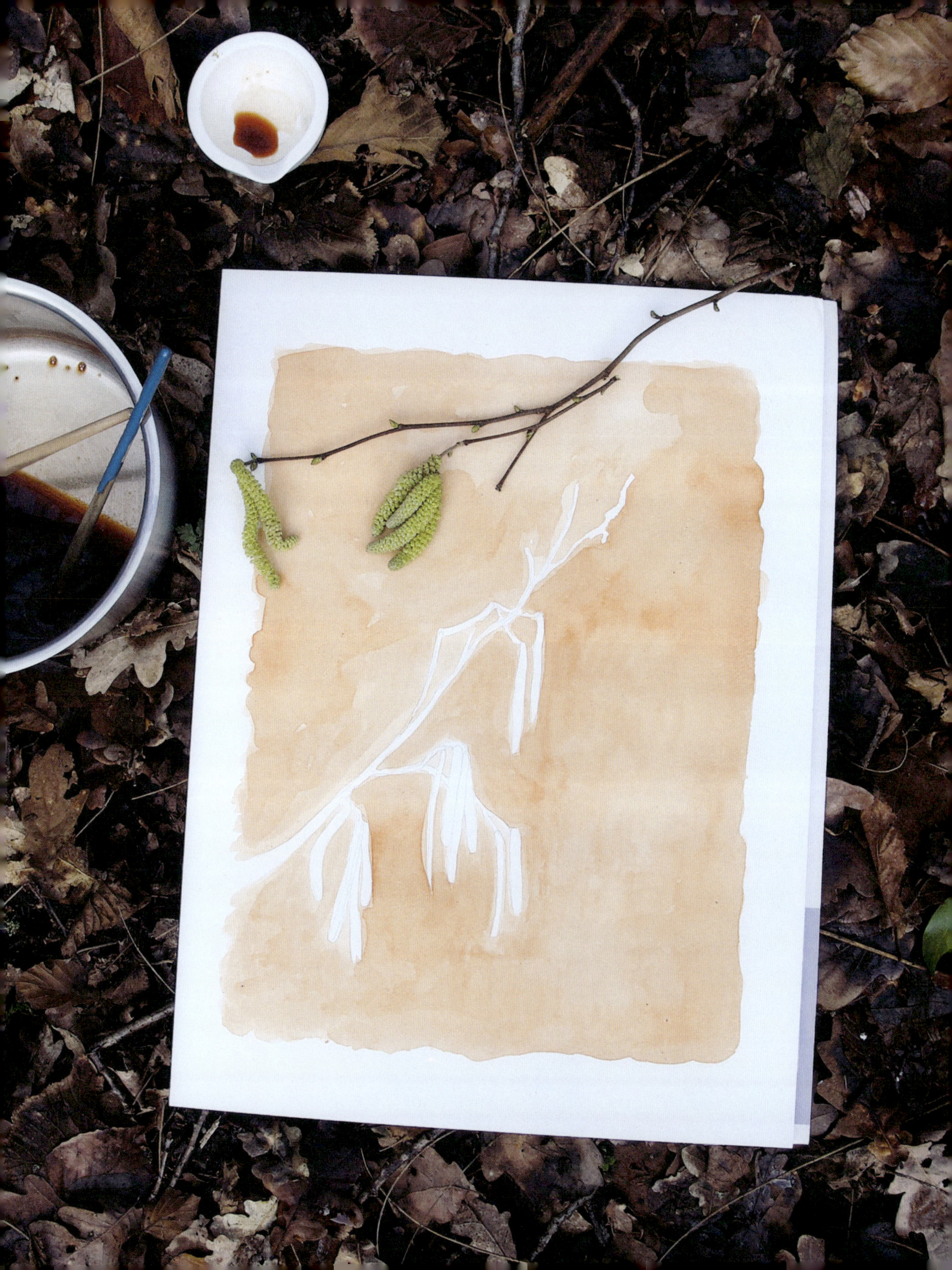

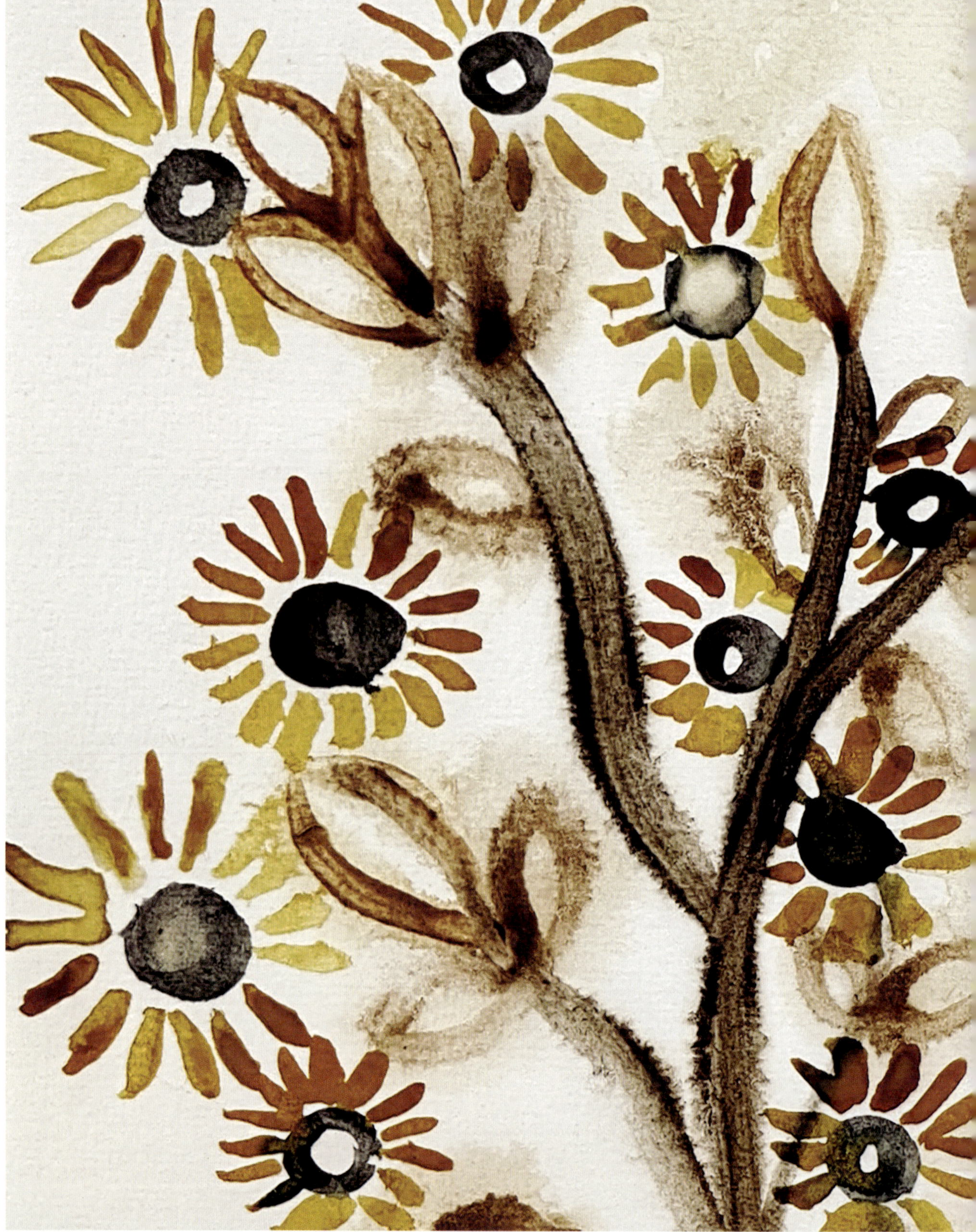

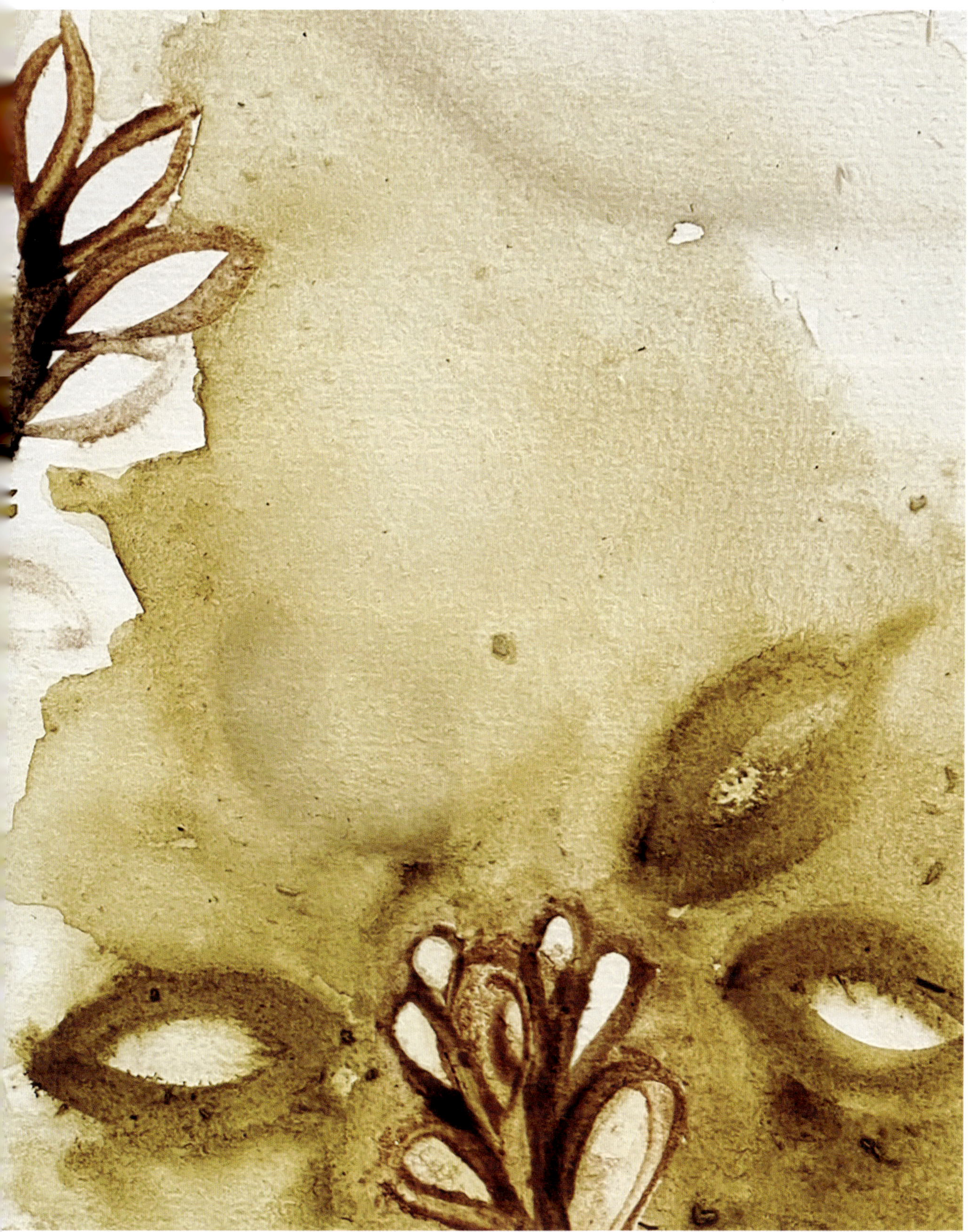

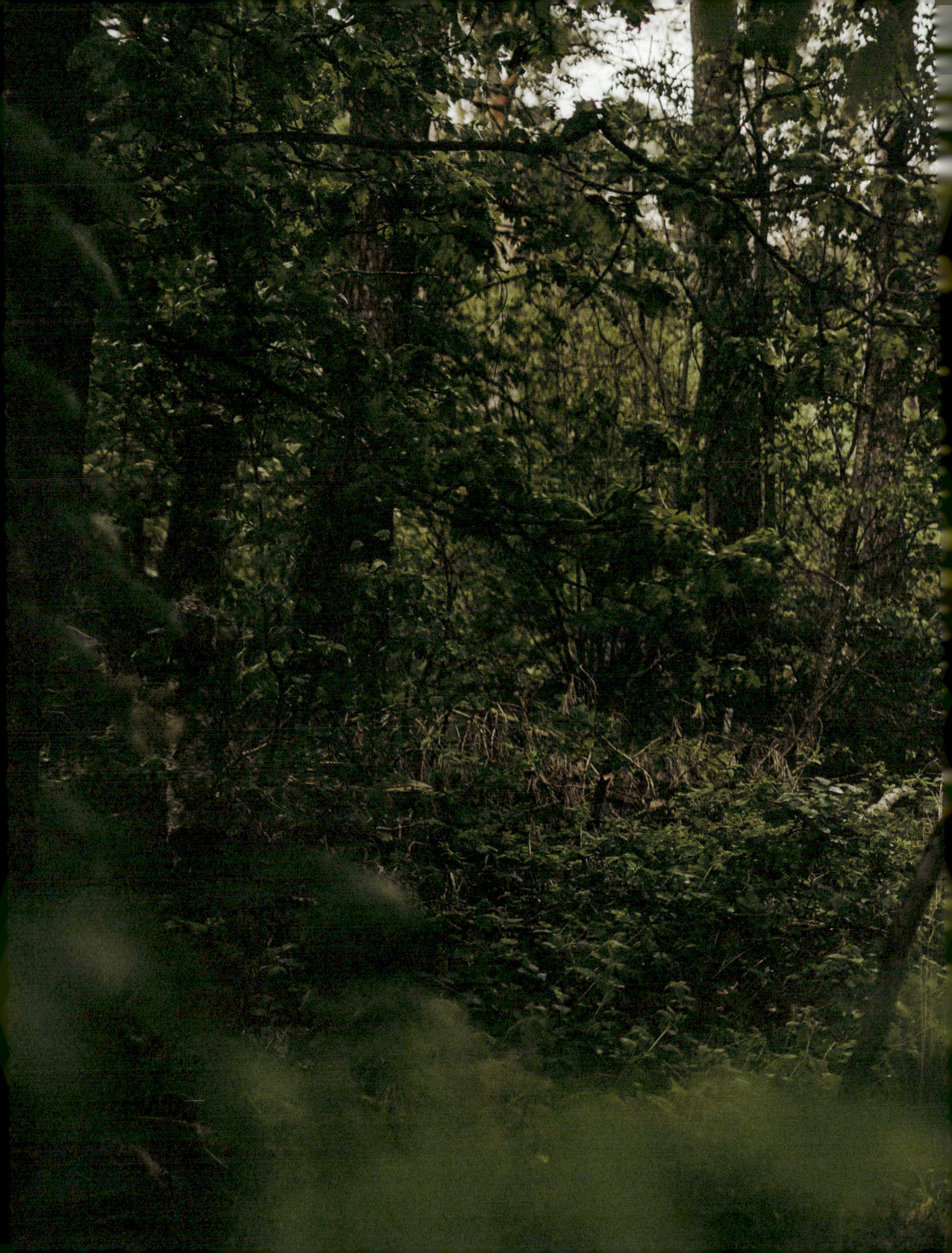

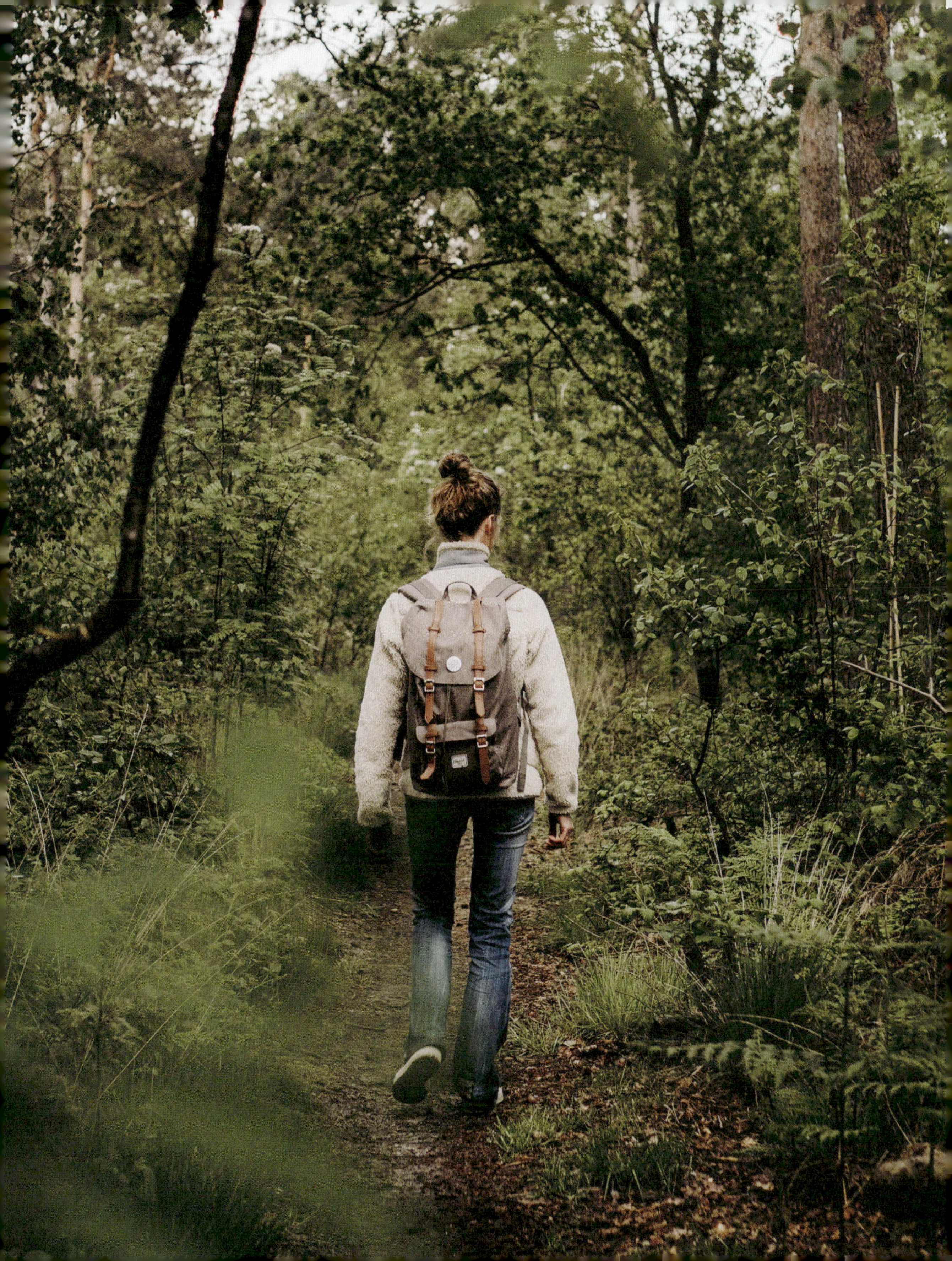

Publication information

First published in the UK in 2025 by
Search Press Limited
Wellwood, North Farm Road,
Tunbridge Wells, Kent TN2 3DR

© 2023, Uitgeverij Terralannoo BV.
Original title: *Planteninkt. Maak je eigen natuurlijke inkt.*
Translated from the Dutch language
www.terralannoo.com
© 2024, Search Press Ltd., for the English edition

English translation by Tankerton Translations

TEXT:
Judith Rosema, Het Inkt Atelier, hetinktatelier.com

EDITORS:
Trijnie Duut and Yulia Knol

INDEX:
Trijnie Duut

PHOTOGRAPHY:
Eva Krebbers, Tumbleweed & Fireflies Photography:
front cover, inside front cover, 2–3, 6–7, 10, 14, 22–23,
27, 32, 34–35, 37, 41, 44, 48–49, 50–51, 52 (tr, bl, br), 56,
59, 70, 74 (li), 76, 86, 89, 94–95, 96 (br), 112, 120, 127
(br), 128–129, 130–131, 132, 134–135, 139, 147, 151,
152–153, 154, 155, 158–159, 161, 162, 165, 166–167,
190–191
Judith Rosema, Het Inkt Atelier: back cover, 8–9,
12–13, 18–19, 24, 28, 30–31, 36, 39, 40, 46–47, 52 (tl),
55, 60, 63, 64, 66–67, 68–69, 73, 74 (tr, br), 79, 81, 82,
85, 90–91, 92–93, 96 (li, tr), 99, 100, 103, 104 (tr), 107,
108–109, 113, 115, 116, 119, 123, 124, 136, 138, 140,
142–143, 144, 148, 156, 165, 168–169, 175, 176–177,
178, 180–181, 182–183, 187
Suzanne van Hees: 110–111, 127 (t, bl)
Carlijn Krielaars: 104 (li, br)

tl = top left; li = left insert; bl = bottom left; t = top;
tr = top right; br = bottom right

COVER AND INSIDE DESIGN:

Jet van der Graaf, vormgraaf.nl

ISBN: 978-1-80092-310-2
ebook ISBN: 978-1-80093-297-5

The Publishers and author can accept no responsibility
for any consequences arising from the information,
advice or instructions given in this publication.

Readers are permitted to reproduce any of the projects
in this book for their personal use, or for the purpose
of selling for charity, free of charge and without the prior
permission of the Publishers. Any use of the projects
or images thereof for commercial purposes, or machine
learning purposes, is not permitted without the prior
permission of the Publishers.

SUPPLIERS:
If you have difficulty in obtaining any of the materials
and equipment mentioned in this book, then please visit
the Search Press website for details of suppliers:
www.searchpress.com

BOOKMARKED HUB:
For further ideas and inspiration, and to join our free
online community, visit www.bookmarkedhub.com

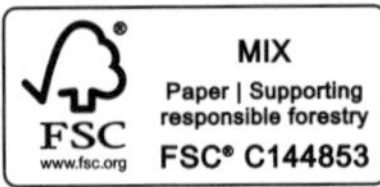